The U.S. Financial Crisis and Economic Recession 2007-2010

Causes, Local and Global Implications, Actions Taken, and the Way Forward

The U.S. Financial Crisis and Economic Recession 2007-2010

Causes, Local and Global Implications, Actions Taken, and the Way Forward

Chiaku Chukwuogor

Eastern Connecticut State University

Global Business Investments and Publications LLC

For product information, contact us at 860 487 9625

For permission to use material from this text or product, submit all requests online to submissions@globip.com

Further permission requests questions can be e-mailed to Chiaku.chukwugor@globip.com

Library of Congress Control Number: 2011931585

ISBN: 978-0-615-39793-1

Printed in the United States

Dedication

This book is dedicated to my children:
Ikechukwu, Udonna, Uchenna, and Kelechi Ndu.

Contents

Preface

A recession is normally associated with lower personal incomes, rising unemployment, and huge declines in business profits because of cuts in consumer and corporate investment spending and increased bankruptcies. The presence of the financial crisis not only escalated these negative macroeconomic indicator variations but also widened the negative impact to include the financial markets, financial institutions, savers, investors, and all levels of government: federal, state, and local. The combined negative impact of the last financial crisis and economic recession is only second to that of the Great Depression. Because of the U.S.'s dominant position in the world and the interconnected nature of the current global economic and financial system, the financial crisis that started in the United States in 2008 became a global phenomenon. Even though the negative financial and economic developments climaxed in 2008 and 2009, the effects still reverberate globally. Global financial flows have slowed significantly. Many countries experienced, and some are still experiencing, exchange rate depreciation. Major capital markets suffered astronomical losses. In addition, many big businesses failed and some were bailed out by their governments. Bank failures have been rampant. As banks struggle to contain their losses and achieve a strong balance sheet, credit for individual consumption and investments has become very tight.

It was obvious that many bureaucrats did not understand how their policies affected not only the economic developments in the U.S. but also such developments globally. Also, professionals in several financial institutions were unaware of the collaborative effect of their actions as they placed more importance on profit maximization. If things must change, students must be aware of the causes of the recent financial crisis and economic recession, the local and global implications, the actions taken by the Government to contain the crises and prevent a future occurrence. This book is written to address these issues and deliberate on the way forward in the final chapter.

Reviewers of this book unanimously agree that the seven chapters of **The U.S. Financial Crisis and Economic Recession 2007-2010:** *Causes, Local and Global Implications, Actions Taken, and the Way Forward* exhibit a deep investigation into the subject matter. The chapters devoted to its impact on the international financial markets, and actions taken by the U.S. Government to correct the effects of the crisis and in particular, the suggestions in Chapter 7 "The Way Forward" are very insightful. This book will make an interesting read for anybody with some background in business and economics as the writing is simple and explanatory.

As a university professor who has taught several courses such as Financial Management, International Financial Management, Bank Management at undergraduate and postgraduate level, Real Estate Finance, Investment Analysis, Financial Institutions Monetary and Fiscal Policy, Advanced Business Concepts and Entrepreneurship, Business Finance, and International Business, I have observed that most books on these topics usually do not go into much detail regarding the financial debacle and the concurrent economic recessions as we have recently experienced. I have also observed that the books often do not connect the contents discussed with the ignominious failure of the financial system in the economy. Therefore the facts presented in this book complement the major publications for undergraduate and post graduate students regarding such courses as Financial Markets, Financial Institutions, Real Estate Finance, Bank Management, Financial Management, Investment Analysis, Financial Institutions Monetary and Fiscal Policy, International Financial Management, Money and Banking, Case Studies in Financial Management, Global Economics, Modern American Economy, Contemporary Economic Problems And Issues, International Monetary Economics, and Public Finance.

xii

Lecturers of the above mentioned courses will no doubt benefit from the depth of the exposition in this book. As the book delves into events leading to the financial crisis and identifies the major causes of the crisis, all who read this book will understand the factors leading to the financial and economic crises. They will appreciate the types of actions taken, and perhaps needed, to remedy the deleterious impacts of such crises. They will understand the domestic impact and the contagion effects of the crisis on other countries. I hope the ideas enunciated in the final chapter regarding the "Way Forward" will motivate further discussions on the topic.

About the Author

Dr. Chiaku Nwamu Chukwuogor is a Professor of Finance at Eastern Connecticut State University. She is the editor of both the *African Journal of Accounting, Economics, Finance and Banking Research* and *Global Journal of International Business Research*; and managing editor of the following journals: the *North American Journal of Finance and Banking Research*, the *Asia Pacific Journal of Finance and Banking Research*, the *European Journal of Finance and Banking Research*, the *Global Journal of Finance and Banking Issues* and the *Global Journal of International Business Research*.

She was conference chairperson of the 2011 Conference on Financial Services, International Trade and Economic Development in Africa in Abuja, Nigeria and the program chairperson of the 2006 International Academy of Business and Technology Business Conference in Mystic, Connecticut.

She has taught several courses in her career including: Financial Management at undergraduate and postgraduate level, International Financial Management, Bank Management at undergraduate and postgraduate level, Real Estate Finance, Investment Analysis at undergraduate and postgraduate level, Financial Institutions Monetary and Fiscal Policy, Advanced Business Concepts and Entrepreneurship, Business Finance, and International Business. Dr. Chukwuogor introduced and developed the post-graduate diploma course in Finance, Banking and Investment Management at the then University of Natal, South Africa in 1997. She also introduced and developed the following courses at the Eastern Connecticut State University in 2005: Real Estate Finance and Bank Management.

Her research on international finance, banking, and real estate finance have been published in numerous journals including the *Journal of Real Estate Finance and Economics, International Journal of Banking and Finance, International Journal of Applied Econometrics and Quantitative Studies,* and *International Research Journal Banks and Bank Systems.*

Acknowledgements

I hereby acknowledge the contributions of my colleagues: Dr. Zakri Bello of Central Connecticut State University and Dr. Augustine Arize of Texas A&M University through discussions, reviews, and comments. The contributions of my student interns and assistants: Pamela Melchior, Melissa Albert, Jessica Adelson, Andzelina Chmielewski, Hannah Hirschfeld, and Peter Meade are highly appreciated. I thank Eastern Connecticut State University for giving me the release time in the spring semester of 2010 that enabled me to start work on this book. Finally, I acknowledge the contributions of my son, Dr. Udonna Ndu, and my sister, Ogoegbunam Chukwuogor, for their excellent editorial reviews.

CHAPTER 1

2008 U.S. FINANCIAL AND ECONOMIC CRISES

INTRODUCTION

The Dow Jones Industrial Average tumbled 504 points on Monday, September 15, 2008, and the S&P 500 suffered its worst decline since September 11, 2001, signaling a financial crisis in U.S. stock markets. How did this happen? The U.S. stock markets had been soaring. From 1998 to 2008 just before the loss on September 15, 2008, the DOW had gained 43.2 percent of its value. It had achieved daily closings of above 12,000 on average. In the first half of October 2007 it had closed at over 14,000. Precisely, it closed at 14,066, 14,164, and at 14,093 on October 5th, October 9th, and October 12th respectively. These robust achievements started to decline in the summer of 2008 amid the ongoing subprime mortgage crisis, the collapse of Bear Stearns, the bankruptcy of Lehman Brothers, the collapse of AIG, Merrill Lynch, and Wachovia, and the failure of many banks, including twenty-five Federal Deposit Insurance Corporation (FDIC) insured banks. The markets continued to react to concerns about unprecedented foreclosures, corporate failures, government bailouts, and the collapse of the banking sector. Between September 9, 2008 and March 9, 2009, the DOW lost 41.85 percent of its value when it closed at 65.44 on March 9, 2009.

As businesses failed and the financial losses of individuals and businesses in the stock market increased, spending power declined, and workers were laid off in the millions. According to the United States Bureau of Labor Statistics, between January 2008 and December 2008, the nation lost a total of 3.6 million jobs.[1] Quarterly gross domestic product (GDP) declined and went to negative territory. According to the Bureau of Economic Analysis, the U.S. Real gross domestic product, that is the output of goods and services produced by labor and property located in the United States decreased at an annual rate of 6.2 percent in the fourth quarter of 2008. Economic recession emanated, although there was some confusion as to exactly when the economic recession started. On Monday, December 1, 2008, the National Bureau of Economic Research (NBER) said that the United States had been in a recession since December 2007.

The NBER, a group of leading economists, is the official business-cycle dating committee in the United States. This committee uses information relating to incomes and other forms of economic malaise, such as increased bankruptcies, unemployment, falling profits, real personal income, industrial production, as well as wholesale and retail sales, and gross domestic product, to reach a decision about the state of the economy. As a result, the presence of a recession is usually announced retrospectively. The rule of thumb method for determining a recession, which is two consecutive quarters of falling real GDP, proved to be right. The U.S. real GDP went from $14.55 trillion in the third quarter of 2008 to $14.15 trillion in the second quarter of 2009. Since then, there have been more than two consecutive quarterly real GDP growths. Technically, the economic recession in the United States is over. However, the huge unemployment situation remains. The stock markets have bounced back and gained significant

---

[1] U.S. Department of Labor, Bureau of Labor Statistics,
http://data.bls.gov/timeseries/CES0000000001?output_view=net_1mth

momentum. Since the DOW's lowest closing value of 65.44 on March 9, 2009 during the financial crisis, it has gained 86.75 as the DOW Industrial closed at 12, 226.64 on January 15, 2011.

Figure 1.1 Historical Daily Stock Price of Lehman Brothers 2005–2010

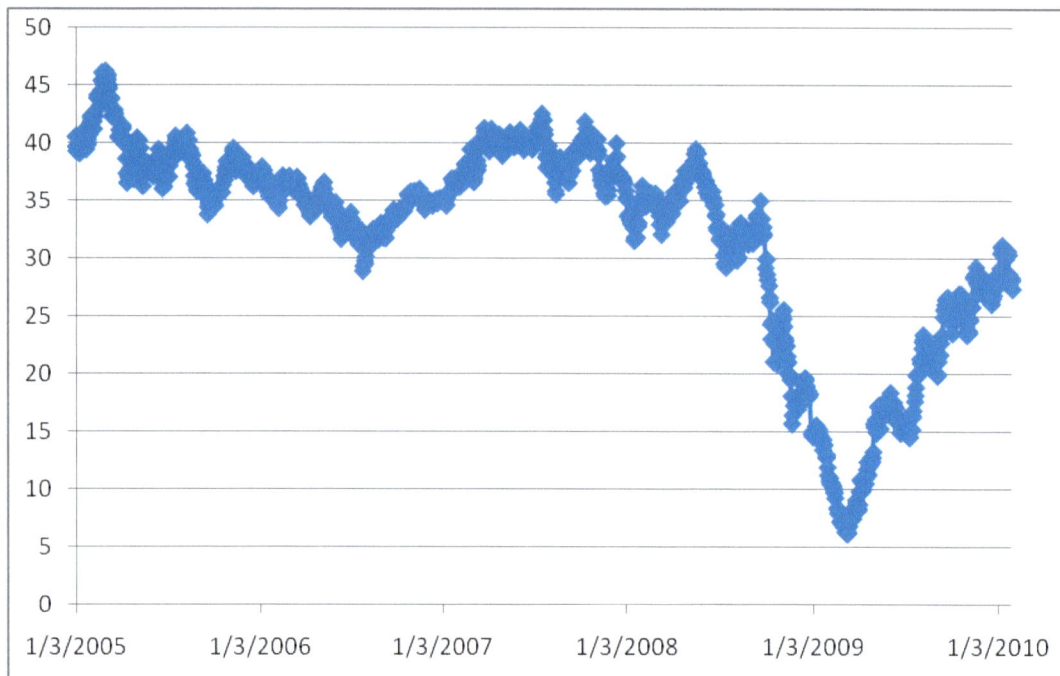

Source: Constructed with data from Yahoo Finance

The U.S. financial crisis metamorphosed into an economic recession. Some described the recession as almost as deep as the Great Depression. The financial crisis and the economic recession had a severe impact on individuals and businesses in the United States and around the world. This book examines the 2008 U.S. financial crisis and ensuing economic recession with particular reference to the causes behind the financial crisis and economic recession, the local and global implications, actions taken by the Government to control the situation, and the way forward. Because of the U.S.'s dominant position in the world and the interconnected nature of the current global economic and financial system, the financial crisis that started in the United States in 2008 became a global phenomenon. Even though the negative financial and economic developments climaxed in 2008 and 2009, the effects still reverberate globally. Global financial flows have slowed significantly. Many countries experienced, and some are still experiencing, exchange rate depreciation. Major capital markets suffered astronomical losses. In addition, many big businesses failed and some were bailed out by their governments. Bank failures have been rampant. As banks struggle to contain their losses and achieve a strong balance sheet, credit for individual consumption and investments has become very tight.

It was obvious that many bureaucrats did not understand how their policies affected not only the economic developments in the U.S. but also such developments globally. Also, professionals in several financial institutions were unaware of the collaborative effect of their actions as they placed more importance on profit maximization. If things must change, students as our future leaders must be aware of the causes of the recent financial crisis and economic recession, the local and global implications, the actions taken by the Government to contain the crises and prevent a future occurrence. This book is written to address these issues and for all of us to deliberate on the way forward.

Chapter 1 contains a discussion of the financial crisis and economic recession. Chapter 2 gives the economic background to the 2008 and 2009 U.S. financial crisis and economic recession, and chapter 3 presents the causes of the financial crisis. Chapter 4 delves into the local impact of the financial crisis and economic recession, whereas chapter 5 looks at the impact of the U.S. financial crisis and economic recession on global financial markets and economies. Chapter 6 discusses actions taken by the Government to stem the crisis/recession, create jobs, and prevent future financial and economic crises. Chapter 7 advances some conclusions drawn from the events of the time and suggests ideas for the way forward.

THE 2008 FINANCIAL CRISIS

A financial crisis reflects the occurrence of a negative event or a series of negative events in the financial services sector or financial markets that leads to a serious loss of value of assets. This loss can be in the value of stocks, bonds, or national currencies. The losses might culminate in a loss of confidence in a country's currency or other financial assets.

A notable financial crisis in recent times was the Asian financial crisis of 1997. The Asian financial crisis was caused by the inability of the Thai Government to successfully defend the value of the Thai Baht that was under attack by speculators who felt that the Thai Baht, pegged at 25 THB = 1 USD in May 1997, was overvalued. Many other Southeast Asian countries, which were similarly vulnerable, joined in the defense of the Thai Baht and of their own currencies; however, these efforts failed, hence the name of the crisis–*Asian financial crisis*.

This resulted in massive unemployment in Thailand, especially in the finance, real estate, and construction sectors. Between May 1997 and January 1998, the Thai Baht lost 75 percent of its value going from 25 THB = 1 USD in May 1997 to about 55 THB = 1 USD in 1998. The loss in the stock market was astronomical. During the period, it declined about 76 percent. Asset values also plummeted. The situation in South Korea was similar. In fact, many countries in the region experienced similar shocks, including Malaysia, Singapore, Philippines, Taiwan, South Korea, and Japan, as a result of contagion effects.

A more than $40 billion program was organized by the International Monetary Fund (IMF) together with other bilateral and multilateral donors and agencies to stabilize the currencies of Thailand, South Korea, Indonesia, and Malaysia to prevent those countries from going bankrupt. The difficult thing to understand about the Asian financial crisis is that most of the governments had been, according to the IMF, implementing sound fiscal policies. So, what caused the financial crisis?

In the decade prior to the crisis, the GDP of most of these countries grew at very high rates. For example, Thailand achieved an average GDP growth rate of about 9 percent during that period. In hindsight, there were allegations of imprudent bank loans because of mismatches of assets and liabilities. It was alleged that governments and banks borrowed funds in U.S. dollars short term for long-term investments. It also was alleged that the incidence of fraud was common. Bank loans to cronies and family members of bank executives were also rampant, all of which contributed to the regulatory failures and the contagion effect.

Soon after the Asian financial crisis, the Russian financial crisis followed, then the Argentine financial crisis in 2002. What about the United States? Have there been recent financial crises prior to the 2008 financial crisis? No, in recent times, there has not been a financial crisis in the United States; however, there have been bubbles (booming economic activity ending in a sudden collapse). Notable among them was the dot-com bubble, the speculative bubble in the IT industry that reached a climax when the bubble burst in 2002. However, it is the bankruptcy of Lehman Brothers Holdings Inc. that is believed to have triggered the U.S. 2008 and 2009 financial crisis.

LEHMAN BROTHERS' BANKRUPTCY

Lehman Brothers Holdings Inc. was listed on the New York Stock Exchange; its ticker symbol was LEHMQ.PK. Although the origin of Lehman Brothers dates back to 1850, the firm Lehman Brothers Holdings Inc., as we knew it, emerged as a traded company with its initial public offering in 1994. It was a global company with headquarters in New York City. It had regional headquarters in London and Tokyo and many offices all over the world. The total capitalization of Lehman Brothers Holdings Inc. on November 30, 2007, was $691.1 billion.

As an investment banker, Lehman Brothers raised capital, traded securities, and organized and managed corporate mergers and acquisitions. Lehman Brothers participated in the issue of equity and fixed-income securities. It traded these securities for its customers on the stock exchanges, managed the investment portfolios of its clients, and engaged in private banking. As a primary dealer, it traded directly with the Federal Reserve Bank (Fed) and made bids or offers when the Fed conducted open market operations, a tool of monetary policy implementation.

The Federal Reserve through its Federal Open Market Committee controls the U.S. money supply by buying and selling government securities or other financial securities. The FOMC meets eight times a year. At these meetings, monetary targets, such as money supply, growth rates, interest rate levels, and exchange rates, are determined and actions are taken to implement these targets. The Federal Reserve's principal tool for implementing monetary policy is the purchase and sale of U.S. Treasury and federal agency securities. For example, the Fed's decision to purchase government debt securities should expand the money supply in the economy and result in an expansionary monetary policy, whereas the sale of government debt securities by the Fed represents a contractionary monetary policy.

Lehman Brothers was a holding company to the following subsidiaries: Lehman Brothers Inc, Lehman Brothers Bank, Aurora Loan Services, Inc., SIB Mortgage Corporation, Neuberger Berman Inc., FSB, Eagle Energy Partners, and the Crossroads Group. The 158-year-old Lehman Brothers filed for bankruptcy under Chapter 11 of the U.S. bankruptcy code. Lehman Brothers was the fourth largest securities firm in the U.S. in 2008, with assets valued at $639 billion and had a total debt of $613 billion, which was owed to more than 100,000 creditors, mainly secured all over the world, including: Tokyo, Hong Kong, New York, Singapore, and Taipei. This became the largest bankruptcy in the United States, pushing into second place that of WorldCom Inc., in July 2002, which had $104 billion in assets. The major shareholders of Lehman Brothers were AXA Equitable Retirement Group (7.3 percent), Clear Bridge Advisors (6.3 percent), and FMR, the parent of Fidelity Investments, (5.9 percent). WorldCom had $150 billion in outstanding bond debt and $138 billion of notes payable. Citigroup Inc. and the Bank of New York Mellon Corp. were the listed creditors of Lehman Brothers.

How did this happen? An examination of the 2007 financial statements of Lehman Brothers Holding Company Inc. shows a higher net income than the preceding two years. However, between 2005 and 2007, there were significant increases in certain risk-sensitive items, such as net receivables (99.96 percent), a 100 percent increase in cash holdings, an increase in accounts payable and other current liabilities, and a 54 percent increase in treasury stock. The greatest indication of financial distress was the increase in net borrowings of 350 percent from $9.7 billion to $43.7 billion between 2005 and 2007. See Table 1.1.

Table 1.1 Lehman Brothers Holdings Summarized Financial Statement 1998–2007, 10 year Summary (in millions)

Income Statement						
Date	Sales	EBIT	Depreciation	Total net income	EPS	Tax Rate (%)
11/07	57,264.0	6,013.0	577.0	4,192.0	7.26	30.28
11/06	45,296.0	5,905.0	514.0	3,960.0	6.73	32.94
11/05	31,476.0	4,829.0	426.0	3,260.0	5.43	32.49
11/04	20,456.0	3,518.0	428.0	2,393.0	3.95	31.98
11/03	17,146.0	2,536.0	326.0	1,771.0	3.17	30.17
11/02	16,696.0	1,399.0	258.0	1,031.0	1.73	26.30
11/01	22,340.0	1,748.0	174.0	1,311.0	2.19	25.00
11/00	26,313.0	2,579.0	102.0	1,831.0	3.19	29.00
11/99	18,925.0	1,631.0	88.0	1,174.0	2.04	28.02
11/98	19,869.0	1,052.0	91.0	736.0	1.30	30.04

Balance Sheet			
	Current Assets	Current liabilities	Long-term debt	Shares outstanding
11/07	691,063.0	668,573.0	123,150.0	531.9 Mil
11/06	503,545.0	484,354.0	81,178.0	533.4 Mil
11/05	410,063.0	393,269.0	53,899.0	542.9 Mil
11/04	357,168.0	342,248.0	56,486.0	548.3 Mil
11/03	312,061.0	297,577.0	43,529.0	533.4 Mil
11/02	260,336.0	250,684.0	38,678.0	462.3 Mil
11/01	247,816.0	238,647.0	38,301.0	475.1 Mil
11/00	224,720.0	216,079.0	35,233.0	472.8 Mil
11/99	192,244.0	185,251.0	30,691.0	479.6 Mil
11/98	153,890.0	148,477.0	27,341.0	454.6 Mil

Source: MSN. Money, 2010 Thomson Reuters,
http://moneycentral.msn.com/investor/invsub/results/statemnt.aspx?Symbol=LEHMQ&lstStatement=1
0YearSummary&stmtView=Ann

As reported by Richard S. Fuld, Jr. and Joseph M. Gregory, Chairman and Chief Executive Officer and President and Chief Operating Officer, respectively, in Lehman Brothers 2007 Annual Report, "The second half of 2007 was very financially challenging as we saw a U.S. housing recession, a credit freeze, and a repricing of credit-related securities. This caused disruptions in the mortgage markets, a sharp decline in liquidity, and a slowing of corporate and institutional activity." In August 2007, Lehman Brothers closed its subprime lender, BNC Mortgage (BNC).

The subprime mortgage crisis began with defaults in 2007. The years of 2004-2006 saw an expansion of these subprime loans. BNC was one of the top subprime producers in 2006, originating over $14 billion in loans. It suffered significant losses in the subprime mortgage crisis. In spite of these hits, Lehman Brothers engaged significantly in long-term investments. As reported in Lehman Brothers 2007 Annual Report, according to the executives of the company, "BNC opened offices in Doha-Qatar, Dubai, Geneva, Istanbul, Lisbon, Moscow, São Paolo, and Shanghai. In connection with the acquisitions of Grange Securities in Australia and Eagle Energy Partners in Texas, they added offices in Sydney, Melbourne, Perth, Brisbane, and Houston." In 2007, BNC also invested in many businesses, including commodities, prime services, investment management, investment banking, emerging markets, and other regions. These investments led to strong revenue growth in those targeted areas. However, this functional and global diversification did not save the company and probably made it more attractive to those seeking its acquisition.

Bank of America, Barclays, and HSBC were all takeover contenders that insisted on funding assistance from their Governments. Both the UK's Financial Services Authority and the U.S. Federal Reserve Bank declined to participate in the proposed takeover or to prevent the bankruptcy of Lehman Brothers. Lehman Brothers and Bear Sterns had similar operations. The Federal Reserve Bank bailed out Bear Sterns but declined to bail out Lehman Brothers. In the United States, this decision was criticized by those who argued that the decision to allow Lehman Brothers to fail instead of financially supporting it to survive or financially supporting a takeover, as was the case with Fannie Mae and Freddie Mac, ignited the financial crisis.

CORPORATE TAKEOVERS AND BAILOUTS IN THE FINANCIAL SERVICES SECTOR

Although the bankruptcy of Lehman Brothers Holding Company Inc. is believed to have precipitated the October 2008 financial crisis, the collapse of Bear Stearns Companies, Inc. certainly signaled the meltdown of the Wall Street investment banking industry. Bear Stearns was founded in 1923 and became a publicly traded Company in 1985 as Bear Stearns Companies, Inc. The 85-year-old American investment bank thrived in the business of financial intermediation. It was involved in all kinds of investment banking operations. Bear Stearns participated in public and private placements of both equity and debt securities in areas of corporate finance. It traded equities and fixed-income securities, such as stocks and bonds, and engaged in financial research. It participated effectively in mergers and acquisitions and was well respected among its peers for innovative techniques and practices.

Bear Stearns pioneered the securitization of mortgages. Bear Stearns Asset Management Inc. (BSAM) was an asset management arm of Bear Stearns Companies Inc. This meant that BSAM provided financial advice to Bear Stearns' clients and made investment decisions on their behalf. The firm also provided sophisticated risk measurement and management capabilities to its clients. It primarily provided its services to high-net-worth individuals. Some believe that its increased exposure to innovative techniques, such as mortgage-backed securities, especially from 2006 to 2007 when investor losses significantly increased due to the subprime mortgage crisis, led the company to huge losses and subsequent insolvency. Before its demise, Bear Stearns was headquartered in New York City, but it also had a substantial international presence in Europe, Asia Pacific, and South America.

In March 2008, Bear Stearns could not borrow money even from its closest associate, J.P. Morgan Chase, to cover what the company perceived as short-term illiquidity. On March 14, 2008, J.P. Morgan Chase, backed by a $30 billion loan from the Fed, took over Bear Stearns Companies. The loan was given to J.P. Morgan Chase to facilitate the takeover. The Reserve Bank rationalized the financial facilitation of this takeover on the grounds that, if it allowed Bear Stearns to become insolvent and declare bankruptcy, the United States would experience a market crash because of the inevitable loss of confidence that such a corporate failure would generate. This was especially so considering that, until this takeover, the stock of Bear Stearns Companies, Inc. had traded at $172 a share in January 2007 and $93 a share in February 2008. The stock had maintained a 52-week high of $133. Bear Stearns' stock had traded at $85 at the New York Stock exchange a couple of days prior to its takeover. The initial takeover deal on March 16, 2008, was that J.P. Morgan Chase would acquire Bear Stearns in exchange for 0.05473 share of J.P. Morgan Chase stock for each share of Bear Stearns, representing an implied merger consideration of $2.00 per share for Bear Stearns at the time of that announcement.

The shareholders of Bear Stearns suspected fraud and mounted a class action suit against Bear Stearns, J.P. Morgan Chase and certain Bear Stearns' officers and directors challenging the terms of J.P. Morgan Chase's previously announced acquisition of Bear Stearns. Seven days later, on March 24, 2008, the merger agreement was amended to, among other things, increase the merger consideration to 0.21753 J.P. Morgan Chase share for each share of Bear Stearns. In addition, the amended merger agreement permitted J.P. Morgan Chase to purchase 95 million newly issued Bear Stearns shares for $10 per share, which conveyed approximately 39.5 percent voting power to J.P. Morgan Chase without the approval of Bear Stearns' shareholders. This constituted a lockup stock sale.

Bear Stearns' shareholders brought a class action law suit against Bear Stearns' directors. They added J.P. Morgan Chase as a defendant for aiding and abetting Bear Stearns. In a revised lawsuit seeking damages, the shareholders alleged that Bear Stearns breached its fiduciary duties, including the duties of loyalty and care, by failing to fully inform them of the value of Bear Stearns. In addition, the shareholders claimed that Bear Stearns failed to act in the best interest of all the shareholders by failing to implement a proper process to evaluate and investigate alternatives to the merger. The stockholders alleged that J.P. Morgan Chase was given a special and favored position with respect to any acquisition of Bear Stearns to the detriment of Bear Stearns' shareholders. They further alleged that J.P. Morgan Chase unfairly exercised its control over Bear Stearns in extracting the terms of the merger. The New York Supreme Court issued an opinion in the case granting a summary judgment to the Defendants on December 4, 2008.[2] The matter is currently under appeal. Moreover, Bear Stearns was certainly no stranger to litigation. In 2006,

> The Securities and Exchange Commission [SEC] announced a settled enforcement action against Bear Stearns & Co., Inc. (BS&Co.) and Bear Stearns Securities Corp. (BSSC), (collectively, Bear Stearns), charging Bear Stearns with securities fraud for facilitating unlawful late trading and deceptive market timing of mutual funds by its customers and customers of its introducing brokers. The Commission issued an Order which found that from 1999 through September 2003, Bear Stearns provided technology, advice and deceptive devices that enabled its market timing customers and introducing brokers to late trade and to evade detection by mutual funds.

> Pursuant to the Order … Bear Stearns will pay 250 million dollars consisting of 160 million dollars in disgorgement and a 90 million dollars penalty.[3]

> Exactly what is late trading and why was there all that fuss?

> Funds can be bought and sold all day. However, unlike stocks, which are priced throughout the trading day, mutual funds are only priced once a day, usually at 4 p.m. Eastern Time. At that point the funds' price, or Net Asset Value (NAV), is determined by adding up the worth of the securities the fund owns, plus any cash it holds minus its liabilities and dividing that by the number of shares outstanding.

---

[2] In re Bear Stearns Litigation, N.Y. Sup. Ct., Index No. 600780/08 12/4/08.
[3] Securities and Exchange Commission, "SEC Settles Fraud Charges with Bear Stearns for Late Trading and Market Timing Violations," March 16, 2006, http://www.sec.gov/news/press/2006-38.htm.

Buy a fund at 2 p.m., and you'll pay a NAV that is determined two hours later. Buy a fund at 5 p.m., and you'll pay a price that won't be set until 4 p.m. the following day. According to ... [the] complaint,... a hedge fund ... took advantage of the way fund prices are set to effectively pick the pockets of long-term shareholders.[4]

FEDERAL NATIONAL MORTGAGE ASSOCIATION (FNMA): FANNIE MAE

James Lockhart, director of the Federal Housing Financing Agency, announced on September 7, 2008, that Fannie Mae and Freddie Mac were being placed into the conservatorship of the FHFA. Conservatorship refers to a situation where an entity or organization is subject to the legal control of an external entity or organization. Fannie Mae was initially established as a federal agency in 1938, and later in 1968 it received a charter from Congress as a private shareholder-owned company. This was considered by many to be one of the most sweeping government interventions in private financial markets since the great depression. Fannie Mae is one of the programs often referred to as the three Rs: relief, recovery, and reform, that is, relief for the unemployed and poor, recovery of the economy to normal levels, and reform of the financial system to prevent a repeat depression that survived the Second World War when many such programs were discontinued. The mission of Fannie Mae is to provide liquidity, stability, and affordability to the U.S. housing and mortgage markets.

Fannie Mae tries to achieve its mission by working with mortgage bankers, brokers, and other primary mortgage market partners to help ensure they have funds to lend to home buyers at affordable rates. For example, this Federal agency sells bonds and uses the funds raised to purchase mortgages originated by mortgage companies, banks and other financial institutions. Together, these businesses contribute to the company's chartered mission to increase the amount of funds available in order to make homeownership and rental housing more available and affordable. Thus, Fannie Mae operates in the U.S. secondary mortgage market by providing liquidity to the market. Fannie Mae and other federal agencies have contributed to the increase in homeownership in the United States.

Before the New Deal, standard mortgages lasted only five to ten years with high interest and huge deposit requirements. Prior to the introduction of the New Deal, only four out of ten Americans owned homes as opposed to two out of every three Americans who owned homes about forty years after the implementation of the New Deal. Improvements that lead to this increase in home ownership included access to thirty-year mortgages, the standardized appraisal and construction standards that helped to open the housing market to more Americans, and a reduction in mortgage rates for many because of government-sponsored programs and increased liquidity in the mortgage market.

Fannie Mae purchases mortgage loans from mortgage lenders, such as mortgage companies, savings institutions, and commercial banks, thereby replenishing those institutions' supply of mortgage funds. Fannie Mae either packages these loans in mortgage-backed securities, which it guarantees for full and timely payment of principal and interest, or purchases these loans for cash and retains the mortgages in its portfolio. Fannie Mae sells mortgage-backed securities, that is, bonds backed by collateral, such as real estate mortgages from which regular payments of principal and interest are paid to the investor or holder of the bond. The investor or holder of the bond is actually loaning money to Fannie Mae in return for the mortgage principal and interest payments paid to the investor. These cash flows come from payments by the mortgage holders.

Moreover, Fannie Mae and Freddie Mac own or guarantee about 50 percent of the nation's $12 trillion mortgage market. Unfortunately, Fannie Mae, a $912.4 billion company, experienced huge

[4] Stone, Amey, "A Primer on the Mutual-Fund Scandal," Bloomberg Businessweek, September 22, 2003, http://www.businessweek.com/bwdaily/dnflash/sep2003/nf20030922_7646.htm.

losses of over $2 billion in 2007 and over $58 billion in 2008. This poor performance resulted mainly from its involvement in the asset securitization of subprime mortgages. The subprime mortgage crisis erupted with an unprecedented default in mortgage payments and huge numbers of foreclosures. This was accompanied with decline in house demand. This led to the inability of financial institutions to sell the repossessed houses. All these negative developments affected the earnings of Fannie Mae, and its income plummeted. The stock market reacted. By August 22, 2008, the stock price of Fannie Mae had tumbled to $5 per share from a previous share price of $66.87 on August 22, 2007. See Figure 1.2. Fannie Mae failed in September 2008, and was seized by the Federal Government.

Figure 1-2. Historical Stock Price of Fannie Mae 2000 to 2009

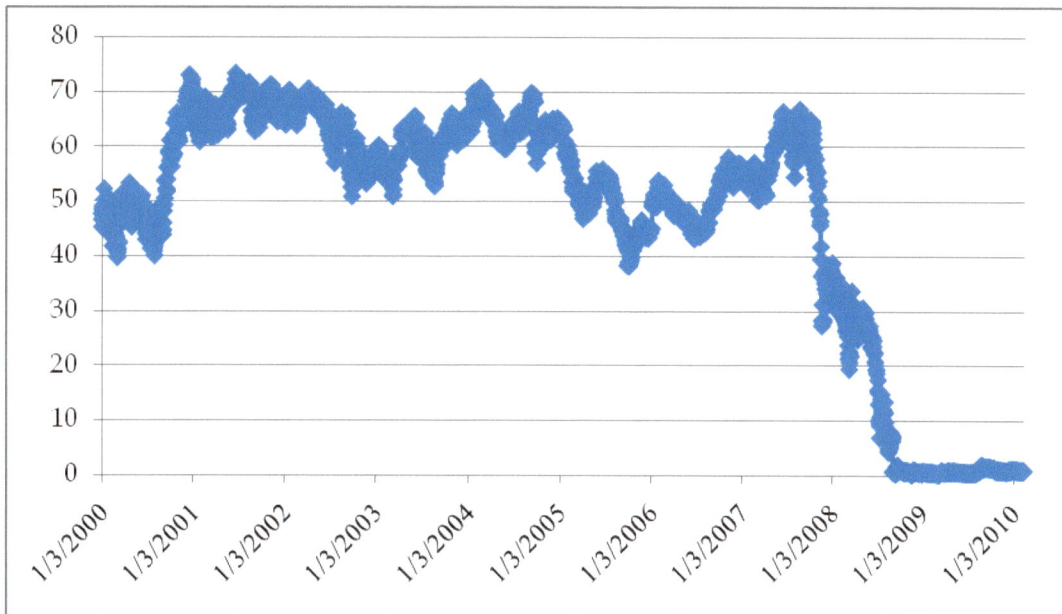

Source: Constructed with data from Yahoo Finance

THE FEDERAL HOME LOAN MORTGAGE CORPORATION (FHLMC): FREDDIE MAC

The Federal Home Loan Mortgage Corporation was established by charter of Congress in 1970 and amended in 2009 as a government-sponsored enterprise of the United States. The purpose of this enterprise is to provide stability in the secondary market for residential mortgages, respond appropriately to private capital markets, and to provide liquidity to the secondary market for residential mortgages. In practice, it increases the supply of money available for mortgage lending and the money available for new home purchases.

Freddie Mac buys mortgages on the secondary market, pools them, and sells them as mortgage-backed securities to investors on the open market. In the process, Freddie Mac claims that it reduces the costs of housing finance and expands housing opportunities for all families, including low-income and minority families. However, this mortgage giant ran into financial difficulty in 2008. The dramatic increase in mortgage defaults threatened to render this mortgage giant insolvent. For the first time in nine years, Freddie Mac recorded negative earnings before interest and tax (EBIT) of $5.977 billion. See Table 1.2. By the end of the third quarter of 2008, the EBIT was negative $9.741 billion. The stock of Freddie Mac plummeted in the stock market. See Figure 1.3.

Table 1.2 Freddie Mac Summarized Financial Statements 1999–2008
10-year Summary (in millions)

			Income Statement			
Date	Sales	EBIT	Depreciation	Total net income	EPS	Tax Rate (%)
12/08	40,436.0	-44,569.0	0.0	-50,119.0	-34.6	0.00
12/07	41,036.0	-5,977.0	0.0	-3,094.0	-5.37	0.00
12/06	40,173.0	2,282.0	0.0	2,327.0	3.00	-1.97
12/05	35,584.0	2,530.0	0.0	2,172.0	2.81	14.15
12/04	35,603.0	3,727.0	0.0	2,937.0	3.94	21.20
12/03	37,098.0	7,018.0	0.0	4,816.0	6.68	31.38
12/02	38,476.0	14,803.0	0.0	10,090.0	14.17	31.84
12/01	35,368.0	4,454.0	0.0	3,115.0	4.16	30.06
12/00	29,182.0	5,170.0	0.0	3,666.0	5.02	29.09
12/99	22,792.0	3,161.0	0.0	2,218.0	2.95	29.83

		Balance Sheet		
Date	Current Assets	Current liabilities	Long-term debt	Shares outstanding
12/08	850,963.0	881,694.0	407,907.0	647.3 Mil
12/07	794,368.0	767,644.0	442,636.0	646.3 Mil
12/06	804,910.0	777,996.0	459,077.0	661.3 Mil
12/05	806,222.0	779,031.0	460,260.0	692.7 Mil
12/04	795,284.0	763,868.0	449,394.0	690.6 Mil
12/03	803,449.0	771,962.0	444,351.0	688.6 Mil
12/02	752,249.0	720,919.0	421,267.0	687.4 Mil
12/01	641,100.0	621,476.0	314,141.0	695.3 Mil
12/00	459,297.0	444,460.0	243,323.0	692.6 Mil
12/99	386,684.0	375,159.0	185,186.0	695.1 Mil

Source: MSN. Money, 2010 Thomson Reuters,
http://moneycentral.msn.com/investor/invsub/results/statemnt.aspx?Symbol=FRE&lstStatement=10YearSummary&
stmtView=Ann

The Federal Government decided to support Freddie Mac and Fannie Mae so that it could weather this difficult period. The U.S. Department of the Treasury acquired $1 billion in Freddie Mac senior preferred stock, paying a rate of 10 percent a year with a total investment value of $100 billion.

Figure 1.3 Freddie Mac Daily Stock Prices 2000–2009

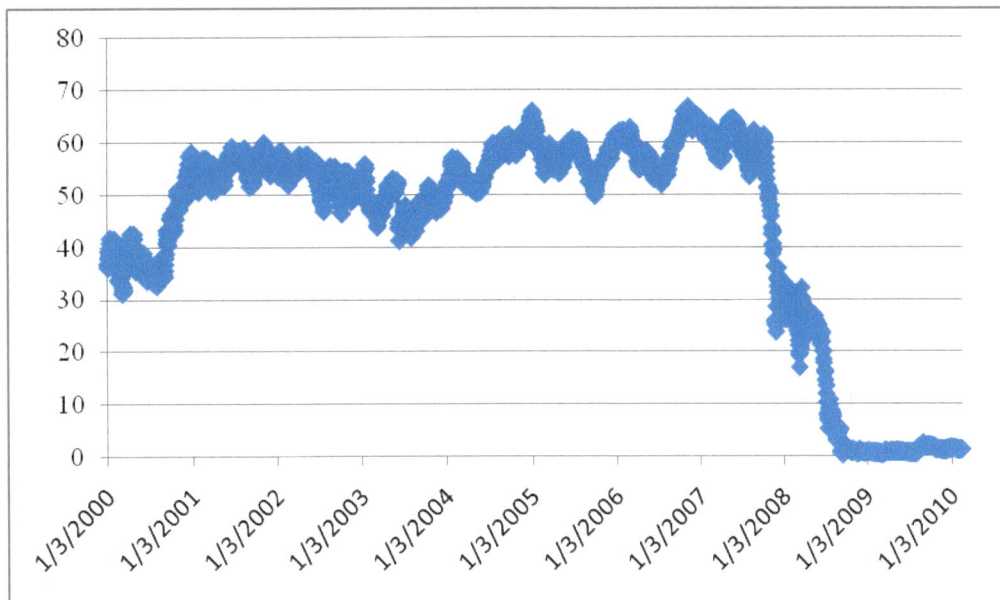

Source: Constructed with data from Yahoo Finance

COLLAPSE OF AMERICAN INTERNATIONAL GROUP (AIG)

In September 2008, three rating agencies, Moody's Investors Service, Standard & Poor's Corporation, and Fitch Investor Service downgraded AIG to below "AA" as AIG tried desperately to raise more capital. One of the rating agencies, Fitch Investor Service, believed that AIG's ability to raise funds was extremely limited because of its plummeting stock price, widening yields on its debt, and difficult capital market conditions.

The 91-year-old American insurance company originated in China when an American, Cornelius Vander Starr, started selling insurance in Shanghai in 1919 before the company relocated to New York City. It expanded regionally and globally through subsidiaries into other markets with the British headquarters in London, the European headquarters in Paris, and its Asian headquarters office in Hong Kong. It also has a presence in other parts of the world such as Africa, Australia, the Middle East, North America, and South America.

As of December 2007, AIG had a net tangible asset of $86.387 billion and net profit of $6.2 billion, down 55. 87 percent from the previous year's $14.048 billion net profit. In 2008, it appeared in Forbes Global2000, a list of the top 2000 public companies in the world. This ranking is based on a mix of four metrics: sales, profit, assets, and market value. The degree of a company's exposure to risk is not included in the matrix. According to the 2008 Forbes Global2000 public companies list, AIG was the eighteenth largest public company in the world. AIG was one of the thirty-one blue-chip companies listed on the DOW Jones Industrial Average Index. So how did this long-established, highly respected, highly capitalized company with a global presence become illiquid? According to the Bank for International Settlement:

> Through its Financial Products Group, headquartered in London, American International Group (AIG) managed to sell enormous amounts of credit risk insurance without the financial resources necessary to cover potential payments. By end-June 2008, AIG had taken $446 billion in notional credit risk exposure as a seller of credit risk protection via *credit default swaps (CDS)*. A CDS contract is a credit derivative that, for a specified bond issuer, protects

the buyer against a default or debt restructuring. AIG's unhedged sales of nearly half a trillion dollars of insurance represented a significant concentration of credit risk in a market participant that ultimately did not have the necessary loss absorption capacity. The widespread bond defaults during the recent crisis imposed substantial losses on AIG and other sellers of risk insurance.[5]

AIG also sold insurance on esoteric asset-backed security pools of collateralized asset obligations, prime mortgages, subprime mortgages, Alt-A mortgages, and collateralized loan obligations. These were sources of premium income that enabled AIG to maintain very robust earnings in the past, and its earnings were robust. However, in this crisis situation of unprecedented bond and mortgage defaults and accumulation of toxic assets and the banks' inability to dispose of these assets, AIG's overwhelming assumption of such credit exposure resulted in the company's liquidity crisis.

AIG's liquidity crisis was not helped when, in 2006, the SEC announced the filing and settlement of charges that AIG had committed securities fraud. The settlement was part of a global resolution of federal and state actions under which AIG had to pay in excess of $1.6 billion to resolve claims related to improper accounting, bid rigging, and practices involving workers' compensation funds. In addition to this, there were fresh charges that were under investigation by the SEC.

The stock market reacted. On September 15, 2008, the share price of AIG slumped by about 61 percent from the last trade of 242.8 on Friday, September 12, 2008, to 95.2 on Monday, September 15, 2008. This slide continued to March 5, 2009, when one share of AIG traded for $7, an all-time low. See Figure 1.4.

Figure 1.4 AIG Daily Stock Prices 2000–2009

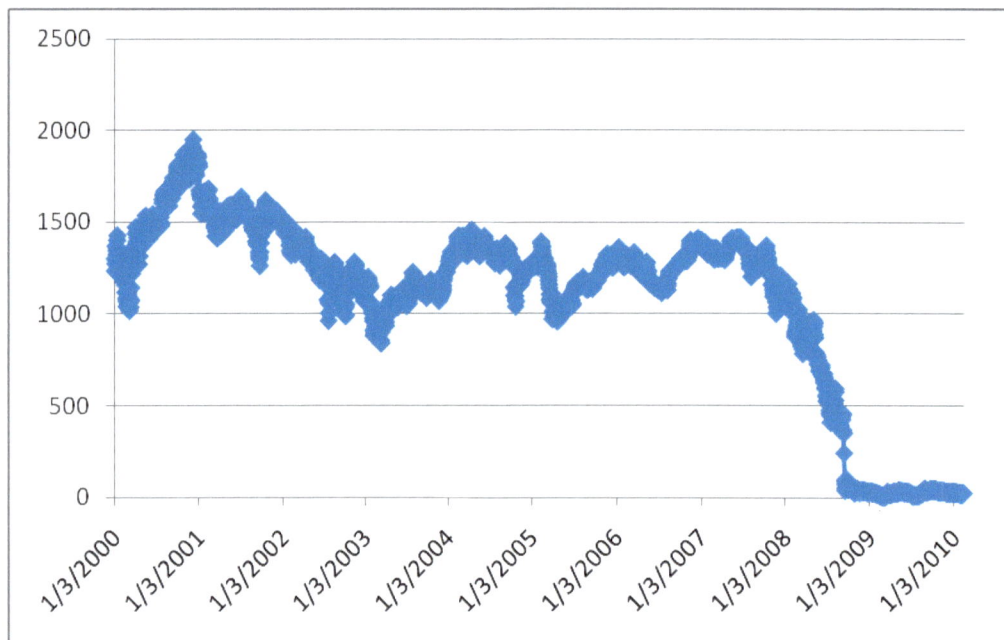

Source: Constructed with data from Yahoo Finance

The Federal Reserve Bank came to the aid of AIG. On September 16, 2008, the Fed created an $85 billion credit facility to enable AIG to meet increased collateral obligations because of the downgrade of its credit rating in exchange for the issuance of a stock warrant to the Federal Reserve Bank for 79

[5] Stephan G. Cecchetti, Jacob Gyntelberg, and Marc Hollanders, "Central counterparties for over-the-counter derivatives," BIS Quarterly Review, September 2009, p, 45, http://www.bis.org/publ/qtrpdf/r_qt0909f.htm.

percent of the equity of AIG. By May 2009, the Federal Reserve Bank n conjunction with the U.S. Treasury had increased the potential financial support to AIG with an investment of as much as $70 billion, a $60 billion credit line, and $52.5 billion to buy mortgage-based assets owned or guaranteed by AIG. This increased the total amount available to AIG to $182.5 billion.

OTHER BANK FAILURES

On September 14, 2008, the 94-year-old Merrill Lynch & Co., a globally renowned full brokerage firm reputed to be the largest U.S. retail investment firm by number of brokers (more than 20,000 brokers in all) with a total of $78.2 billion in assets as of December 2007, agreed to sell itself to Bank of America Corp. for $50 billion. The banking giant had suffered significant losses from its involvement in investments in the subprime mortgage crisis.

At the end of 2007, the company had recorded net earnings of over $1 billion. That performance represented a 37 percent decline from the previous year's earnings. The reported record loss of $16.7 billion was after write-downs on assets infected by subprime mortgages. Merrill Lynch reported a first quarter 2008 net loss from continuing operations of $1.97 billion. It is believed that it was this challenging market environment, which continued to deteriorate throughout 2008, that forced Merrill Lynch to accept the takeover by Bank of America.

Many banks, such as Merrill Lynch, that were seriously involved in subprime lending experienced severe financial difficulties. Wachovia was not an exception. On September 29, 2008, Citigroup announced it would buy Wachovia's banking operations for $2.1 billion in stock. It would also assume another $53 billion in debt. Many other FDIC insured banks also failed. In 2009 and 2010, according to the FDIC updated information, more than 170 and 353 banks failed respectively.

The Glass-Steagall Act (48 Stat. 162), also known as the Banking Act of 1933, established the FDIC as an independent agency of the U.S. Government that protects depositors' funds placed in FDIC insured institutions. The FDIC deposit insurance is backed by the full faith and credit of the U.S. Government. Because of the Federal Deposit Corporation Improvement Act of 1991 (P.L. 102-242, 105 Stat. 2236), the FDIC also maintains stability and public confidence in the nation's financial system by insuring deposits, examining and supervising financial institutions for safety, soundness, and consumer protection, and managing receiverships. It guarantees the safety of deposits in member banks, currently up to $250,000 per depositor per bank. This maximum FDIC insurance coverage is temporary and expires on December 31, 2013. After that date, the maximum FDIC insurance coverage for a depositor's funds in one FDIC bank reverts to the limit before 2008, which is $100,000 for all account categories except IRAs and certain other retirement accounts; these remain at $250,000 per depositor.

The presence of the FDIC during this crisis and economic recession is helping to smooth the negative impact of bank failures on depositors. During the Great Depression, the official unemployment rate was 25 percent. It is estimated that 4,000 banks failed during the year 1933 alone. In all, 9,000 banks failed during the decade of the 1930s. By 1933, an average depositor had lost $140,000. The stock market had declined 75 percent since 1929, and bank runs were common. There was no insurance for customers' deposits in banks until 1993.

ECONOMIC RECESSION

In 2008, the DOW lost 48.63 percent of its value. There were bank failures and takeovers, jobs were lost in the hundreds of thousands, and, in the presence of unprecedented foreclosures, housing prices collapsed in the mortgage market. It was not surprising that the U.S. economy sank into a recession. On December 1, 2008, the NBER announced that the United States had been in a recession since December 2007. The NBER cited the deterioration in the labor market as the key for its decision that the recession started in 2007. Since the Second World War, there have been several recessions, but none has been as severe or as long as the last recession.

CONCLUSION

In the fall of 2008, the stock markets in the United States plummeted, and for several months continued to react to concerns about unprecedented foreclosures, corporate failures, government bailouts, and the collapse of the banking sector. The negative effect of the financial crisis was exacerbated as more businesses continued to fail. Huge financial losses suffered by individuals and businesses in the stock market led to a decline in spending. Businesses laid off workers in the millions resulting in a very high unemployment rate. All these culminated in a deep recession.

It has been argued that the decision to allow Lehman Brothers to fail instead of financially supporting its survival or financially supporting a takeover, as was the case with Fannie Mae and Freddie Mac, ignited the financial crisis. Perhaps, that is one of the immediate causes of the financial crisis. We will learn in Chapter 3 that many factors caused the financial crisis. Before examining those factors, it is important to understand the economic background underlying the financial crisis and economic recession. Chapter 2 examines the economics behind financial crises and economic recessions.

BIBLIOGRAPHY

A Glossary of Political Economy Terms, S.V. "Open Market Operation," http://www.auburn.edu/~johnspm/gloss/open_market_operations (accessed March 7, 2010).

Cecchetti, Stephen G., Jacob Gyntelberg, and Marc Hollanders. "Central Counterparties for Over-the-Counter Derivatives." *BIS Quarterly Review*, September 2009, http://www.bis.org/publ/qtrpdf/r_qt0909f.htm.

Chasan, Emily. "UPDATE 1-Lehman Brothers Examiner Ends Probes of Collapse." *Reuters*, February 8, 2010. http://www.reuters.com/article/idUSN0820300520100208.

"Farming in the 1930's, Bank Failures." *Wessels Living History Farm*, March 7, 2010. http://www.livinghistoryfarm.org/farminginthe30s/money_08.html.

FDIC. "Deposit Insurance Simplification Fact Sheet." March 7, 2010. http://www.fdic.gov/deposit/deposits/difactsheet.html.

FDIC. "Mission, Vision, and Values." March 7, 2010. http://www.fdic.gov/about/mission/index.html

Federal Home Loan Mortgage Corporation Act of 1970. Public Law No. 91-351, 84 Stat. 450, Approved July 24, 1970, As amended through July 21, 2010.

Federal Reserve Bank. "U.S. Treasury and Federal Reserve Board Announce Participation in AIG Restructuring Plan," press release, March 2, 2009. http://www.federalreserve.gov/newsevents/press/other/20090302a.htm.

"Freddie Mac Quarterly Statements." *Yahoo Finance*, http://finance.yahoo.com/q/is?s=Fmcc.ob, last modified January 20, 2009.

Geisst, Charles. *The Last Partnerships: Inside the Last Wall Street Money Dynasties*. McGraw-Hill Professional, 2001.

Karnitschnig, Matthew, Carrick Mollenkamp, and Dan Fitzpatrick. "Bank of America to Buy Merrill." *Wall Street Journal Digital Network*, September 15, 2008, http://online.wsj.com/article/SB122142278543033525.html?mod=special_coverage.

Keoun, Bradley. "Merrill Posts Record Loss on $16.7 Billion Writedown (Update6)." *Bloomberg*, January 17, 2010. http://www.bloomberg.com/apps/news?pid=20601087&sid=ap70wMBpqI4Q.

"Lawsuit Threat to Merrill Lynch." *BBC News*, August 16, 2008. http://news.bbc.co.uk/2/hi/business/7564630.stm.

"Lehman Brothers Annual Report 2007." http://www.slideshare.net/QuarterlyEarningsReports3/lehman-brothers-annual-report-2007 (accessed March 7, 2010).

Luhby, Tami. "AIG: Pressure Mounts with Downgrades." *CNNMoney*, September 21, 2008. http://money.cnn.com/2008/09/15/news/companies/AIG/?postversion=2008091519.

Malloy, Michael P., Glass-Steagall Act (1933), Major Acts of Congress, 2004, *Encyclopedia.com*, October 10, 2010, http://www.encyclopedia.com (accessed October 7, 2010).

Merrill Lynch. "2008 First Quarter Report," press release, http://www.ml.com/index.asp?id=7695_7696_8149_88278_95339_96026 (accessed March 7, 2010).

Merrill Lynch Bank. "2007 Financial Statement." http://ir.ml.com/phoenix.zhtml?c=231864&p=financialsSub (accessed March 7, 2010).

"Profile: American International Group, Inc. (AIG.N)." *Reuters*, http://www.reuters.com/finance/stocks/companyProfile?symbol=AIG (accessed March 7, 2010).

Son, Hugh. "AIG Trustees Shun 'Shadow Board,' Seek Directors (Update 2)." *Bloomberg*, May 13, 2009. http://www.bloomberg.com/apps/news?pid=newsarchive&sid=aaog3i4yUopo&refer=us

Securities and Exchange Commission v. American International Group, Inc., Case No. 06 CV 1000 (S.D.N.Y.) (2006).

Securities and Exchange Commission v. Bear, Stearns & Co. Inc., 03 CV 2937 (WHP) (S.D.N.Y.) (2003).

Securities and Exchange Commission. "SEC Settles Fraud Charges with Bear Stearns for Late Trading and Market Timing Violations, Firm To Pay $250 Million in Disgorgement and Penalties," press release, March 16, 2006, http://www.sec.gov/news/press/2006-38.htm.

Stone, Amey. "A Primer on the Mutual-Fund Scandal." *Bloomberg Businessweek*, September 22, 2003, http://www.businessweek.com/bwdaily/dnflash/sep2003/nf20030922_7646.htm.

U.S. Department of Labor, Bureau of Labor Statistics, http://data.bls.gov/timeseries/CES0000000001?output_view=net_1mth, (accessed October 26, 2011)

CHAPTER 2

ECONOMIC BACKGROUND TO THE 2008 U.S. FINANCIAL CRISIS AND ECONOMIC RECESSION

INTRODUCTION

It is important to review the financial and economic situation prior to the financial crisis and economic recession. In this chapter, we discuss the economic data relating to gross domestic product, (GDP), balance of payments, employment, personal income situation, mortgage statistics, corporate income, industry performance, stock market performance, and property values.

ANALYSIS OF THE U.S. ECONOMIC TRENDS FROM 1999–2008

The United States is one of the largest and most technologically developed countries in the world. Its economy is about three times that of Japan, the second largest economy in the world. The U.S. economy is approximately equal to the economy of the "eurozone" or the euro area.

The euro is one of the world's most powerful currencies. It is used by more than 320 million Europeans in twenty-two countries. The sixteen Member States of the European Union, that use the euro as their sole legal currency are Austria, Belgium, Germany, Ireland, Greece, Spain, France, Italy, Cyprus, Luxembourg, Malta, The Netherlands, Portugal, Slovenia, Slovakia, and Finland. Some countries not in the EU also use the euro as a legal tender in one form or the other. Such countries include Andorra, Kosovo, Monaco, Montenegro, San Marino, and Vatican City. Countries in the eurozone that do not use the euro as their single currency include Bulgaria, Czech Republic, Denmark, Estonia, Latvia, Lithuania, Hungary, Poland, Romania, Sweden, and the United Kingdom.

The United States is a market-driven economy where private individuals and businesses make most of the decisions, and the Federal and State Governments buy needed goods and services predominantly in the private marketplace. The GDP of the United States grew by 50 percent from $9.2 trillion in 1999 to $14.2 trillion in 2008. Taxation is responsible for much of this. The various sources of income include taxes on individual income: social security/social insurance; corporate, excise, estate, and gift taxes. Personal income and security/social insurance taxes make the greatest contribution of over 40 percent.

In 2001, a recession began. According to the NBER, the recession lasted from March to November 2001, or eight months. The NBER determined that the expansion of the U.S. economy, which started in 1991, ended in March 2001 and a recession began. The expansion in the last decade lasted exactly ten years, the longest in the NBER's chronology.

We often refer to the 2001 recession as the dot.com bubble, because we attribute the cause of this recession to the collapse of a technology bubble. Many of these technology companies were listed on the NASDAQ. Between 1995 and 2000, there were sharp increases in the stock price of many of these companies. The technology boom of the 1990s was accompanied by intense speculative activities that unfortunately reached unsustainable heights. This occurred in a period of liberal Federal Reserve Bank monetary policies that created huge increases in the money supply and loanable funds, which boosted speculative tendencies. As the stock prices of the companies in the technology sector fell amid several instances of corporate misconduct, accounting irregularities, and fraud, the dampening of investor confidence was inevitable. Investors abandoned the stock market by dumping their stock.

The terrorist attack on the United States on September 11, 2001, further exacerbated the already gloomy situation. For example, between January 1995 and March 2000, the NASDAQ index increased from 743.58 to 5048.62, an increase of 578.88 percent. It declined to 1820.57 by March 29, 2001, a decline of about 64 percent. This signaled a recession. The loss of value due to the dot.com bubble crash is estimated at $5 trillion. See Figure 2.1. Even though the recession ended in November 2001, many of the dot.com companies failed. Approximately 50 percent of them survived. The investment climate remained pessimistic and unemployment remained high.

Figure 2.1 NASDAQ Daily Index Values January 3, 1995 to March 30, 2001

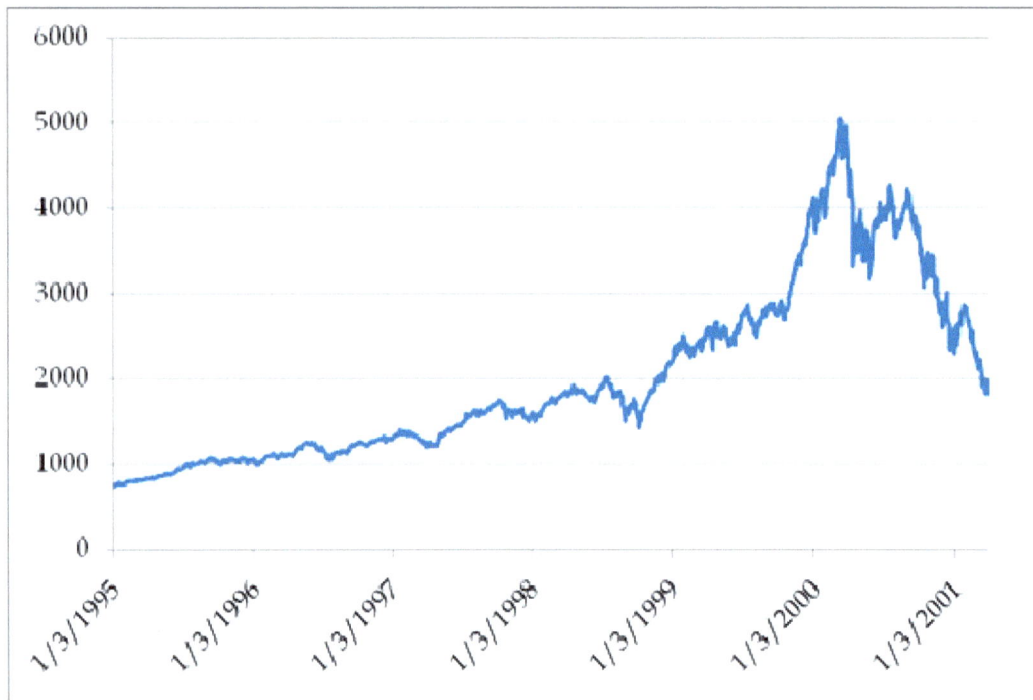

Source: Constructed with data from Yahoo Finance

After this short decline in GDP, the GDP continued to expand. Every quarterly GDP reflected a growth over the previous quarter until the first quarter of 2008, when the U.S. economy experienced a decline in GDP growth. See Figure 2.2.

Figure 2.2 U.S. Quarterly GDP 1999 to 2009(in billions)

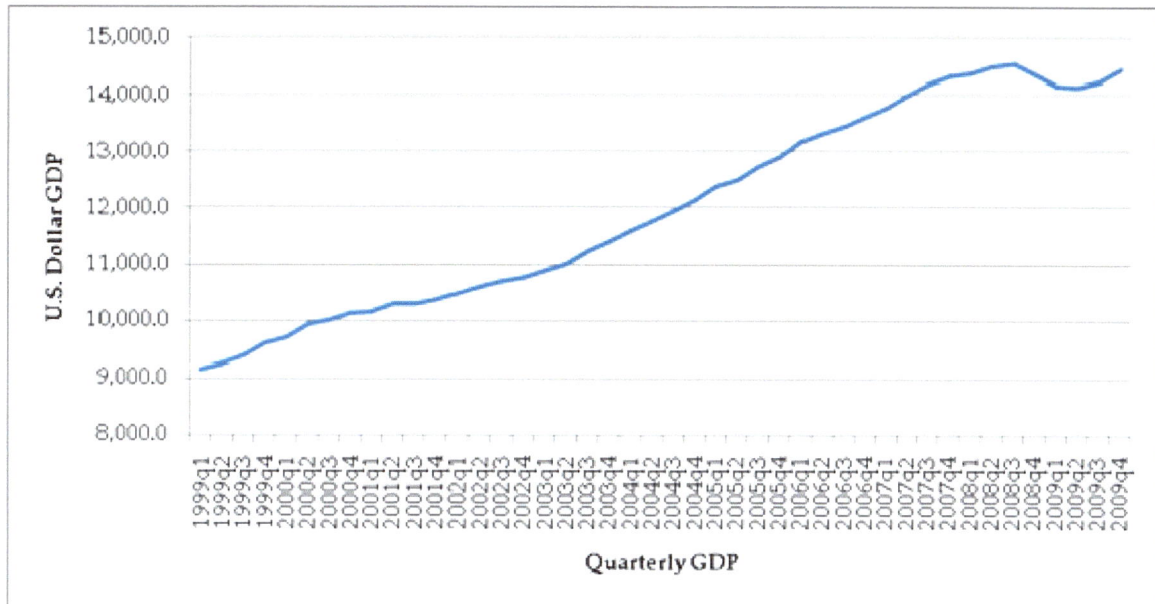

Source: Constructed with data from the Bureau of Economic Analysis, http://www.google.com/publicdata?ds=wb-wdi&met=ny_gdp_mktp_cd&idim=country:USA&dl=en&hl=en&q=us+gdp+chart

The enormous increase in personal income during the period contributed to this growth in GDP. Because the tax on personal income is the greatest component of the GDP, as the income from this source increased so did the GDP. There was generally lower unemployment in the United States since 1980, except for 2003 when the unemployment rate jumped to 6 percent. See Figure 2.3.

Figure 2.3 U.S. Unemployment Rates 1999–202008

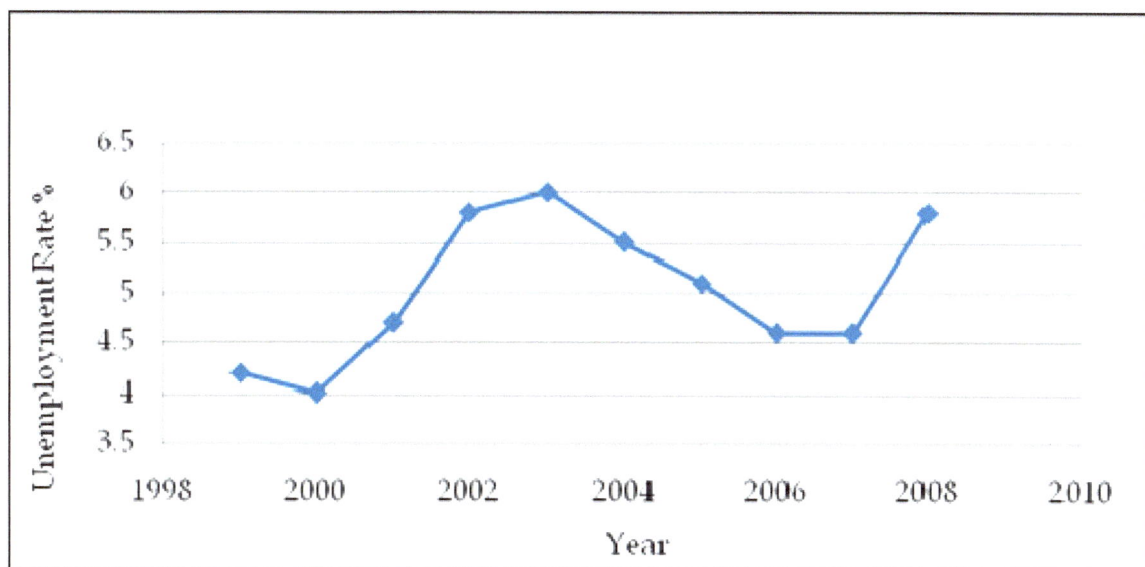

Source: Constructed with data from the Bureau of Labor Statistics, http://data.bls.gov/PDQ/servlet/SurveyOutputServlet

In addition, the population of the United States increased significantly from 227,225,000 in 1980 to 304,059,724 in 2008. The percentage of the total population that was employed did not differ significantly between 1999 and 2008, but the number of employed workers increased from 139,368,000 in 1999 to 154,287,000 in 2008.

Personal income grew in the United States from $7.91 trillion in 1999 to $12.2389 trillion in 2008, an increase of about 55 percent. As more people gained employment and kept their jobs, payments into the social security/social insurance taxes increased. Another factor that contributed to the increases in GDP was an increase in corporate profits. Total corporate profits were $720.6 billion in 1999, and they increased to $1.0723 trillion in 2007, representing an increase of 49 percent. This surge in corporate profits declined to $791.3 billion, just a little over the 1999 level of profits. The year 2006 recorded the highest level of corporate profits. See Figure 2.4.

Figure 2.4 U.S. Corporate Profits 1999 to 2008(in billions)

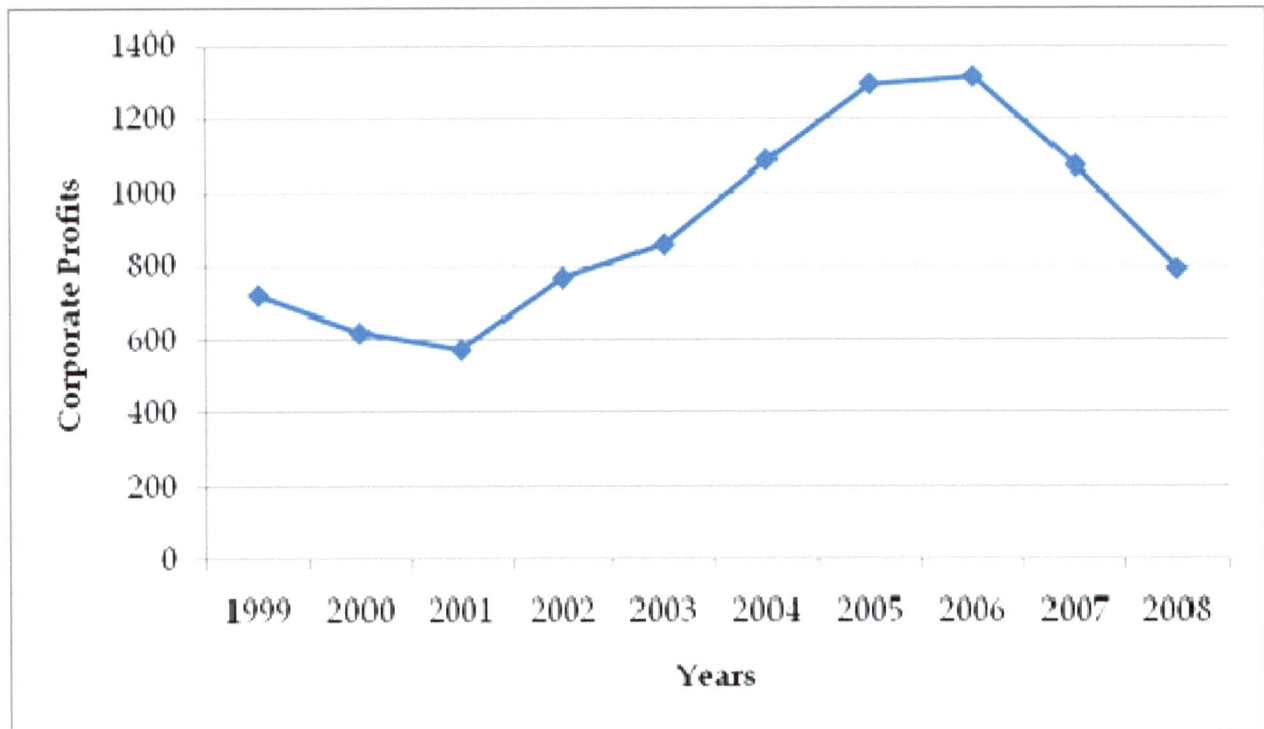

Source: Constructed with data from the Bureau of Economic Analysis,
           http://www.bea.gov/national/nipaweb/TableView.asp?SelectedTable=51&ViewSeries=NO&Java=no&Request3P
           lace=N&3Place=N&FromView=YES&Freq=Qtr&

The best performing industries in the past five years include: electric utilities, copper, agricultural chemicals, steel and iron, online retail, health information services, consumer services, oil and gas drilling and exploration, cigarettes, and beverages/brewers. The great performance of companies in these industries is probably necessity driven. Consumers must buy what they need. The elasticity of demand of certain products such as utilities, commodities, and beverages is very low. An increase in the population increases demand and turnover. The convenience of delivery and the reduced cost of substitute products account for some of the success of consumer services and online retail. See Table 2.1 for the five-year percentage return for these industries.

Table 2.1 Top Ten Performing Industries in the Past Five Years

Industry	5-year return in %
Electric utilities	31.72
Copper	28.19
Agricultural chemicals	23.83
Steel & iron	21.02
Online retail	22.01
Health information services	17.17
Consumer services	17.15
Oil & gas drilling & exploration	15.48
Cigarettes	15.46
Beverages – brewers	14.85

Note: Data through 2/26/2010; returns are market-cap weighted.

Source: Morningstar, http://news.morningstar.com/stockReturns/CapWtdIndustryReturns.html

The worst performing industries in the past five years were music and video stores, toy and hobby stores, mortgage investment, broadcasting/radio, resorts and casinos, manufactured housing, reinsurance, residential construction, and publishing/newspapers. Not surprisingly, many housing-related industries, such as mortgage investment, manufactured housing, residential construction, and reinsurance, performed badly in the ten years prior to the financial crisis. This was probably due to the implications of the subprime mortgage crisis that started in 2006. In Chapter 4, I discuss the subprime mortgage crisis and its implications in detail. The introduction of cheaper online marketing of videos negatively affected performance of music and video stores. A typical example is Netflix where a consumer, for $18 a month, can watch ninety movies on a laptop.

Table 2.2 Worst Ten Performing Industries in the Past Five Years

Industry	5-year return in %
Music & video stores	-44.11
Toy & hobby stores	-31.81
Mortgage investment	-27.65
Broadcasting – radio	-27.32
Resorts & casinos	-23.99
Manufactured housing	-22.90
Reinsurance	-22.49
Insurance – title	-21.81
Residential construction	-20.39
Publishing – newspaper	-19.31

Note: Data through 2/26/2010; returns are market-cap weighted.

Source: Morningstar, http://news.morningstar.com/stockReturns/CapWtdIndustryReturns.html

BUDGET DEFICITS

The huge increase in budget deficits during the period 1999 to 2008 helped to fuel the economic expansion that occurred during the period. The budget deficit in any fiscal year is the difference between the U. S. Government's receipts from taxes and other revenues and the amount of money the Government spends, called outlays. The items included in the deficit are considered on either budget or off budget. The total debt normally represents accumulated deficits plus accumulated off-budget surpluses. The on-budget deficits require the U.S. Treasury to borrow money to raise cash needed to keep the Government operating. The Government, through the Treasury and the Reserve Bank, borrows the money needed by selling securities like Treasury bills, notes, bonds, and savings bonds to the public (individuals, companies, and governments, including foreign governments). The Treasury securities issued to the public and to government trust funds (intra governmental holdings) then become part of the total debt.

The surplus in 1999 was U.S. $1,873 million. The estimated budget deficit for 2007 was –$465,878 billion. The U.S. total public debt outstanding by the end of 1999 was $5.78 trillion. By the end of 2007, it had increased to $9.229 trillion and to $10.7 trillion by the end of 2008. The public holds about 60 percent of this outstanding total debt and 40 percent is intergovernmental holdings. Many individuals and companies that purchased U.S. securities are our creditors along with many foreign governments. Some of the foreign governments that hold treasury securities are Japan and the People's Republic of China (mainland) with the highest holdings of 21.27 percent and 20.90 percent, respectively.[6] Other foreign government holders of U.S. Treasury securities are the United Kingdom (including the Channel Islands and the Isle of Man), several oil exporting countries,[7] Brazil, Hong Kong, Russia, Luxembourg, Taiwan, Switzerland, Germany, Canada, Ireland, North and South Korea, Singapore, France, Thailand, Mexico, Norway, India, Turkey, Egypt, The Netherlands, Sweden, Italy, Colombia, Israel, Belgium, Australia, Chile, Philippines, Malaysia, and others. See Table 2.3 for the dollar value of U.S. securities held by foreigners.

Table 2.3 Major Foreign Holders of Treasury Securities (in billions)

Country	December 31 2009
Japan	768.8
Peoples Republic of China (mainland)	755.4
United Kingdom (including Channel Islands and Isle of Man)	302.5
Oil Exporting countries	186.8
Caribbean Banking Centers	184.7
Brazil	160.6
Hong Kong	152.9
Russia	118.5
Luxembourg	99.9

[6] Estimated foreign holdings of U.S. Treasury marketable and nonmarketable bills, bonds, and notes reported under the Treasury International Capital (TIC) reporting system are based on annual Surveys of Foreign Holdings of U.S. Securities and on monthly data.
[7] Oil exporters include Ecuador, Venezuela, Indonesia, Bahrain, Iran, Iraq, Kuwait, Oman, Qatar, Saudi Arabia, the United Arab Emirates, Algeria, Gabon, Libya, and Nigeria.

Country	December 31 2009
Taiwan	79.6
Switzerland	76.0
Germany	52.7
Canada	48.3
Ireland	39.3
South Korea	39.2
Singapore	38.1
France	37.5
Thailand	35.4
Mexico	31.1
Norway	29.7
India	29.6
Turkey	28.3
Egypt	24.8
Netherlands	19.8
Sweden	19.1
Italy	18.7
Colombia	15.8
Israel	15.3
Belgium	15.2
Australia	14.1
Chile	12.5
Philippines	12.2
Malaysia	11.0
Other countries	140.7
Total	3614.0

Source: Department of the Treasury/Federal Reserve Board, February 16, 2010, http://www.ustreas.gov/tic/mfh.txt; http://www.investorwords.com/5200/U.S._Treasury_Securities.html

The increase in the U.S. budget and consequent total debt has been a source of great concern especially with regard to the huge number of foreign participants. Between 2001 and 2008, our total public debt increased from $5.8 to $10 trillion, an increase of 72 percent. The increase in gross public debt between 1990 and 2000 of 76 percent is equally alarming. Since the 1980s, the acceleration in the increase in public debt has been very worrisome. The increase in gross public debt between 1980 and 1990 was 252.7 percent, which almost tripled the 1980 public debt level. Public debt has been a factor of U.S. fiscal policy since the American Revolution when the government borrowed significantly to finance the war.

The reasons why governments borrow are very similar to why individuals borrow. Imagine for a second that you just graduated from college and you were lucky enough to get a job. You want to buy a house in a better neighborhood than where your parents lived; you want to buy a car, and you want to go to a graduate school. You desire these things because you want to maintain a good quality of life. You are likely to borrow to do some of these things. The reason for government borrowing may be different because of governmental responsibilities such as protecting the sovereignty of the nation and ensuring national security, which may include financing a war effort. In addition to these responsibilities, governments have social responsibilities, and they may sometimes borrow to finance public works, especially when widespread unemployment exists. This form of public debt is justified in part by its long-term social utility. The best way, in normal situations, to finance government activities is through taxation and other sources of government revenue. Because of the negative political consequences of increasing taxation and reducing spending in a recession, most governments normally choose to increase governmental spending. They normally justify this action, because it has expansionary effects on employment and production during times of high unemployment.

Some of these normal reasons apply to the period of 1999 to 2008. There was a recession in 2001. There was an act of terrorist aggression against the United States on September 11, 2001. This led to a flight of investors in the U.S. inbound Foreign Direct Investments (FDI) to the U.S. which declined from $321.3 billion in 2002 to $63.8 billion in 2003.[8] This development might have helped to precipitate the 2001 recession. Therefore, there is justification for the huge increase in public debt between 1999 and 2010. Factors that increased our public debt include the following: reduction in corporate and personal income taxation, financing of two wars in Afghanistan and Iraq, increased expenditures on national security following September 11, 2001 attack, and unfavorable economic cycles such as a recession.

Tax cuts may act as an incentive for investment and increased consumption. This depends, on the original tax rate. Increased investment and consumption on the part of the individual are likely to contribute to increased economic activity, thus stimulating the economy. A tax cut has two effects. It generally increases the real income of those who have benefitted from the tax cut and reduces the real income of the Government, because the Government will not receive the income that would have been the basis of a tax. Free market economists argue that the effect of a tax cut is likely to be neutral, if the Government does not borrow money to make up for the lost revenue. In addition, if we assume that the individuals who befitted from the tax cut purchased goods solely from within the country, a tax cut improves economic welfare as individuals are empowered to consume what they want. On the other hand, supply-side economists argue that if the Government increases spending in spite of the tax cut and individuals spend their income resulting from the tax cut on commodities or services sourced from within the country, the economy will receive a stimulus. When the Government increases spending and the recipients of the tax cut spend the additional money mainly on goods and services from outside the country, a deflation can occur and balance of payments difficulties may result.

During his first term in office, President George W. Bush introduced an across-the-board federal tax cut. The exercise created a new lowest tax rate, 10 percent for the first $8,350 of taxable dollars earned. Between 2000 and 2003, the tax cut reduced the rate of tax on taxable income between $33,950 and $82,250 from 28 percent in 2000 to 25 percent in 2003. The Government reduced the personal income tax rate for taxable income of $82,250 and $171,550, from 31 percent to 28 percent in 2003. For the top brackets of taxable income $171,550 to $372,950 and $372,950 and above, the rates were reduced between 2000 and 2003 to 33 percent and 35 percent, respectively. In addition to these incremental tax cuts, it was expected that the child tax credit would double from $500 to $1,000 by 2011. See Table 2.4.

---

[8] Organization for International Investment, Foreign Direct Investment in the United States, March 18, 2010, http://www.ofii.org/docs/FDIUS_2010.pdf

Table 2.4 Federal Personal Income Tax Rates Structure between 1993 and 2010

Personal income	Taxable income between			
	1993–2000	2001	2002	2003–2010
0 – 8,350	-	-	10%	10%
8,350 – 33,950	15%	15%	15%	15%
33,950 – 82,250	28%	27.5%	27%	25%
82,250 – 171,550	31%	30.5%	30%	28%
171,550 – 372,950	36%	35.5%	35%	33%
372,950 – above	39.6%	39.1%	38.6%	35%

Source: Federal Income Tax Guide, 2010.

The Economic Growth and Tax Relief Reconciliation Act of 2001 introduced these tax cuts. The Jobs and Growth Tax Relief and the Reconciliation Act of 2003 accelerated these tax reductions. The estimated savings for taxpayers was $1.3 trillion over ten years. The Jobs and Growth Tax Relief and Reconciliation Act of 2003 also reduced the top tax rate for both capital gains and dividends to 15 percent. Two tax bills signed in 2005 and 2006 extended through to 2010 the favorable rates on capital gains and dividends introduced by legislation in 2003. This raised the exemption levels for the Alternative Minimum Tax, and enacted new tax incentives designed to persuade individuals to save more for retirement. All these personal income tax modifications that are favorable to individuals, promoted savings and consumption that energized the economy and the stock market boom.

BALANCE OF PAYMENTS 1999–2008

What is the balance of payments? Individuals and businesses resident in a country, and the country's government at all levels can do business by buying and selling goods and services, engage in establishing businesses overseas (foreign direct investments), and foreign individuals and businesses can similarly do business with that country. Each country maintains a record of the transactions with residents of other countries for a period of time, usually a quarter or a year. The balance of payments is a summary of these transactions between domestic and foreign residents for a specific country over a period. If the total receipts for a particular country from all transactions from overseas exceed the total payments to foreign countries, that county will have a surplus balance of payments. However, if the total payments to foreign countries for all transactions during the period exceed the total receipts of that country from all overseas transactions, that country will have a deficit balance of payments or a negative balance of payments.

The balance of payments has various components. The current and the capital accounts usually receive the greatest attention. The current account records the flow of funds from the purchase of goods and services or the provision of income in financial assets between one country and all other countries over a specified period. The goods are often referred to as merchandised exports and imports, and examples are shoes, cars, computers, machinery, and television sets, to name a few. The balance of trade is a key component of the current account. The balance of trade represents the difference in all exports and imports, including merchandised exports and imports and exports and imports of services. Another component of the current account is the factor income. This represents income received by investors on foreign investments in financial securities. This income will be in the form of interest on debt securities, such as bonds, or dividends on equity investments, such as stock. A transfer payment is another component of the current account. It includes grants, aid, and gifts exchanged between countries. The capital account, on the other hand, records the flow of funds from the sale of assets between one country and other countries over a specified period.

The United States is very active in international trade and other business transactions across many countries and regions of the world. It has an export-import relationship for goods and services with many countries in Europe, North America, Asia, Latin America, and Africa. However, its main trading partners are Canada, China, Mexico, Japan, United Kingdom, Germany, and France. In 1999, the United States exported $966 billion worth of goods and services and imported goods and services valued at $1.23 trillion. By 2007, total exports had increased to over $1.6 trillion and total imports had increased to $2.3 trillion. In recent times, except for 2002, there was a slight decline in both imports and exports. After 2002, the volume of goods and services imported and exported by United States continued to increase with the volume of imports exceeding exports. See Figure 2.5.

Figure 2.5 U.S. Balance of Trade 1999 to 2008(in billions)

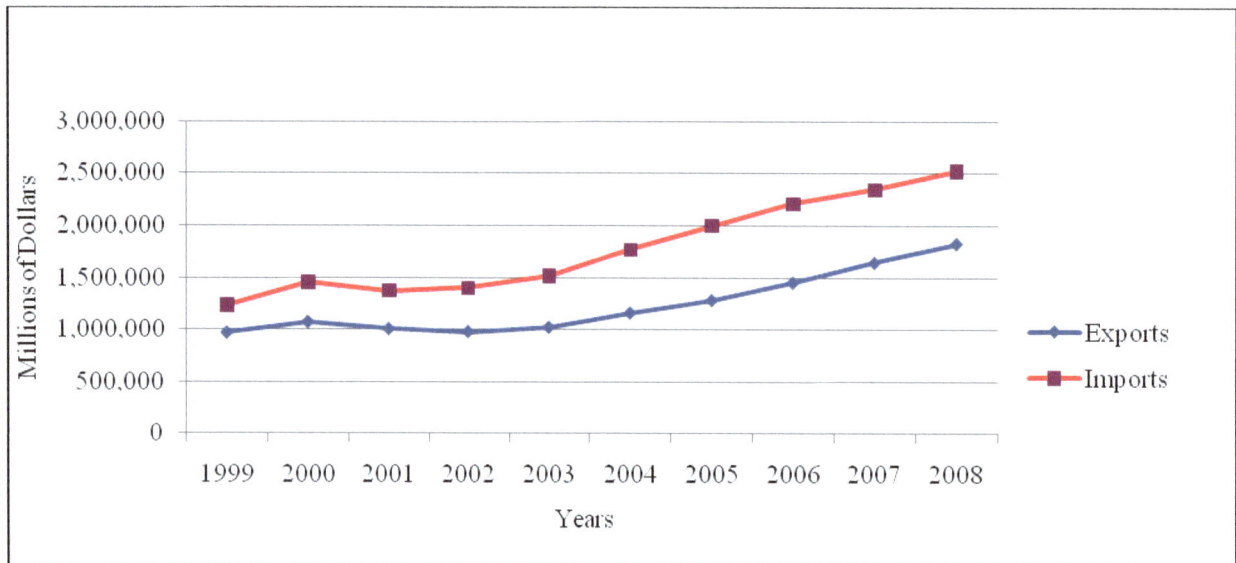

Source: Constructed with data from the Bureau of Economic Analysis,
            http://www.bea.gov/newsreleases/international/trade/trad_time_series.xls

Notice the substantial growth of both imports and exports in recent times. The amount of goods imported by the United States always exceeded the amount of goods exported to other countries. It is important to note that the value of services exported by the United States always exceeded the value of services imported by the United States. For example, in 1992, the United States exported services to the value of about $282 billion and imported services to the tune of about $199 billion. By 1997, the value of exported services had risen to approximately $506 billion and the value of imported services had risen to $375 billion.

The United States has recorded an excess in the value of U.S. imports over exports, thus achieving a balance of payments deficit since 1976. The balance of trade was just over $39 billion in December 1992, but by December 2008, it had exceeded $701 billion. This contributed significantly to the U.S. deficit depicted in Figure 2.6.

Figure 2.6 U.S. Trade Deficit 1999 to 2008(in millions)

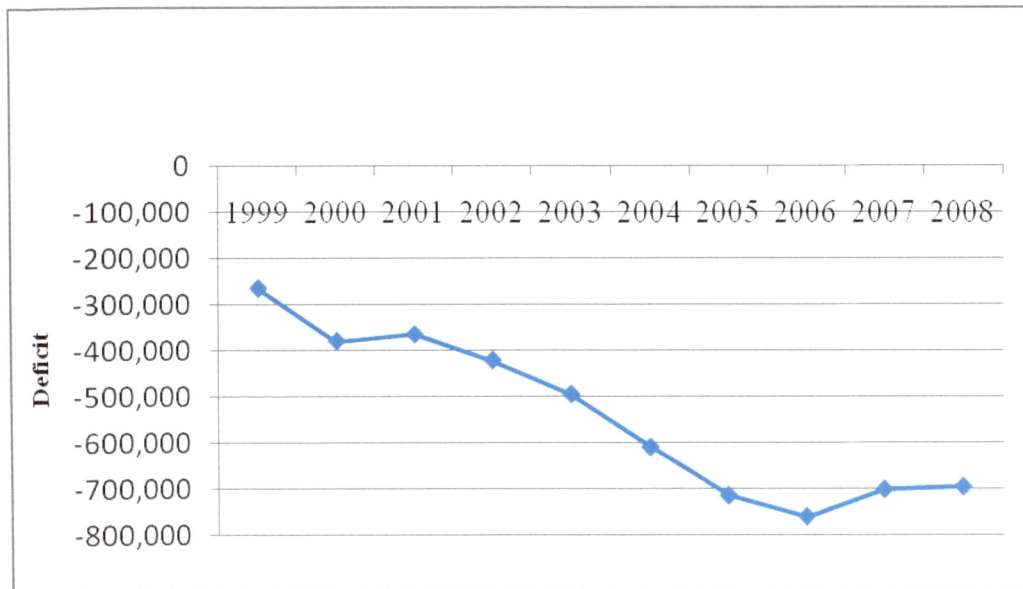

Source: Constructed with data from the Bureau of Economic Analysis, http://www.bea.gov/newsreleases/international/trade/trad_time_series.xls

This U.S. trade deficit situation seems to be attributable to trade imbalances with China and Japan. U.S. imports from China have not been in labor-intensive sectors; however, some are in office and data processing machines, telecommunications and sound equipment, electrical machinery, and appliances. Since 2000, the United States has incurred its largest bilateral trade deficit with China. Between 1999 and 2008, this deficit almost quadrupled from the 1999 deficit amount of $68.677 billion to $268.04 billion in 2008.

In 2003, China replaced Mexico as the second largest source of imports for the United States. China runs a trade surplus with the world's three major economic regions: the United States, the European Union, and Japan. The United States imports almost as much from Canada as from China. However, Canada reciprocates by importing from the United States almost in the same proportion. In 2008, the share of Chinese goods in U.S. imports was 13.4 percent, whereas the proportion of exports to China in U.S. total exports for 2008 was 3.8 percent. See Table 2.5 and Figures 2.7 and 2.8.

Table 2.5 U.S. Trade in Merchandized Goods with China 1999–2009
(in millions)

Year	Exports	Imports	Balance
1999	13,111.10	81,788.20	-68,677.10
2000	16,185.20	100,018.20	-83,833.00
2001	19,182.30	102,278.40	-83,096.10
2002	22,127.70	125,192.60	-103,064.90
2003	28,367.90	152,436.10	-124,068.20
2004	34,427.80	196,682.00	-162,254.30
2005	41,192.00	243,470.10	-202,278.10

Year	Exports	Imports	Balance
2006	53,673.00	287,774.40	-234,101.30
2007	62,936.90	321,442.90	-258,506.00
2008	69,732.80	337,772.60	-268,039.80
2009	69,576.00	296,402.10	-226,826.10

Source: U.S. Census Bureau, Foreign Trade Division, Data dissemination Branch, Washington D.C. 20233.

Figure 2.7 U.S. Exports in 2008

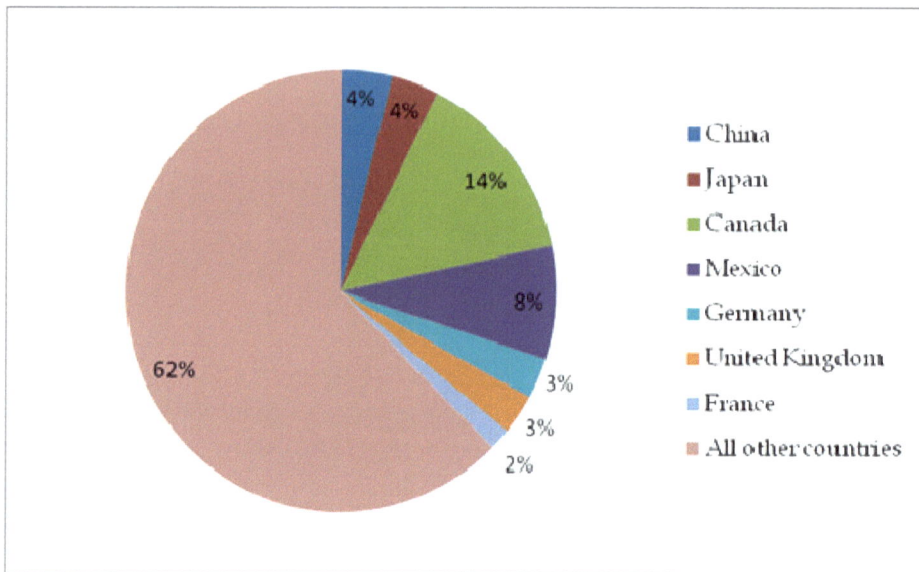

Figure 2.8 U.S. Imports in 2008

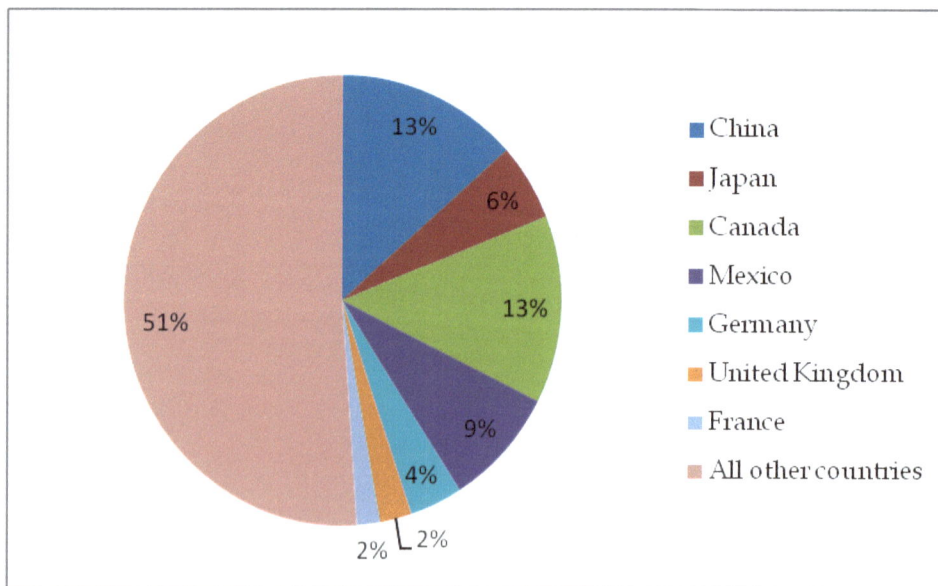

According to the Report to Congress, updated in 2007,[9] this U.S. trade imbalance with China is of great concern to the U.S. Congress because the development poses a threat to some U.S. industries and manufacturing employment. Therefore, the U.S. Congress has begun to focus on not only access to the Chinese market and intellectual property rights (IPR) protection but also the mounting U.S. trade deficit with China as well as allegations that China is selling its products on the international market at below cost (dumping), engaging in "currency manipulation," and exploiting its workers for economic gain.

The United States has also consistently maintained a negative trade balance with Japan. Between 1999 and 2008, the average U.S. trade deficit with Japan was approximately $77 billion. The highest trade deficit of about $90 billion occurred in 2006. See Table 2.6.

Table 2.6 U.S. Trade in Merchandized Goods with Japan 1999–2009 (in millions)

Year	Export	Import	Balance
1999	57,466.00	130,863.80	-73,397.80
2000	64,924.40	146,479.40	-81,555.00
2001	57,451.50	126,473.10	-69,021.60
2002	51,449.20	121,428.60	-69,979.40
2003	52,004.30	118,036.60	-66,032.40
2004	53,568.70	129,805.20	-76,236.50
2005	54,680.60	138,003.70	-83,323.10
2006	58,459.00	148,180.80	-89,721.80
2007	61,159.60	145,463.30	-84,303.80
2008	65,141.80	139,262.20	-74,120.40
2009	51,179.60	95,949.00	-44,769.40

Source: U.S. Census Bureau, Foreign Trade Division, Data dissemination Branch, Washington D.C. 20233.

The huge size of the bilateral trade imbalances, obvious evidence of unfair trading practices, has been a source of contentious bilateral discussions between the United States and Japan. Japan is a developed economy but has a serious cost advantage over the United States, especially with regard to wages. In 2008, 6 percent of U.S. total imports were from Japan. In the same year, exports to Japan constituted 4 percent of total U.S. exports. See Figures 2.7 and 2.8.

There was no serious imbalance in trade between the U.S. and its major trading partners, except for China and Japan, until 2008. A new pattern developed in 2008. Other major U.S. trading partners also recorded huge bilateral trade imbalances with the United States: Canada $78 billion, Mexico $65 billion, Germany $43 billion, France $15 billion and the United Kingdom $5 billion. This development was probably due to the huge increase in U.S. imports between 1999 and 2008. The value of U.S. imports increased from $1.2 trillion in 1999 to $2.5 trillion in 2008.

---

[9] Thomas Lum and Dick K. Nanto, "China's Trade with the United States," Congressional Research Service, (CRS) Report to Congress updated 2007, http://www.fas.org/sgp/crs/row/RL31403.pdf.

THE HOUSING MARKET

This unprecedented price increase in housing prices started in 1997 and peaked in 2006. See Table 2.7 and Figure 2.9. According to the S&P/Case-Shiller National Home Price Indexes, the price index for homes increased from 92.08 percent in the first quarter of 1999 to 189.93 percent in the second quarter of 2006 and 206 percent between 1999 and 2008.

Table 2.7 S&P/Case-Schiller National Home Price Index

Year	Quarter	Index
1999	Q1	92.08
1999	Q2	94.75
1999	Q3	97.03
1999	Q4	98.29
2000	Q1	100.00
2000	Q2	103.77
2000	Q3	106.33
2000	Q4	107.90
2001	Q1	109.27
2001	Q2	112.69
2001	Q3	115.50
2001	Q4	116.23
2002	Q1	118.00
2002	Q2	122.24
2002	Q3	126.13
2002	Q4	128.58
2003	Q1	130.48
2003	Q2	134.20
2003	Q3	138.41
2003	Q4	142.29
2004	Q1	146.26
2004	Q2	152.92
2004	Q3	158.53
2004	Q4	163.06
2005	Q1	169.19
2005	Q2	176.70
2005	Q3	183.08

Year	Quarter	Index
2005	Q4	186.97
2006	Q1	188.66
2006	Q2	189.93
2006	Q3	188.11
2006	Q4	186.44
2007	Q1	184.83
2007	Q2	183.16
2007	Q3	179.94
2007	Q4	170.39
2008	Q1	159.17
2008	Q2	155.68
2008	Q3	150.29
2008	Q4	139.18
2009	Q1	128.81

Source: S&P/Case-Schiller National Home Price Index,
http://www2.standardandpoors.com/spf/pdf/index/csnational_value_052619.xls

Table 2.8 U.S. Median and Average Sales Price of New Homes 1999 to 2009

Year	Median	Average
1999	161000	195600
2000	169000	207000
2001	175200	213200
2002	187600	228700
2003	195000	246300
2004	221000	274500
2005	240900	297000
2006	246500	305900
2007	247900	313600
2008	232100	292600
2009	215900	270400

Source: U.S. Census Bureau, http://www.census.gov/const/uspriceann.pdf

Figure 2.9 U.S. Median and Average Sales Price of New Homes 1999 to 2009

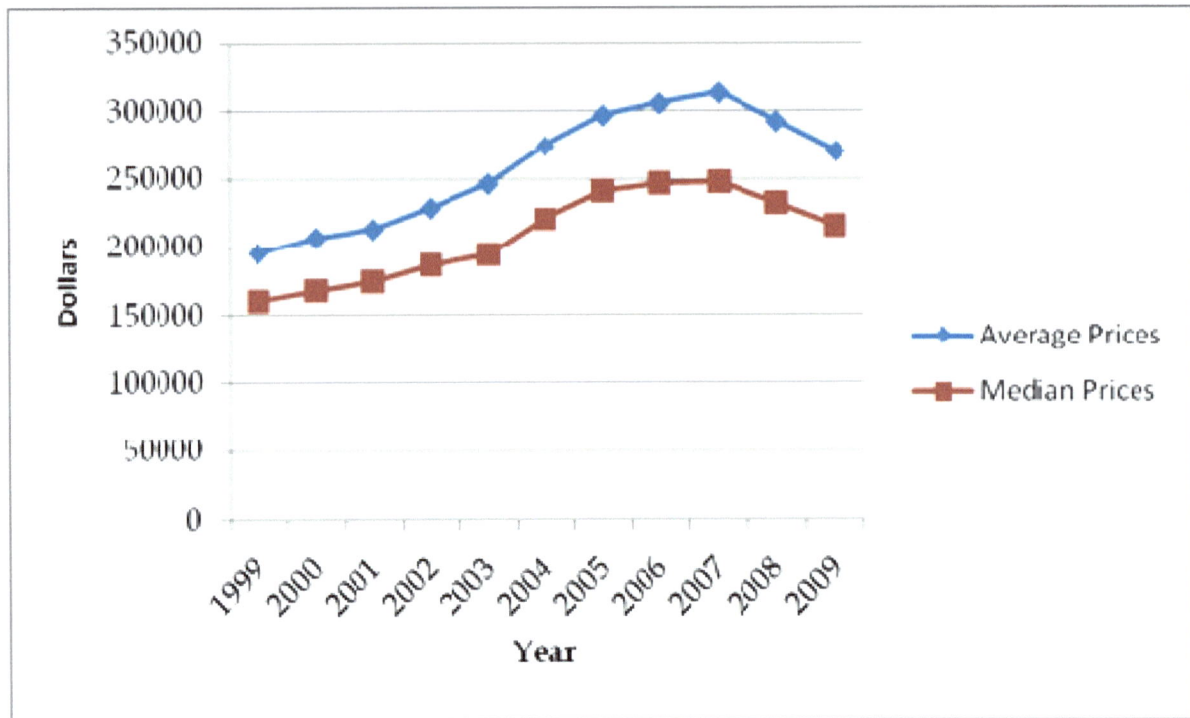

Source: Constructed with data from U.S. Census Bureau,
           http://www.census.gov/const/uspriceann.pdf

These huge increases in housing prices over a short period resulted in a bubble. A housing bubble is an unexplainable, rapid, huge increase in the price of all property that sometimes occurs in local or global real estate markets. If this rapid increase in the valuation of real property continues, it results in unsustainable levels in prices in relation to incomes and other indicators of affordability. When this occurs, rapid decreases in home prices result. Very often mortgage debt becomes higher than the value of the property. When mortgage holders realize that they are making mortgage payments on houses that are worth less than the balance outstanding on the mortgage and that they will not be able to cash out any equity on the mortgage, many will default. When this happens, the market usually corrects itself. Starting in 2006, many mortgage holders defaulted on their mortgages.

SUBPRIME MORTGAGE CRISIS

When the housing bubble burst, it affected virtually every part of the United States; however, the situation was more severe in some areas and states than in others. Some areas and states experienced unusually large increases and severe declines in home prices such as California, Colorado, Arizona, Florida, Michigan, Nevada, New Mexico, the Northeast, Oklahoma, Oregon, Texas, and Utah. According to the Case-Shiller House Price Index, by December 2007, house prices in Las Vegas had declined by about 18 percent. By December 2009, they had declined by 55.9 percent. Other cities that suffered huge declines in house prices include Phoenix (Arizona), Miami (Florida), and Detroit (Michigan), among others. See Figure 2.9.

Figure 2.10 Case-Schiller Price Decline from Peak through December 2009 for Selected U.S. cities

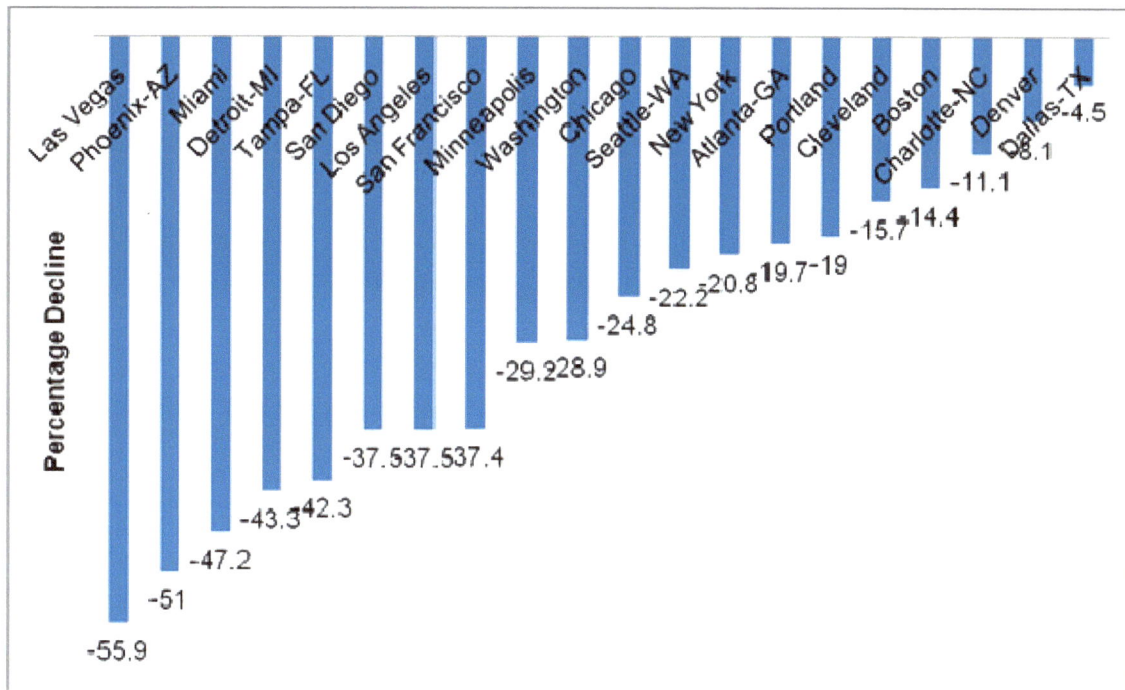

Source: Constructed with data from the Case-Shiller House Price Index, http://www.calculatedriskblog.com

There were many new houses in many of the cities, built by builders hoping to take advantage of the high prices in the housing market. Unfortunately, when interest rates started going up in 2005, mortgage holders, especially those with adjustable rate mortgages, started to refinance to secure fixed rates and cash out on the equity in their homes. Adjustable rate mortgages (ARMs), after the initial teaser rates, went up much higher, so high that many borrowers could no longer meet their new mortgage payments. See Figure 2:10. In addition, many potential house buyers could not afford to buy at the new higher interest rates. The demand for houses started to decline. When the housing bubble ended in the midst of unprecedented foreclosures, the builders could not sell the newly constructed houses at the high prices they had hoped to get, especially as interest rates started to increase. There was too much supply of foreclosed homes at very low bargain prices. The increased high rate of unemployment in many cities exerted more pressure on the housing market, precipitating more foreclosures. The newly constructed buildings and the foreclosures significantly increased the supply of houses in the market amid reduced demand. A slump in the real estate market resulted.

In Chapter 3, we will discuss in more detail the causes of the subprime mortgage crisis.

CONCLUSION

After a ten-year economic expansion in the United States during the 1990s, the United States experienced a recession starting in March 2001 that lasted until November 2001. In the same year, the United States suffered a terrorist attack on September 11. This development further exacerbated an already gloomy situation. The two wars in Iraq and Afghanistan that erupted because of the terrorist attack on the United States contributed significantly to the U.S. deficit situation. Furthermore, the actions the Government took to stimulate the economy, such as the Economic Growth, and Tax Relief Reconciliation Act of 2001, the Jobs and Growth Tax Relief and the Reconciliation Act of 2003, also contributed to both the huge 2008 Federal Government deficit and the huge economic expansion experienced after 2001 until 2008. Personal incomes and corporate profits soared.

The real estate sector boomed. This bubble reflected unexplainable rapid, huge increases in the price of property all over the United States. All this occurred in the face of a huge, unfavorable U.S. balance of payments situation. The United States has recorded a balance of payments deficit since 1976. When the housing bubble ended in 2007 in the midst of unprecedented foreclosures, builders could not sell the newly constructed houses at the high prices that they had hoped to get. This was even more farfetched, because interest rates started to increase. There were too many foreclosed homes on the market at very low, bargain prices. The increased high rate of unemployment in many cities exerted more pressure on the housing market as this precipitated more foreclosures. Consequently, the U.S. economy went from a boom to a financial crisis and a deep economic recession.

BIBLIOGRAPHY

Bianco, Katalina M. The Subprime Lending Crisis: Causes and Effects of the Mortgage Meltdown, http://business.cch.com/bankingfinance/focus/news/Subprime_WP_rev.pdf.

Bianco, Katalina M., J.D., CCH Writer Analyst, CCH Federal Banking Law Reporter, CCH Mortgage Compliance Guide and Bank Digest, The Subprime Lending Crisis: Causes and Effects of the Mortgage Meltdown, http://business.cch.com/bankingfinance/focus/news/Subprime_WP_rev.pdf.

Bureau of Economic Analysis, International Economic Accounts, http://www.bea.gov/international/index.htm#trade.

Bureau of Economic Analysis, National Economic Accounts, http://www.bea.gov/.

Bureau of Labor Statistics, United States Department of Labor, February 23, 2010, http://www.bls.gov/eag/eag.us.htm.

Executive Office of the President, Summary of Receipts, Outlays, and Surpluses or Deficits (-): 1789–2009, http://www.gpoaccess.gov/usbudget/fy05/hist.html.

Heilbroner, R., and P. Bernstein, The Debt and the Deficit (1989); D. Stabile, The Public Debt of the United States (1991); J. S. Gordon, Hamilton's Blessing: The Extraordinary Life and Times of Our National Debt (1997), http://www.encyclopedia.com/topic/public_debt.aspx.

Household Data Annual Averages, Employment status of the civilian non-institutional population, ftp://ftp.bls.gov/pub/special.requests/lf/aat1.txt/and http://www.bls.gov/cps/eetech_methods.pdf.

International Monetary Fund, http://www.imf.org/external/data.htm#data.

Lum, Thomas, and Dick K. Nanto, (2007), China's Trade with the United States, *Congressional Research Service, (CRS) Report to Congress updated 2007*, http://www.fas.org/sgp/crs/row/RL31403.pdf.

National Bureau of Economic Research, http://www.nber.org/cycles/november2001.

National Census Bureau, http://www.census.gov/statab/hist/HS-01.pdf.

Organization for International Investment, Foreign Direct Investment in the United States, March 18, 2010 [sighted February 16, 2011], http://www.ofii.org/docs/FDIUS_2010.pdf

Stein, Herbert. Balance of Payments, Library of Economic Liberty, [sighted February 16, 2011], http://www.econlib.org/library/Enc/BalanceofPayments.html.

Tax_Policy_Center:_Urban_Institute_and_Brookings_Institution, Department of the Treasury/Federal Reserve Board, February 16, 2010, http://www.ustreas.gov/tic/mfh.txt.

Treasury Direct, Bureau of Public Debt, Annual History of Debt Returns, http://www.treasurydirect.gov/govt/resources/faq/faq_publicdebt.htm#DebtOwner.

United States Public Debt, http://en.wikipedia.org/wiki/United_States_public_debt.

U.S. Census Bureau, Foreign Trade Statistics, http://www.census.gov/foreign-trade/balance/c4279.html#2008.

CHAPTER 3

CAUSES OF THE FINANCIAL CRISIS AND ECONOMIC RECESSION

INTRODUCTION

In Henry M. Paulson Jr.'s testimony before the Senate Banking Committee on the turmoil in U.S. credit markets, he noted that the events leading up to the U.S. financial crisis began many years ago. The financial crisis started with bad lending practices by banks and financial institutions, and by borrowers taking out mortgages they could not afford. Mr. Paulson identified the root cause of the financial crisis as the housing correction that resulted in illiquid mortgage-related assets now choking off the flow of credit, which is so vitally important to our economy.

Many critics disagreed with Mr. Paulson on the events that led to the crisis and the root causes of the crisis. The reason for this disagreement is that so many factors, not exclusively those mentioned by Paulson, contributed to the financial crisis: Factors such as an inadequate regulatory framework and oversight of the financial services sector; regulatory compliance failures, such as the failure of the Reserve Bank and the Securities Exchange Commission to introduce and implement appropriate policies and surveillance to achieve long-term goals of price stability and sustainable economic growth; unchecked corporate greed; easy credit conditions; excessive subprime lending and predatory lending practices; increased debt burden and overleveraged and poor pricing of risk that subsequently led to the collapse in house prices; unprecedented foreclosures and unavoidable illiquidity in the financial institutions; and the clogging of the financial system. In this chapter, we discuss some of the factors that contributed to the financial crisis starting with the immediate cause, the subprime mortgage crisis.

SUBPRIME LENDING

It is often difficult to explain subprime loans because they mean different things to different people. To grasp the meaning of a subprime loan, one needs to understand customary underwriting standards. In mortgage lending, for example, these standards include the borrower making a down payment of about 20 percent of the face value of the mortgage loan and providing evidence of sufficient funds to accommodate the closing costs, which can be as high as $6,000 or more. Lenders expect the borrower's FICO score to be well above 700. The borrower must show evidence that the take-home monthly income after deducting existing monthly financial liabilities covers the expected monthly mortgage payment by a great margin. Any mortgage loan where the borrower is not subjected to these stringent criteria can be referred to as a subprime mortgage loan. In most subprime mortgage lending, as little as 3 percent or no down payment is acceptable. Sometimes relatives of the borrower can contribute to the down payment as long as they understand that these contributions will not be refunded by the borrower. Lower FICO scores are acceptable. The lender may not require the borrower to finance the closing costs, which can be capitalized. Very often in these situations, the lender examines the borrower's income in its gross form, sometimes ignoring important prior financial commitments.

In general, someone with a poor credit history and a FICO score of less than 620 or 640 is considered subprime. The reason we have 620 and 640 as the cutoff point is because what constitutes subprime is a grey area. In addition, banks use other criteria to determine subprime, such as the person's income, length of employment, and monthly expenses relative to gross income. Recent credit history can include late payments or defaults. Even though a subprime borrower is assumed to have a higher credit risk than someone with average or above average credit, banks still lend to subprime borrowers for many different purposes, such as for the purchase of a house or automobile, or for credit card payoffs, and consumer installment loans. Banks penalize the subprime borrowers by charging them higher interest on loans than they would charge a prime borrower because of the risk involved.

Therefore, subprime lending refers to extending high risk loans to borrowers with a history of high default rates. It also can refer to lending to borrowers who already have excessive debt or lending to borrowers who have a documented history of missed payments or have experienced defaults or recorded bankruptcies. Such loans have interest rates higher than regular loans.

THE SUBPRIME MORTGAGE CRISIS

The assumed fundamental security of investing in property encouraged banks to lend to subprime borrowers. The lending bank always had a lien on the financed property, and so as long as the property was adequately valued in the event of the borrower's default the bank could always repossess, sell the property, and recover its investment. The financing of home mortgages increased significantly in the 1990s. The total value of home mortgage originations in the U.S. grew from $773 billion in 1994 to $1.5 trillion in 1998, an increase of 88 percent. The value of subprime home mortgage originations accounted for 4.5 percent of total originations in 1994 and $35 billion. Subprime home mortgage originations accounted for 10.3 percent of total home mortgage originations in 1998, valued at $149 billion. Between 1994 and 1998, the value of subprime home mortgage originations increased by 329 percent, more than triple the previous rate. The value of subprime home mortgage originations in 2006 was more than sixteen times the value in 1994. See Table 3.1.

Table 3.1 Growing Importance of Subprime and Securitization of Home Mortgage Originations 1994–2006
(in billions of dollars)

Year	Total originations	Prime market share of all originations	Prime market originations in dollars	Subprime originations share	Subprime originations in dollars	Subprime MBS share of SP originations	Subprime MBS share of SP in dollars
1994	773	94%	726.62	4.50%	34.785	31.60%	10.99206
1995	639	86.90%	555.291	10.20%	65.178	28.40%	18.510552
1996	785	83.20%	653.12	12.30%	96.555	36.40%	35.14602
1997	859	78.30%	672.597	14.50%	124.555	50%	62.2775
1998	1,450	84%	1218	10.30%	149.35	55.10%	82.29185
1999	1,310	83.20%	1089.92	12.20%	159.82	37.90%	60.57178
2000	1,048	81.50%	854.12	13.20%	138.336	40.50%	56.02608
2001	2,215	87.90%	1946.985	7.80%	172.77	55.20%	95.36904
2002	2,885	88.40%	2550.34	7.40%	213.49	57.10%	121.90279
2003	3,945	86.50%	3412.425	8.40%	331.38	61%	202.1418
2004	2,920	68.10%	1988.52	18.20%	531.44	75.70%	402.30008
2005	3,120	62.40%	1946.88	21.30%	664.56	76.30%	507.05928
2006	2,980	63.70%	1898.26	20.10%	598.98	80.50%	482.1789

Source: The 2007 Mortgage Market Statistical Annual, Inside Mortgage Finance

The dramatic increase in subprime lending for home purchases also was accompanied by huge increases in the securitization of these subprime mortgages to develop and market mortgage-backed securities. A mortgage-backed security is a type of asset-backed security or debt obligation that has a claim on the cash flows from mortgage loans, especially home mortgages. The main debt instrument used is a bond. As cash flows are received from mortgage coupon payments, principal repayments are made to investors in these mortgage-backed securities. Government sponsored agencies and some private entities, including the Federal National Mortgage Association, Federal Home Loan Mortgage Corporation, and Government National Mortgage Association, purchase mortgage loans from regulated and authorized banks, mortgage companies, and other originators. These loans are then assembled into pools that must be rated by an accredited credit rating agency. These mortgaged-backed securities are marketed to investors for the various benefits of future payments and capital payments. Thus, the mortgage-backed securities derive their value from the underlying assets in these home mortgages. If the holders of the various mortgages default, the mortgage-backed securities will be affected. If they foreclose, the banks and financial institutions repossess the houses. If the banks are unable to sell the houses, the mortgage-backed securities are negatively affected.

It is not by accident that most issuers of mortgage-backed securities are government-sponsored enterprises such as Fannie Mae, Freddie Mac, and Ginnie Mae. These government-sponsored enterprises were established to provide liquidity in the mortgage market. Ginnie Mae is backed by the full faith and credit of the U.S. Government. Ginnie Mae guarantees that investors receive timely payments. Before the 2008 financial crisis, Fannie Mae and Freddie Mac were not backed by the full faith and credit of the U.S. Government. Instead, Fannie Mae and Freddie Mac provided certain guarantees and had special authority to borrow from the U.S. Treasury.

The value of the subprime mortgage-backed security portion of subprime mortgages increased from $11 billion in 1994 to $482 billion in 2006. In the decade prior to the crisis, there was excessive subprime lending and predatory lending practices. These practices increased the debt burden, over-leverage, and poor pricing of risk. The rating agencies failed to adequately rate the risks inherent in subprime loans as a whole and, more importantly, for the mortgage-backed securities. All these occurrences subsequently led to the collapse in housing prices, unprecedented foreclosures, unavoidable illiquidity in financial institutions, and clogging of the financial system. The rate of subprime foreclosures decreased from 23.88 percent in 1999 to 10.25 percent in 2006. Because of the huge increases in total subprime mortgage originations, which reflect aggressive bank lending to high risk borrowers, the total number of subprime foreclosures increased from 188,000 in 1999 to 231,000 in the 2005. See Table 3.2.

Table 3.2 National Subprime Foreclosures* 1999 to 2006

Year	Total Number of Foreclosures	Total Number of Originations	Foreclosure Rates
1999	188,026	787,420	23.88
2000	165,801	739,749	22.41
2001	140,195	620,945	22.58
2002	124,781	797,625	15.64
2003	127,100	1,143,037	11.12
2004	176,729	1,716,141	10.3
2005	231,360	1,925,780	12.01
2006	140,278	1,368,706	10.25

Source: Loan Performance

* Foreclosure rates are based on the number of loans starting foreclosure

The rate of subprime foreclosures was not uniform across the nation. In 2006, when the national subprime foreclosure rate was 10.25 percent, California recorded a subprime foreclosure rate of 19.3 percent.

What precipitated these aggressive lending activities by U.S. banks and other financial institutions that specifically targeted subprime borrowers? There seems to be a legislative initiative for this trend, at least for increased lending to subprime borrowers.

COMMUNITY REINVESTMENT ACT OF 1977

The Community Reinvestment Act (CRA) of 1977 was introduced by the Federal Government. Section 802 subsections (a) and (b) clearly state the intent of this Act.

(a) The U.S. Congress finds that-

    (1) Regulated financial institutions are required by law to demonstrate that their deposit facilities serve the convenience and needs of the communities in which they are chartered to do business;

    (2) The convenience and needs of communities include the need for credit services as well as deposit services; and

    (3) Regulated financial institutions have continuing and affirmative obligation to help meet the credit needs of the local communities in which they are chartered.

(b) It is the purpose of this title to require each appropriate Federal financial supervisory agency to use its authority when examining financial institutions, to encourage such institutions to help meet the credit needs of the local communities in which they are chartered consistent with the safe and sound operation of such institutions.

The Community Reinvestment Act therefore is intended to encourage depository institutions to help meet the credit needs of the communities in which they operate, including low- and moderate-income neighborhoods, consistent with safe and sound operations. The Act also requires that the records of institutions responsible for meeting the credit needs of an entire community be evaluated periodically. The financial institutions' performance in this regard is supposed to be evaluated by the relevant agencies. The results of the records and evaluations are to be taken into account when considering an institution's application for deposit facilities.

To ensure compliance, the records kept by depository financial institutions must be examined for adherence to the provisions of the Community Reinvestment Act. The Federal Reserve examines state-chartered banks that are members of the Federal Reserve. Other depository institutions are examined by Federal Deposit Insurance Corporation, the Office of the Comptroller of the Currency, and/or the Office of Thrift Supervision.

Some have blamed the CRA for indirectly causing the financial crisis. It is important to understand the reasons behind the decision of Congress to develop the CRA. Ben S. Bernanke, Chairman of the Reserve Bank, very clearly explained this decision in his speech delivered in 2007 at the Community Affairs Research Conference in Washington, D.C. According to Bernanke[10]:

> Several social and economic factors help explain why credit to lower-income neighborhoods was limited at that time. First, racial discrimination in lending undoubtedly adversely affected local communities. Discriminatory lending practices had deep historical roots. The term "redlining," which refers to the practice of designating certain lower-income or minority neighborhoods as ineligible for credit, appears to have originated in 1935, when the Federal Home Loan Bank Board asked the Home Owners' Loan Corporation to create "residential

---

[10] http://www.federalreserve.gov/newsevents/speech/bernanke20070330a.htm

security maps" for 239 cities that would indicate the level of security for real estate investments in each surveyed city. The resulting maps designated four categories of lending and investment risk, each with a letter and color designation. Type "D" areas, those considered to be the riskiest for lending and which included many neighborhoods with predominantly African-American populations, were color-coded red on the maps–hence the term "redlining" (Federal Home Loan Bank Board, 1937). Private lenders reportedly constructed similar maps that were used to determine credit availability and terms. The 1961 Report on Housing by the U.S. Commission on Civil Rights reported practices that included requiring high down payments and rapid amortization schedules for African-American borrowers as well as blanket refusals to lend in particular areas.

The Chairman went on to cite other factors that were responsible for the relative unavailability of credit in lower-income neighborhoods. Those other factors included the economic, institutional, and regulatory environment. The rudimentary secondary market for mortgages limited local loan originators' access to capital and reduced their ability to diversify credit risks geographically. Inadequate appraisal information and great diversity in the nature of home sales among neighborhoods might have discouraged interested depository institutions from moving in. In addition, credit evaluations tended to be more costly for lower-income borrowers, who are relatively more likely to have short or irregular credit histories. The absence of uniform national depositories of information on the credit experiences of consumers further worsened informational barriers to lending. There was no reliable credit reporting system as the credit reporting system at that time was still at a rudimentary stage, which made information gathering very difficult, time consuming, and costly.

There were also some regulatory obstacles to lending. For example, the regulatory environment of the period was yet another factor limiting broad access to credit. State and federal rules prohibited interstate branching or acquisitions and in some cases restricted even intrastate branching, which reduced competition and the ability of lenders to diversify risk geographically. In addition, interest rate ceilings on mortgages in some locations effectively blocked lending to potential borrowers judged to pose higher risks. Furthermore, interest rate ceilings on deposits (notably, the infamous Regulation Q) led to periodic episodes of disintermediation (a situation where surplus funds in the economy did not flow to deficit units requiring funds) and reduced availability of mortgage credit. In his speech, Bernanke reminded listeners that the Community Reinvestment Act, enacted in 1977, affirming the obligation of federally insured depository institutions to help banks meet the credit needs of communities in which they were chartered, is consistent with safe and sound banking operations. The objectives of the Community Reinvestment Act are laudable, but there is some question as to whether the implementation was carried out in a safe and sound operational manner by the depository institutions and regulatory bodies.

AMERICAN DREAM DOWNPAYMENT ACT OF 2003

The American Dream Downpayment Initiative (ADDI) was created in 2003 to help low-income and first-time homebuyers to purchase homes. The U.S. Congress followed this by passing the American Dream Downpayment Act, which was signed into law on December 16, 2003. The Act authorized $200 million a year in funding between 2004 and 2007, which was available to towns in all fifty states with jurisdictions exceeding a population of 150,000. The purpose of this funding was to increase home ownership for low-income and minority households, as well as to stabilize communities. First-time homebuyers whose income did not exceed 80 percent of the median income for the area were eligible for this funding. The funding per person was limited to 6 percent of the purchase price of the property, up to a maximum of $10,000 and had to be used as part of closing costs, down payment, or rehabilitation. A first-time homebuyer is defined as an individual and spouse who have not owned a home during the three-year period prior to the purchase of a home with ADDI assistance It is believed that this was responsible for the spike in subprime lending starting in 2003. As shown in Table 3.1, the total value of subprime loan originations was $213.5 billion in 2002, and it increased to $599 billion in 2006, an unprecedented increase of 180.6 percent.

FEDERAL HOUSING ADMINISTRATION (FHA) LOANS

Another program that might have encouraged more lending to subprime borrowers is the FHA loan. During the Great Depression of the 1930s, many people defaulted on mortgages, and there were high rates of foreclosure in a mortgage market where there was no insurance. About two million construction workers lost their jobs. The terms for borrowing to buy a house were stiff. Institutions financing mortgages required huge down payments, as much as 50 percent of the property's market value, with a repayment schedule spread over three to five years and ending with a huge balloon payment. At that time, the U.S. was primarily a nation of renters. Only four out ten households owned homes.

The FHA was created in 1934 to mitigate some of the previously stated problems by increasing home construction, reducing unemployment, and operating various loan insurance programs. The FHA does not make loans. Specifically, the FHA is a Federal Government program that guarantees loans extended to consumers by private lending institutions, especially to low- and medium-income buyers. The FHA investigates the applicant, and it determines if the risk of the borrower is acceptable. If the risk is acceptable, the FHA insures the lending institution against its loss of principal, in case the borrower fails to meet the terms and conditions of the mortgage. The FHA gets involved either at the request of the borrower or because the lender insists on FHA's involvement. FHA loans usually receive lower interest rates. The applicant also receives the benefit of a careful appraisal of the property by an FHA inspector. In return, the homebuyer pays a monthly insurance premium of one-half of 1 percent on declining balances for the lender's protection. This is usually organized as an escrow account where the annual or semiannual amount is paid in advance to the mortgage company, typically in the monthly payment. FHA-insured borrowers require very little cash investment to close their loans. There is more flexibility in calculating household income and payment ratios. Most beneficiaries of FHA protection are low- and medium-income people.

It is easier to qualify for FHA loans than other types of home loans. The FHA guidelines for loan qualification are the most flexible of all mortgage loans and require less than a 5 percent downpayment. Basic FHA loan qualification guidelines include:

- Two years of steady employment, preferably with the same employer
- Last two years of income should be the same or increasing
- Credit reports should typically have less than two, thirty-day late payments in the last two years with a minimum credit score of 620 or higher or in some cases no credit score at all
- If there was bankruptcy, it must be at least two-years old with perfect credit since discharge
- If there was foreclosure, it must be at least three-years old with perfect credit since the occurrence of foreclosure
- The new mortgage payment should be approximately 30 percent of gross (before taxes) income

Many lending institutions will verify employment, income, credit score, any late payments, and obtain explanations for the relevant late payments and monthly obligations as recorded in the credit report. Some banks did verify employment, income, and credit scores. With respect to the affordability of the mortgage by the borrower, the focus was on the FHA requirement that the new mortgage payment should be approximately 30 percent of gross (before taxes) income. This provision is highly inadequate. There could be a great disparity between a person's gross pay and take home pay.

The FHA and HUD have insured over 34 million home mortgages and 47,205 multifamily home mortgages since 1934. The FHA currently has 4.8 million insured single-family mortgages and 13,000 insured multifamily homes in its portfolio.

RATING AGENCIES

Some of the U.S. based rating agencies are A.M. Best, Fitch Ratings, Moody's Investors service, Standard and Poor's, and Egan-Jones Rating Company. Other well-known rating agencies that operate in the U.S. include the Australian-owned Baycorp Advantage, Canadian-owned Dominion Bond Rating Service, Japanese-owned Japan Credit Rating Agency and Chinese-owned China Credit information Service. The largest rating agencies in the U.S. are Moody's Investors service, Standard and Poor's, and Fitch Ratings.

Rating agencies use quantitative and qualitative methods to give an indication of the borrower's default risk to the lender. Bond issuers use rating agencies extensively as an independent verification, and sometimes validation, of a borrower's credit worthiness. For example, for any bond issue to have credibility among the investing public, such an issue must be accompanied by at least one credit rating of the issue from a recognized credit rating agency. A "BBB," rating is usually considered investment grade. All ratings below that are considered speculative grade. Rating agencies also rate the quality of underlying assets in mortgaged-backed securities and collateralized debt obligation (CDOs).

Credit rating agencies have been accused of contributing to the subprime mortgage crisis because of their failure to recognize the higher risk inherent in CDOS, including adjustable-rate and other mortgage-backed securities that included subprime loans in their mortgage pools. Such CDOS and mortgage-backed securities that included subprime loans in their mortgage pools should have been given a lower rating than the "AAA" reserved for much higher quality tranches or class of bonds. It is argued that, if investors had been warned of the higher risk of some of these assets, some investors might not have invested in them. This argument seems to have some credibility. In 2003, the U.S. Securities and Exchange Commission submitted plans to Congress indicating its intention to launch an investigation into the anticompetitive practices of credit-rating agencies and other issues relating to conflicts of interest. This was in the wake of several bankruptcies and corporate malpractices in investment banking and accounting industries. With regard to the SEC's concern of conflicts of interest, it is important to note that a rating agency's remuneration is fee based. It is possible that a debt-issuing company can take its business elsewhere if it is not satisfied with the rating a rating agency assigns to it or any of the debt instruments it issues.

Adjustable-rate, subprime, and other mortgages were packed into mortgage-backed securities of great complexity. Rating agencies underestimated the risk of these securities either because of a lack of competition, poor accountability, or most likely the inherent difficulty in assessing risk due to the complexity of these financial assets. Perhaps, they compromised and failed to flash a red light on the risk inherent in these assets in order to safeguard their assured income. It is possible that a full disclosure of the risk inherent with these financial assets might have discouraged some risk-averse investors from investing in them. Speculative investors might have demanded high returns that would have included a high risk premium.

INADEQUATE REGULATORY FRAMEWORK AND OVERSIGHT OF FINANCIAL SERVICES SECTOR PRIOR TO THE FINANCIAL CRISIS

Since the financial crisis, so many questions have arisen. Why were consumers allowed to borrow huge amounts of money for home mortgages even though there was evidence they could not afford to service such loans? Why were some financial institutions allowed to engage in predatory lending practices? Why were mortgage brokers and bank officials allowed to exploit the situations for personal gain? Were the rating agencies not regulated? Was the securitization of assets not regulated? Why did so many banks fail? Is the bank capital requirement adequate? Were there not enough regulations? Perhaps, there was not adequate supervision. Were the federal and state regulators not aware of what was going on?

The Government admitted that, in some of our most sophisticated financial firms, risk management systems did not keep pace with the complexity of new financial products. The lack of transparency and standards in markets for securitized loans helped to weaken underwriting standards. Market discipline broke down as investors relied excessively on credit rating agencies. Compensation practices throughout the financial services industry rewarded short-term profits at the expense of long-term value. Although this crisis had many causes, it is clear now that the Government could have done more to prevent many of these problems from growing out of control and threatening the stability of our financial system. Gaps and weaknesses in the supervision and regulation of financial firms presented challenges to our Government's ability to monitor, prevent, or address risks as they built up in the system. No regulator saw its job as protecting the economy and financial system as a whole. Existing approaches to bank holding company regulation focused on protecting the subsidiary bank, not on comprehensive regulation of the whole firm. Investment banks were permitted to opt for a different regime under a different regulator and, in doing so, escaped adequate constraints on leverage. Other firms, such as AIG, owned insured depositories but escaped the strictures of serious holding company regulation, because the depositories that they owned were technically not "banks" under relevant law.[11]

Efforts have been made by the U.S. Congress to introduce and improve the regulations under which financial institutions must operate since the National Currency and Bank Acts (1863–1864) were introduced in 1983. Many subsequent acts seem to have been introduced in reaction to certain observed negative developments. The Federal Reserve System (commonly known as the Fed), was created in 1913 to act as the central bank of the United States. This was in response to the financial crisis that led to banking panics in the late 19th and early 20th centuries. The Federal Reserve System was charged with fostering a sound banking system and a healthy economy, serving as a lender of last resort by providing temporary loans to depository institutions facing financial emergencies and stabilizing the financial markets and the economy in order to preserve public confidence. In addition to these roles, the Fed was also expected to develop a system to collect and clear checks. This is now being done electronically. The Federal Reserve System focuses on controlling money supply and credit conditions to ensure economic stability. Today, the Fed describes its duties in four broad areas:

- Conducting the nation's monetary policy by influencing the monetary and credit conditions in the economy in pursuit of maximum employment, stable prices, and moderate long-term interest rates
- Supervising and regulating banking institutions to ensure the safety and soundness of the nation's banking and financial system and to protect the credit rights of consumers
- Maintaining the stability of the financial system and containing systemic risk that may arise in financial markets
- Providing certain financial services to the U.S. Government, to the public, to financial institutions, and to foreign official institutions, including playing a major role in operating the nation's payments systems

The Federal Reserve Bank currently is a well-funded quasi-government institution but independent from Congress. Alan Greenspan was the Chairman of the Federal Reserve System from 1987 to 2006. So for almost twenty years prior to the crisis, Mr. Greenspan could have used the powers given to the Federal Reserve to shape the economy a different way and could have asked for more powers to enable it to achieve more financial security and stability for consumers and the country. During his testimony to Congress in 2008, some politicians accused him of encouraging the bubble in housing prices by keeping interest rates too low for too long and for failing to rein in the explosive growth of risky and often fraudulent mortgage lending. Congress insisted that he had the authority to prevent irresponsible lending

---

[11] U.S. Department of Treasury, Financial Regulatory Reform, a new Foundation, Rebuilding Financial Supervision and Regulation,http://www.treasury.gov/initiatives/wsr/Documents/FinalReport_web.pdf.

practices that led to the subprime mortgage crisis, and he failed to do anything about it, even though he was advised by many others to stop it. Mr. Greenspan admitted to the House Committee on Oversight and Government Reform that he had put too much faith in the self-correcting power of free markets and had failed to anticipate the self-destructive power of excessive mortgage lending.[12]

Prior to the crisis, from 2001 to 2005, the federal funds rate and the prime lending rate were low. The federal funds rate is the interest rate at which depository institutions lend balances to each other temporarily, sometimes overnight. However, loans in the federal funds market are normally for one to seven days. The Federal Open Market Committee responsible for the nation's monetary policy establishes the target rate for trading in the federal funds market. See Figures 3-1 to 3-3.

Figure 3.1 U.S. Discount Rate 1999 to 2008

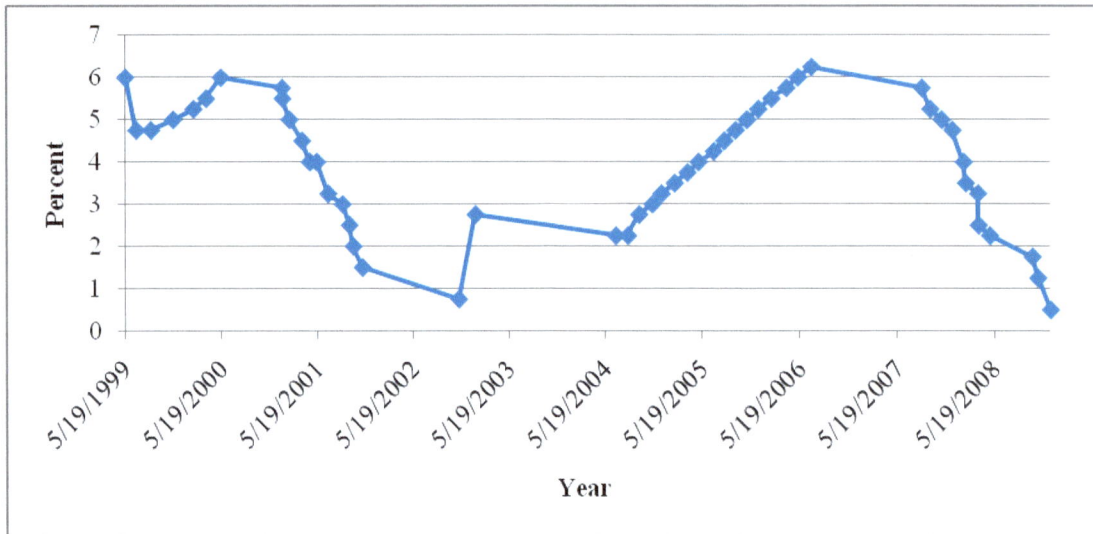

Source: Constructed with data from Federal Reserve

Figure 3.2 Federal Funds Rate 2000 to 2008

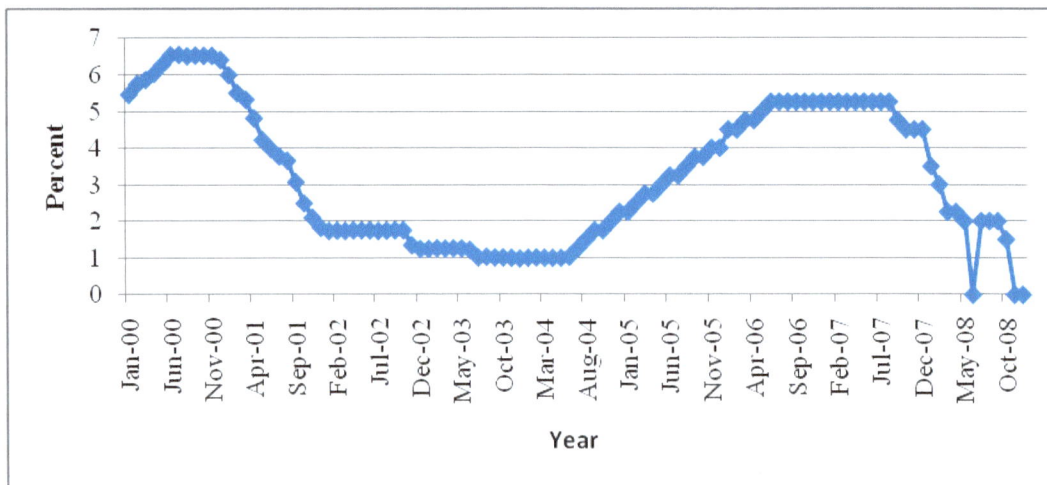

Source: Constructed with data from Federal Reserve

---

[12] Edmund L. Andrews, Greenspan Concedes Error on Regulation, New York Times, October 23, 2008, http://www.nytimes.com/2008/10/24/business/economy/24panel.html.

Figure 3.3 U.S. Prime Lending Rate 1998 to 2008

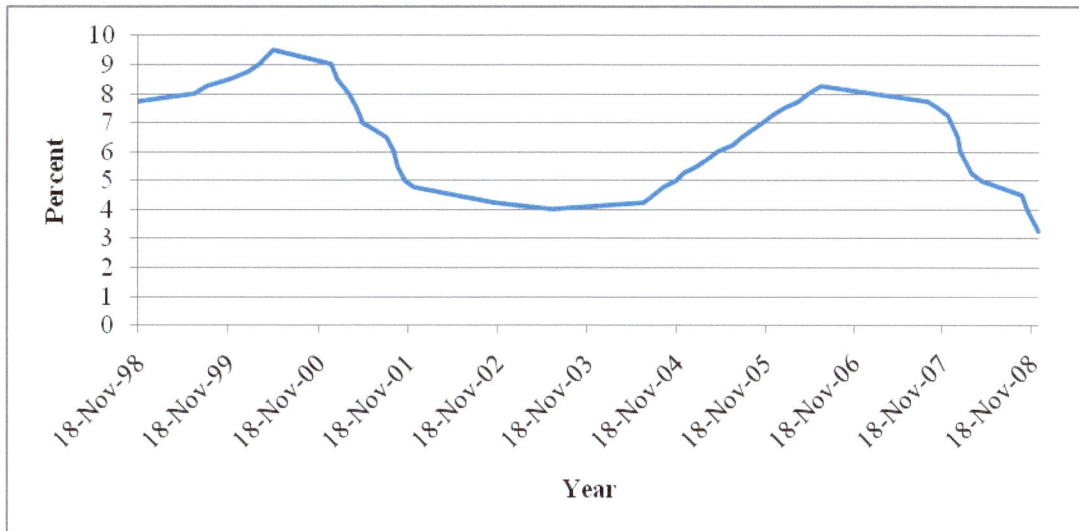

Source: Constructed with data from Federal Reserve

Mr. Greenspan noted that the immense and largely unregulated business of spreading financial risk widely through the use of exotic financial instruments called derivatives had gotten out of control and had added to the havoc of today's crisis. Mr. Greenspan stated that the multi-trillion dollar market for credit default swaps, originally created to insure bond investors against the risk of default, needed to be restrained. He argued that the low level of interest rates between 2001 and 2005 were not solely responsible for the hike in subprime lending. Other factors were responsible, including an unexpected increase in the supply of loanable funds from overseas, especially from some emerging economies where the savings ratio had significantly increased in the decade prior to the financial crisis. The current Chairman of the Federal Reserve System, Ben S. Bernanke, in his speech at the Council on Foreign Relations in Washington, D.C. in March 2009, emphasized the need for the Federal Reserve to do better. He said, "We must strengthen what I will call the financial infrastructure–the systems, rules, and conventions that govern trading, payment, clearing, and settlement in financial markets–to ensure that it will perform well under stress.… We should review regulatory policies and accounting rules to ensure that they do not induce excessive procyclicality–that is, do not overly magnify the ups and downs in the financial system and the economy. Finally, we should consider whether the creation of an authority specifically charged with monitoring and addressing systemic risks would help protect the system from financial crises like the one we are currently experiencing."

The bankruptcy examiner, Anton Vakulas reported that the Federal Reserve's shortsighted approach toward Lehman Brothers was instrumental in its collapse. The Fed had more information on Lehman than the SEC. The Fed was focused on Lehman's health and simply was not interested in Lehman from a regulatory or compliance standpoint.

Therefore, it is obvious that the Federal Reserve failed to implement an effective regulatory compliance system and failed to introduce the right policies to control the excess liquidity in the system that had prevailed some years before the financial crisis. The Fed also failed to introduce and implement the appropriate policies and surveillance to achieve the long-term goals of price stability and sustainable economic growth.

THE U.S. SECURITIES AND EXCHANGE COMMISSION (SEC)

It has been alleged that the regulatory compliance failure that existed prior to the financial crisis was a result of the failure of the SEC to introduce and implement the appropriate policies and surveillance to achieve long-run goals. These long-term goals were price stability, sustainable economic growth, and corporate integrity. The absence of appropriate policies and effective surveillance created a fertile ground for unchecked corporate greed and easy credit conditions.

According to the SEC, its mission is to protect investors; maintain fair, orderly, and efficient markets; and facilitate capital formation. The role of the SEC has evolved over a long period of time.

The stock market crash in October 1929 caused a severe loss of public confidence. All categories of investors and banks lost huge sums of money. Congress acted on the public's consensus that, for the economy to recover, the public's faith in the capital markets needed to be restored. In 1933, Congress passed the Securities Act of 1933 (as amended through P.L. 111-229, approved August 11, 2010). This Act was to ensure that companies publicly offering securities for investment dollars must inform the public of the truth about their businesses, the securities they are selling, and the risks involved in investing. In other words, these companies are required to fully disclose all relevant financial information about them and the securities they plan to issue.

Congress passed the Securities Exchange Act of 1934 (as amended through P.L. 111-257), and approved on October 5, 2010. This Act was supposed to ensure that those who sell and trade securities, such brokers, dealers, and exchanges, must treat investors fairly and honestly, putting investors' interests first. Congress established the SEC in 1934 to enforce the newly passed securities laws, to promote stability in the markets, and most importantly, to protect investors.

The SEC is another federal supervisory authority that has come under attack for failure to perform its job efficiently. In particular, many have questioned the ability of the SEC to: monitor and supervise the over-the-counter derivatives, securities, hedge funds, brokers/dealers and investment advisers, credit rating agencies, and its ability to identify and address emerging systematic risks that pose a threat to the stability of our financial system.

In her testimony, before the U.S. House of Representatives Committee on Financial Services in 2009 on "Regulatory Perspectives on the Obama Administration's Financial Regulatory Reforms Proposals," the SEC Chairman, Mary L. Schapiro, explained that there was a lack of regulation of Over-the-Counter (OTC) derivatives. OTC derivatives are financial instruments that derive their value from other financial instruments, events, or conditions, but are not traded on an exchange. Apparently, the OTC derivatives were excluded from the securities regulatory framework by the Commodity Futures Modernization Act of 2000.[13] Specifically, Section 2A of the Securities Act and Section 3A of the Securities and Exchange Act and other related provisions prohibit the SEC from promulgating, interpreting, or enforcing rules in a manner that imposes or specifies reporting or recording requirements, procedures, and standards as prophylactic measures against fraud or manipulation with respect to any security-based swap agreement. The SEC is further prohibited from registering or requiring the registration of any security-based swap agreement. Therefore, the SEC was not able to prevent certain activities in the OTC derivatives markets from posing risks in the financial system. Consequently, the SEC could not promote transparency or efficiency in these markets, and it was not able to prevent any possible market manipulation, fraud, abuses, or protect unsophisticated parties from inappropriate marketing. It is important to note that some OTC derivative instruments, such as certain equity linked notes, have always been considered securities and are currently covered by the securities regulatory regime.

Rules regarding short sales still contained loopholes that allowed the manipulation of the markets. There was still not enough reporting on money market mutual funds, and there was also not enough regulation to prevent extreme turbulence in the money market mutual funds market. There were also issues surrounding dark pools and stock lending. Dark pools generally refer to automated trading systems that do not display quotes in the public quote system. The concerns about dark pools relate to the possibility of their leading to a lack of transparency, significant private markets, and the potential impairment of the public price discovery function.

---

[13] H.R. 5660: Commodity Futures Modernization Act of 200

Security brokers or dealers sometimes loan a security to another security dealer or a trader and the borrower is required to return the same security as payment. This loan may be collateralized and very often is. This is called security lending, and it allows the broker or dealer in possession to earn high returns on the security through finance. How does this work? The lending agent and the borrower negotiate the terms of the loan. These terms normally include collateral that can be cash or non-cash assets, rebate rate for cash transactions or premium for non-cash transactions, duration of the loan, dividend, and reclaim rate. The market supply and demand for the loanable securities determines the rebate rate. The cash collateral is normally invested. In the case where the borrower presents non-cash collateral, the borrower pays the lending agent a fee or premium, and there is no investment of cash; hence, no rebate will be paid to the borrower. A third-party custodian may be involved and is usually a bank. In this case, the lending agent must send delivery instructions to the sub-custodian. The borrower must also send receipt instructions to the sub-custodian. There is a requirement that the lending agent should perform a daily mark-to-market to ensure that the collateral is adjusted based on the market value of the borrowed securities. On expiration of this security loan, the borrower must return the securities to the lending institution through the sub-custodian. If cash was used as security, that amount must be returned to the borrower, the accrued rebate having been paid on a monthly basis. To settle the account, the investment earnings minus the borrower's rebate are shared between the lender and the lending agent on a predetermined basis, often 60 percent for the lender and 40 percent for the lending agent.

Prior to the financial crisis, the SEC did not have full supervisory oversight over the participants in securities lending. As the principal regulator for broker-dealers in the U.S., the SEC has oversight of securities borrowing and lending activities of these entities. The SEC does not directly regulate the non-broker-dealer entities that participate in these securities lending. Some of the non-broker-dealer entities are regulated by other bodies, including the Federal Reserve Bank. It is important to note that there were not effective or appropriate controls on short selling to reduce or minimize the potential risks that could affect the orderly and efficient functioning and stability of financial markets. There was no regulatory reporting requirement for short sales and credit-default swaps.

The securities laws seem to be trailing the growth and market significance of hedge funds and other private funds. As a result, the SEC has very little oversight or authority over these important sources of capital and investment vehicles of choice for many institutional investors. In 2008, Advisors of hedge were managing funds valued at almost $1.4 trillion. Hedge funds control about 20 percent of all trading in the New York Stock Exchange. Venture capital manages about $257 billion of assets. Private equity funds raised about $256 billion in 2008. Some of these instruments are not regulated and advisers and managers are not accountable to any federal or state supervisory agency. There are no regulations specifically targeting these funds. They are also ways to organize affairs that fall within certain exemptions to the registration requirements of the Federal Securities laws.

The SEC only has the authority to conduct compliance examinations of those funds and advisers that are registered under one of the statutes administered by the SEC. However, certain exemptions from the registration of the offer or sale of securities made possible by the Securities Act of 1933, the Investment Company Act of 1940, and the Investment Advisers Act of 1940 offer private funds and investment advisers opportunities for exemption.

In 2008, Christopher Cox, then acting SEC Chairman, acknowledged that the voluntary supervision program's (Consolidated Supervised Entities Program) failure contributed to the global financial crisis. The program was "fundamentally flawed from the beginning" as investment banks were able to opt in or out of supervision voluntarily.[14]

This program allowed the SEC to monitor the parent companies of major Wall Street firms, even though the agency technically had authority over only the firms' brokerage components. The primary

---

[14] Labaton, Stephen. "S.E.C. Concedes Oversight Flaws Fueled Collapse," *New York Times*, September 26, 2008.http://www.nytimes.com/2008/09/27/business/27sec.html

focus of the regulatory program was on the investment banks' liquidity and risk management. Recognizing the banks' vulnerability to liquidity crisis, the program ostensibly required the banks to maintain sufficient liquid assets to survive a year without access to unsecured funding and without having to liquidate a substantial position. Under the program, the banks were also required to have internal risk controls that the SEC approved and monitored, theoretically to prevent the banks from taking on more risk than they could handle. Finally, firms in the regulatory program had to assess their soundness by undergoing regular stress tests.

The bankruptcy examiner, Anton Vakulas, reported that the SEC failed to regulate Lehman Brothers. According to Vakulas' findings, none of these very important regulations was meaningfully enforced with Lehman Brothers.[15]

In 1975, the SEC began an informal process of recognizing rating agencies. It introduced the designation Nationally Recognized Statistical Rating Organizations (NRSROs). This permitted regulated entities, such as brokerage companies and mutual funds, to rely on their ratings to satisfy specific regulatory requirements. This designation involved minimal, informal oversight, because it relied on market acceptance rather than regulatory standards. Later, in 2006, after a series of corporate scandals such as Enron and WorldCom, Congress passed the Credit Rating Agency Reform Act. The Act provided the SEC with explicit legal authority to require rating agencies electing to be treated as NRSROs to register with it. This meant that the registered credit rating agencies must comply with certain requirements, such as periodic reporting on activities and the public disclosure of information on internal standards and policies as well as rating methodology and performance. The Act also empowered the SEC to conduct on-site inspections of rating agencies and to take disciplinary action for violations of the law. However, it prohibited the SEC from regulating the credit rating process, including the procedures and methodologies used. Note that there was not a mandatory registration of all rating agencies operating in the U.S. There was limited transparency. The conflict of interest remained. For example, a registered rating agency could still issue a rating for a structured finance product paid for by the product's issuer, sponsor, or underwriter. The SEC could still not examine the credit rating agencies' rating methods.

FEDERAL DEPOSIT INSURANCE CORPORATION

The Banking Act of 1933, known also as the Glass-Steagall Act, established the Federal Deposit Insurance Corporation (FDIC) as an independent agency of the U.S. Government to protect the funds that depositors place in FDIC insured institutions. The FDIC's deposit insurance is backed by the full faith and credit of the U.S. Government. Due to the 1991 Federal Deposit Corporation Improvement Act, the FDIC also maintains stability and public confidence in the nation's financial system by insuring deposits, examining and supervising financial institutions for safety and soundness and consumer protection, and managing receiverships. It guarantees the safety of deposits in member banks, currently up to $250, 000 per depositor per bank. This maximum FDIC insurance coverage is temporary and expires on December 31, 2013. After that date, the maximum FDIC insurance coverage for a depositor's funds in one FDIC bank will revert to the limit before 2008 or $100,000 for all account categories except IRAs and certain other retirement accounts, which will remain at $250,000 per depositor. The presence of the FDIC during this crisis and economic recession is helping to smooth the negative impact of bank failures on depositors. Should the FDIC have done more to prevent the banking crisis in which over 353[16] banks have failed since 2008?

---

[15] Field, Abigail. "Lehman Report: Were Securities Regulators Out to Lunch?" *Daily Finance.* December 28, 2010. http://www.dailyfinance.com/story/investing/lehman-report-were-securities-regulators-out-to-lunch/19397816/
[16] FDIC List of Failed Banks, http://www.fdic.gov/bank/individual/failed/banklist.html, [May 29, 2011]

The FDIC, in its summer 2009 report, listed factors that caused the banking crisis. It highlighted weak underwriting standards, Alt-A mortgages, and excessive reliance on financial leverage as the main causes of the banking crisis. The FDIC hopes to promote some of the old banking basics such as prudent loan underwriting, strong capital and liquidity, and the fair treatment of customers.

Because the 1991 Federal Deposit Corporation Improvement Act empowered the FDIC to maintain stability and public confidence in the nation's financial system by insuring deposits as well as examining and supervising financial institutions for safety and soundness and consumer protection, it is obvious that the magnitude of underwriting failures that occurred indicates that the FDIC failed in its duty. It also failed to maintain stability and public confidence in the nation's financial system by allowing FDIC insured banks to engage excessively in subprime mortgage lending and embarking on huge leveraged positions. Adequate examination of the banks could have revealed these negative tendencies, which could have been checked by administering existing regulation or by introducing new regulations.

CONCLUSION

It is true that bad lending practices by banks and financial institutions, whereby borrowers took out mortgages that they could not afford, were some of the immediate causes of the financial crisis and economic recession. The unprecedented foreclosures caused illiquid mortgage-related assets which choked off the flow of credit that is so vitally important to any economy. Broadly speaking, some factors that directly or indirectly contributed to the maladies of the financial crisis and economic recession were: the inadequate regulatory framework and oversight of the financial services sector, regulatory compliance shortcomings and failure of the Federal Reserve Bank and the Securities Exchange Commission to introduce and implement appropriate policies and surveillance to achieve long-run goals of price stability and sustainable economic growth, unchecked corporate greed, easy credit conditions, excessive subprime lending, predatory lending practices, increased debt burden and over-leverage, poor pricing of risk that subsequently led to the collapse in real estate prices, unprecedented foreclosures, and unavoidable illiquidity in the financial institutions and the clogging of the financial system. This chapter examined some of the factors that contributed to the financial crisis and economic recession.

BIBLIOGRAPHY

Alembakis, Rachel. "SEC lending in the spotlight." *Global Pensions,* March 2, 2009. http://www.globalpensions.com/global-pensions/feature/1558880/sec-lending-spotlight.

Amel, Dean F., and Daniel G. Keane. "State Laws Affecting Commercial Bank Branching, Multibank Holding Company Expansion, and Interstate Banking," *Issues in Bank Regulation* 10,1986 (Autumn): 30–40.

Andrews, Edmund L. "Greenspan Concedes Error on Regulation," *New York Times*, October 23, 2008. http://www.nytimes.com/2008/10/24/business/economy/24panel.html

Apgar, William, and Mark Duda. (2003). "The Twenty-fifth Anniversary of the Community Reinvestment Act: Past Accomplishments and Future Regulatory Challenges" (209 KB PDF), *FRBNY Economic Policy Review*, 2003 (June): 169–191.

Avery, Robert B., Raphael W. Bostic, and Glenn B. Canner. "CRA Special Lending Programs" (115 KB PDF), *Federal Reserve Bulletin* 86,2000 (November): 711–731.

Avery, Robert B., Kenneth P. Brevoort, and Glenn B. Canner. "Higher-Priced Home Lending and the 2005 HMDA Data" (580 KB PDF), *Federal Reserve Bulletin* 92, 2006. www.federalreserve.gov/pubs/bulletin.

Avery, Robert B., Paul S. Calem, and Glenn B. Canner. "The Effects of the Community Reinvestment Act on Local Communities" (89 KB PDF). Paper presented at Sustainable Community Development: What Works, What Doesn't and Why, a conference sponsored by the Board of Governors of the Federal Reserve System, March 27–28, 2003.

Avery, Robert B., Glenn B. Canner, Shannon C. Mok, and Dan S. Sokolov."Community Banks and Rural Development: Research Relating to Proposals to Revise the Regulations that Implement the Community Reinvestment Act" (149 KB PDF), *Federal Reserve Bulletin* 91, 2005.www.federalreserve.gov/pubs/bulletin.

Barr, Michael S. (2004). "Banking the Poor," *Yale Journal on Regulation* 21, 2004 (Winter): 121–237.

Barth, James R., Tong Li, Triphon Phumiwasana, and Glenn Yago, "A Short History of the Subprime Mortgage Market Meltdown," *Milken Institute*, January 2008. http://www.milkeninstitute.org/pdf/SubprimeMeltdownv2.pdf.

Bernanke, Ben S. "The Community Reinvestment Act: Its Evolution and New Challenges," Presented at the Community Affairs Research Conference, Washington, D.C., March 30, 2007. http://www.federalreserve.gov/newsevents/speech/bernanke20070330a.htm.

Bernanke, Ben S. "Financial Reform to Address Systemic Risk." Presented at the Council on Foreign Relations, Washington, D.C., March 10, 2009. http://www.federalreserve.gov/newsevents/speech/bernanke20090310a.htm.

Board of Governors of the Federal Reserve System, "Federal Reserve's Duties," November 6, 2009. http://www.federalreserve.gov/aboutthefed/mission.htm.

Board of Governors of the Federal Reserve System Federal Reserve Bank, "Intended federal funds rate, Change and level," January 26, 2010. http://www.federalreserve.gov/fomc/fundsrate.htm.

Chomsisengphet, Souphala, and Anthony Pennington-Cross. "The Evolution of the Subprime Market" (553 KB PDF), *Federal Reserve Bank of St. Louis Review* 88 2006 (January/February):31–56.

Data Explorers, Data & Analysis, "Analysis and Insight into Short Selling and Securities Financing"6 October 2009. http://www.redorbit.com/news/entertainment/1765698/data_explorers__shines_a__light_on_securities_financing_and_shortselling/index.html

(accessed December 28, 2010)

Department of the Treasury, *Financial Regulatory Reform*. http://financialstability.gov/docs/regs/FinalReport_web.pdf.

FDIC. "A Year in Bank Supervision: 2008 and a Few of Its Lessons, Supervisory Insights," Vol. 6, Issue 1. http://www.fdic.gov/regulations/examinations/supervisory/insights/sisum09/si_sum09.pdf.

FDIC."Statement of Sheila C. Bair, Chairman, Federal Deposit Insurance Corporation on the Causes and Current State of the Financial Crisis before the Financial Crisis Inquiry Commission, Room 1100, Longworth House Office Building," Washington D.C., January 14, 2010.http://www.fdic.gov/news/news/speeches/chairman/spjan1410.html.

FDIC. *Federal Deposit Insurance Corporation, Community Reinvestment Act of 1977*, Pub. L. No. 95–128; 91 Stat. 1147, effective October 12, 1977.http://www.fdic.gov/regulations/laws/rules/6500-2515.html#6500hcda1977.

Federal Reserve Bank of Minneapolis, "Born of a Panic: Forming the Fed System," August 1988. http://www.minneapolisfed.org/publications_papers/pub_display.cfm?id=3816.

FHA. "FHA Home Loans, FHA Loan Qualifying Summary." http://www.fha-home-loans.com/loan_qualifying_fha_loans.htm

Field, Abigail. "Lehman Report: Were Securities Regulators Out to Lunch?" *Daily Finance.* December 28, 2010. http://www.dailyfinance.com/story/investing/lehman-report-were-securities-regulators-out-to-lunch/19397816/

Henderson, David. "Don't Blame Greenspan," *Wall Street Journal*, March 27, 2009. http://online.wsj.com/article/SB123811225716453243.html.

Homes and Communities, U.S. Department of Housing and Urban Development. "The Federal Housing Administration (FHA)." http://www.hud.gov/offices/hsg/fhahistory.cfm.

Homes and Communities, U.S. Department of Housing and Urban Development. "American Dream Downpayment Initiative. http://www.hud.gov/offices/cpd/affordablehousing/programs/home/addi/index.cfm.

Labaton, Stephen. "S.E.C. Concedes Oversight Flaws Fueled Collapse," *New York Times*, September 26, 2008.http://www.nytimes.com/2008/09/27/business/27sec.html (accessed February 10, 2010).

Mishler, Lon, and Robert H. Cole. *Consumer and Business Credit Management*. Homewood, IL: Irwin, 1995.

Nelson, Leslie S. "SEC Securities Lending and Short Sale Roundtable," September 29, 2009. http://www.sec.gov/comments/4-590/4590-29.pdf.

Pagano, Claire E., George P. Attisano, and Joanne A. Skerr. "SEC Proposes Revisions to Money Market Fund Rules" *K&L Gates Newsstand*, July 7, 2009. http://www.fmocklaw.com/newsstand/Detail.aspx?publication=5763.

SEC. "The Investor's Advocate: How the SEC Protects Investors, Maintains Market Integrity, and Facilitates Capital Formation." http://www.sec.gov/about/whatwedo.shtml#create.

Shapiro, Mary L. "Testimony Before the United States House of Representatives Committee on Financial Services, 'Regulatory Perspectives on the Obama Administration's Financial Regulatory Reform Proposals,'" July 22, 2009. http://www.house.gov/apps/list/hearing/financialsvcs_dem/schapiro_testimony.pdf.

Shearman & Sterling LLP, "SEC Proposed Revisions to Rule 105: Short Selling in Connection with a Public Offering," March 2007. http://www.shearman.com/files/Publication/0aa24e08-6957-4ff4-b74c-21a13ef37147/Presentation/PublicationAttachment/3282f38a-e275-4b8d-99a6-228903a23e1b/SEC%20Proposed%20Revisions%20to%20Rule%20105%20032007.pdf.

Taylor, John B. "How Government Created the Financial Crisis, Research shows the failure to rescue Lehman did not trigger the fall panic." *Wall Street Journal*, February 9, 2009. http://online.wsj.com/article/SB123414310280561945.html.

Teather, David. "SEC Seeks Rating Sector Clean-up," *Guardian*, January 28 2003. http://www.guardian.co.uk/business/2003/jan/28/usnews.internationalnews.

U.S. Department of the Treasury. "Testimony by Secretary Henry M. Paulson, Jr. before the Senate Banking Committee, on Turmoil in US Credit Markets: Recent Actions regarding, Government Sponsored Entities, Investment Banks and, other Financial Institutions," September 23, 2008. http://www.treas.gov/press/releases/hp1153.htm.

U.S. Department of Treasury, Financial Regulatory Reform, a new Foundation, Rebuilding Financial Supervision and Regulation, June 17, 2009. http://www.financialstability.gov/latest/tg_06172009.html. (Accessed December 28, 2010)

CHAPTER 4

LOCAL IMPACT OF THE FINANCIAL CRISIS AND ECONOMIC RECESSION

INTRODUCTION

A recession is normally associated with generally lower personal incomes, rising unemployment, and huge declines in business profits because of cuts in consumer and corporate investment spending and increased bankruptcies. The presence of the financial crisis not only escalated these negative macroeconomic indicator variations but also widened the negative impact to include the financial markets, the financial institutions, savers, investors, and all levels of governments: federal, state, and local. The combined negative impact of the last financial crisis and economic recession is only second to that of the Great Depression.

In this chapter, we examine the local impact of the financial crisis and economic recession by looking at the implications on the financial system, investors, savers, businesses, employment, and different levels of government.

IMPACT OF THE FINANCIAL CRISIS/ECONOMIC RECESSION ON THE FINANCIAL SYSTEM

In every economy, at any point in time, there are those who have more funds than they need and may wish to lend these excess funds or invest them in equities (ownership interests) for benefits including interest income or dividend income, and appreciation in asset values, as in the case of equities and fixed income securities. The people who have excess funds are called surplus units in the economy. On the other hand, at any point in time, there are those who need funds and are willing to borrow and pay varying levels of interest for the use of the borrowed funds. These are called deficit units. The problem has always been how to efficiently coordinate the flow of funds from surplus units to deficit units so that the deficit units can obtain the funds they need for the right length of time at competitive interest rates.

The financial system provides a mechanism whereby an individual surplus unit (firm or household) can easily make funds available to deficit units who plan to spend more money than they intend to generate. The financial system consists of the financial markets, such as the New York Stock Exchange and NASDAQ as well as financial institutions, such as commercial banks, thrifts, mutual funds, pension funds, etc., that act as financial intermediaries. Financial intermediation in our economy is not exclusive to these institutions, but these are good examples. In a well-developed financial system, there are two main ways in which funds flow from surplus to deficit units. The first method is through the financial markets where deficit units issue financial instruments to surplus units called investors. These financial instruments include bonds and common stock.

For example, if Wal-Mart wants to establish another store, it needs to raise two million dollars by issuing bonds and another two million dollars by issuing stock. It can do so by making seasoned issues of bonds and stock in the financial markets. Investors who have excess funds may purchase these issues. These investors can be individual investors, or institutional investors such as mutual funds. Thus, the proceeds flow from the investors (surplus units) to Wal-Mart (deficit unit), in exchange for bond certificates and stock certificates. The bond certificates acknowledge the long-term debt and promise to make coupon payments and the principle on maturity. The stock certificate is evidence of the investor's ownership right to dividends and stock appreciation that may accrue to the investor. This method of funds transfer from surplus units to deficit units is referred to as direct finance. Normally companies like Wal-Mart sell these securities in the primary market through investment bankers. This is indirect transfer. Sometimes the indirect transfer occurs through other institutions such as mutual funds.

Funds can also flow from the surplus units to deficit units through financial institutions. Because households, individuals, businesses, and governments deposit surplus funds in saving accounts with financial institutions, these financial institutions accumulate funds that they extend as loans to deficit units. When surplus units deposit funds with banks, those funds are assets to the surplus units and liabilities to the banks. However, when the banks use these funds to extend loans, the loans extended become assets to banks and liabilities to the deficit units that receive the loans. There is no problem as long as the loans extended by the financial institutions to individuals are repaid in a timely manner because checking account deposits at financial institutions must be paid back to depositors on demand. The deposits at saving accounts must be returned to the depositors with interest as agreed.

Unfortunately, this was not the case during the subprime mortgage crisis that started in 2006. Many financial institutions had extended huge sums of money to many risky borrowers to purchase homes in fulfillment of the American Dream initiative or under FHA conditions. Many of them also had mortgages with adjustable rates that started with very low initial interest rates. When the interest rates started to go higher and higher for these borrowers, amidst the housing bust and slump in home prices, many borrowers holding mortgages from financial institutions could no longer pay their mortgages, and the financial institutions foreclosed on their homes. Some home owners abandoned their homes, because the homes were worth less than the mortgage, and the banks foreclosed on these homes. In the presence of declining home prices, there was not much hope for accumulating any equity on their homes.

In a good housing market, the banks would have been able to sell the foreclosed homes and recover their money. However, they could not sell most of the foreclosed homes because of the low demand for homes, and there was no financing available for the little demand that did exist. The foreclosed houses had become toxic assets. Many of the small financial institutions that participated substantially in subprime lending failed, because their funds were tied up in these toxic assets, and they could not extend more loans. Because loans constitute about 60 percent of bank assets, it meant that the financial institutions' ability to generate earnings was diminished. In addition, their ability to service saving and other deposit accounts, pay deposits back to depositors as agreed, and pay back checking accounts on demand also were diminished.

These so-called toxic assets have generated intense conversation nationwide. How do we identify them? How much are they worth? Initially, they were estimated at two trillion dollars. However, when the Obama Administration decided to tackle the clogging of the U.S. credit system, Treasury Secretary Tim Geithner announced on March. 23, 2009, a plan to buy the toxic assets in the form of bad mortgage securities estimated at one trillion dollars.

IMPACT OF THE FINANCIAL CRISIS/ECONOMIC RECESSION ON FINANCIAL INSTITUTIONS

The first banks to show severe signs of financial stress were the banks that were involved in excessive lending for construction and mortgages. For example, IndyMac Bank was taken over by federal regulators on Friday, July 11, 2008.[17] IndyMac Bank operated as a hybrid thrift/mortgage banker that provided cost-efficient financing for the acquisition of single-family homes. IndyMac also provided financing secured by single-family homes and other banking products to facilitate consumers' personal financial goals. At the point of collapse IndyMac had assets of $32.01 billion and deposits of $19.06 billion and was one of the nation's largest home lenders.

David Loeb and Angelo Mozilo, who also founded Countrywide, another big mortgage lender whose loans helped fuel the housing boom, founded IndyMac in 1985.[18] Countrywide used IndyMac as a means of collateralizing Countrywide Financial loans that were too big to be sold to Freddie Mac and Fannie Mae. In 1997, Countrywide spun off IndyMac as an independent company.[19]

Countrywide had to do this because of the criteria set by the Office of Federal Housing Enterprise Oversight (OFHEO) regarding what constitutes a conforming loan and limiting what the two Government enterprises, Fannie Mae and Freddie Mac, can buy. The criteria include documentation requirements, debt-to-income ratio limits, and maximum loan amounts.

Fannie Mae, for example, can only purchase mortgage loans made to individuals from financial institutions. Fannie Mae inspects the property being used as collateral for the mortgage loan in order to have an accurate and reliable appraisal by an appraiser licensed in accordance with Fannie Mae's guidelines. The first or front ratio represents the housing expense to income ratio. In other words, the proposed mortgage payment, such as the principle, interest, taxes, and insurance, divided by the gross monthly income must not exceed 36 percent. The total debt to income ratio must not exceed 28 percent. In addition to all this, the price of the house for certain descriptions must not exceed a certain amount. According to the information available at the Fannie Mae website,[20] in 1998, the Fannie Mae mortgage loan limits were $227,150 for a single-family home, $290,650 for a two-family home, $351,300 for a three-family home, $436,600 for a four-family home, and $113,575 for a second home. In 2008, the Fannie Mae mortgage loan limits were $417,000 for a single-family home, $533,850 for a two-family home, $645,300 for a three-family home, $801,950 for a four-family home, and $208,500 for a second home. An adjustment is usually made upwards, about 50 percent, for high cost areas such as Alaska, Hawaii, the Virgin Islands, and Guam. The Virgin Islands was designated a high cost area in 1992 and Guam in 2001. Prior to 1984, second mortgage limits were the same as first mortgage limits. The provisions in the Economic Stimulus Act of 2008 reduced the limits to 50 percent of first mortgage limits. Fannie Mae had no second mortgage program before 1981. Fannie Mae uses the October-to-October changes in median home price to set the maximum loan amount per loan it purchases from financial institutions. Fannie Mae does not purchase jumbo loans from financial institutions. Because these are loans above these established limits and usually considered more risky, they have higher rates. These regulations are similar to the regulations under which Freddie Mac purchases loans from financial institutions.

As IndyMac operated in the subprime mortgage market and delivered services in the securitization of mortgage securities, including the risky and non-conforming jumbo loans, the company flourished. In 2006, the net income of IndyMac Bank Corp Inc. had increased to US$300,000 from US$34,000 in 2005. Because of the subprime mortgage crisis, IndyMac Bank Corp Inc. sustained the first annual loss of US$614.8 million in 2007.[21]

[17] See Catherine Clifford and Chris Isidore, CNNMoney.com
[18] See Jon-Christopher Bua, Sky News, Sunday July 13, 2008.
[19] See Damian Paletta and David Enrich Crisis, *Wall Street Journal*, July 12, 2008.
[20] See Fannie Mae, http://www.fanniemae.com/aboutfm/pdf/historicalloanlimits.pdf;jsessionid=AWTNF2FMES3RTJ2FQSHSFGI.
[21] See Los Angeles Times, IndyMac Bancorp posts first annual loss, http://articles.latimes.com/2008/feb/13/business/fi-indy13

2006 was the best year for IndyMac. The stock price of the company soared in the stock market from $12.18 on January 5, 1998, to $45.01 on May 8, 2006, and then it declined to $0.08 on June 26, 2008. See Figure 4.1.

Figure 4.1 IndyMac Bank Corporation Daily Stock Prices 1998 to 2008

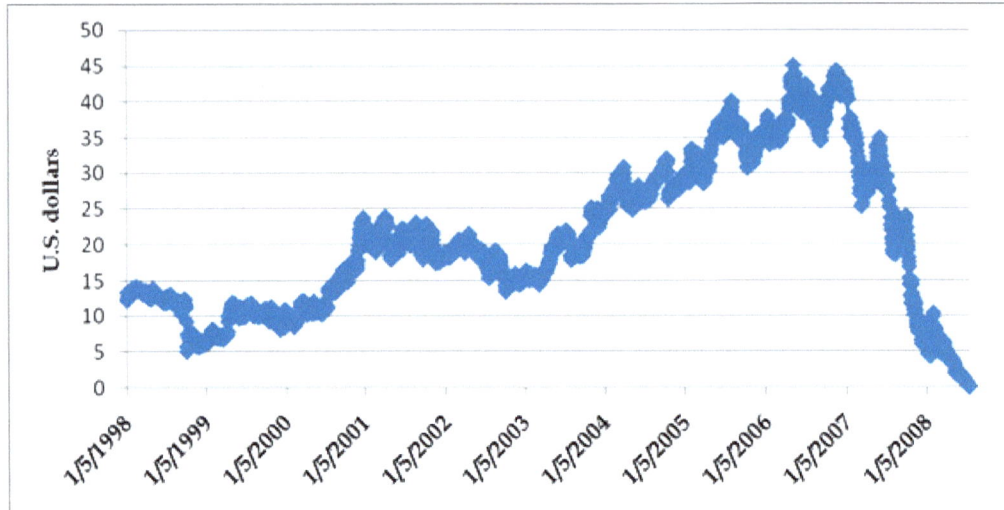

On Thursday, July 31, 2008, IndyMac Bancorp filed for Chapter 7 protection with the Federal Bankruptcy Court in Los Angeles. With a stunning $32 billion in assets, this is by far one of the largest failures in decades, the second largest savings and loan failure in history, and the third largest banking failure in U.S. history. In addition to engaging in risky subprime lending and securitization of jumbo loans, IndyMac also acquired Financial Freedom in 2004 that specialized in the reverse mortgage business.

A reverse mortgage allows senior citizens to access a portion of their home equity. The senior citizen maintains the title to the home and can continue to live in it without having to make monthly reverse mortgage payments. Proceeds from the reverse mortgage loan can be used for a variety of things such as covering medical costs, prescription drugs, long-term care costs, home improvements, or any unexpected expenses. The money received under a reverse mortgage arrangement is tax free. In the event of a sale of the property or death of the senior citizen holding the mortgage, the proceeds are used to repay the balance of the loan to the financial institution. All remaining equity goes to the estate of the deceased. The estate is not liable if the home sells for less than the balance of the reverse mortgage. Reverse mortgages are very appealing to seniors who are experiencing cash flow problems but have equity in their homes. The only problem with a reverse mortgage is that there has to be equity in the home, which of course was very rare when the housing bubble collapsed.

When IndyMac the mortgage lender failed, it had about $32 billion in assets and about $19 billion in deposits. Most of the deposits were insured but approximately $1 billion of that did not fall within FDIC insured protection. Therefore, depositors were impacted by this financial crisis, and many banks suffered a similar fate. Between April 2008 and May 2011, more than 353[22] FDIC banks failed.

IMPACT OF THE FINANCIAL CRISIS/ECONOMIC RECESSION ON THE CREDIT MARKETS

Bank credit to the private sector exceeded 100 percent of GDP between 2001 and the first quarter of 2003. The highest amount of bank credit to the private sector before the crisis occurred in the third

---

[22] FDIC List of Failed Banks, http://www.fdic.gov/bank/individual/failed/banklist.html, [May 29, 2011]

quarter of 2006 was in the amount of about $11.3 trillion. As the crisis ensued, many financial institutions lost billions of dollars, bank credit to the private sector contracted by about $2.7 trillion to the amount of $9.8 trillion in the fourth quarter of 2008. Table 4.1 contains the data and Figure 4.2 depicts the trend in the growth and decline of bank lending to the private sector in the U.S. The highest growth period coincided with the period of the highest growth in subprime lending.

Table 4.1 Bank Credit to Private Sector in the U.S., 2001 to 2009

Quarters	GDP (billions of dollars)	Bank Credit as Proportion of GDP	Bank Credit to Private Sector (billions of dollars)
2009 Q4	13,149.50	0.782721	10292.38979
2009 Q3	12,973.00	0.793718	10296.90361
2009 Q3	12, 901.50	0.795831	10,267.41
2009 Q1	12,925.40	0.804576	10399.46663
2008 Q4	12,141.90	0.808247	9813.654249
2008 Q3	13,324.60	0.813374	10837.8832
2008 Q2	13,415.30	0.823801	11051.53756
2008 Q1	13,366.90	0.823557	11008.40406
2007 Q4	13,391.20	0.826545	11068.4294
2007 Q3	13,391.20	0.83126	11131.56891
2007 Q2	13,204.00	0.845127	11159.05691
2007 Q1	13,099.90	0.860168	11268.11478
2006 Q4	13,060.70	0.862003	11258.36258
2006 Q3	12,965.90	0.870932	11292.41722
2006 Q2	11,291.70	0.889741	10046.68845
2006 Q1	11,217.30	0.894475	10033.59442
2005 Q4	11,086.10	0.895426	9926.782179
2005 Q3	11,505.00	0.90426	10403.5113
2005 Q2	10,954.10	0.913479	10006.34031
2005 Q1	10,878.40	0.933177	10151.47268
2004 Q4	10,796.40	0.936975	10115.95689
2004 Q3	10,728.70	0.952315	10217.10194
2004 Q2	10,671.50	0.952873	10168.58422
2004 Q1	10,612.50	0.96888	10282.239
2003 Q4	10,502.60	0.968529	10172.07268
2003 Q3	10,410.90	0.977815	10179.93418
2003 Q2	10,230.40	0.989043	10118.30551
2003 Q1	10,138.60	1.006457	10204.06494
2002 Q4	10,095.80	1.006471	10161.12992
2002 Q3	10,090.70	1.027305	10366.22656
2002 Q2	10,031.60	1.03787	10411.49669
2002 Q1	9,977.30	1.059027	10566.23009
2001 Q4	9,910.00	1.063016	10534.48856
2001 Q3	9,971.10	1.080367	10772.44739

Quarters	GDP (billions of dollars)	Bank Credit as Proportion of GDP	Bank Credit to Private Sector (billions of dollars)
2001 Q2	9,905.90	1.095052	10847.47561
2001 Q1	9,875.60	1.108047	10942.62895

Source: U.S. Bureau of Economic Analysis and Bank for International Settlement (BIS), World Bank, http://www.bea.gov, http://www.jedh.org/jedh_dbase.html

Figure 4.2 U.S. Bank Credit to the Private Sector, 2001 to 2009

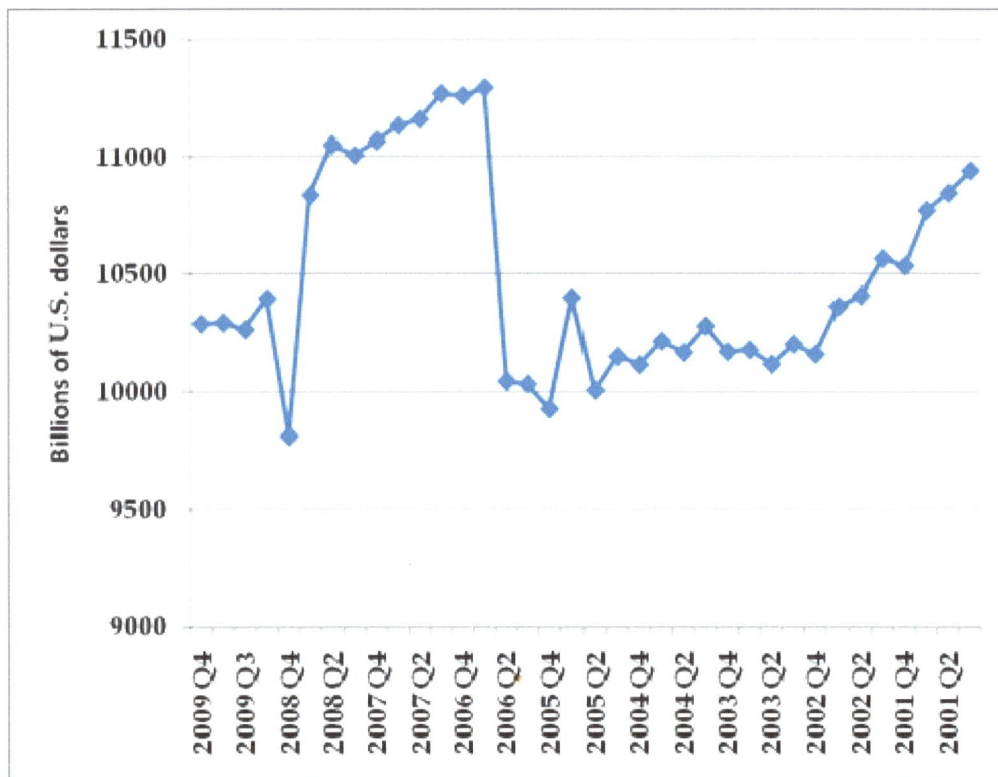

This decline in bank lending to the private sector created a severe credit crunch. The huge losses sustained by many banks led to the failure of many of them, thus reducing the number of lending banks and the amount of loanable funds. The huge losses suffered by many banks put some on the brink of bankruptcy and severely limited their ability to continue their lending function. The two mortgage giants, Fannie Mae and Freddie Mac who were responsible for ensuring liquidity in the mortgage market and that guaranteed almost 50 percent of total U.S. home loans worth more than $5 trillion, were on the brink of collapse in the summer of 2008. This was due to their involvement in the sale of risky asset-backed subprime mortgage securities. Some of the big banks that suffered huge losses had enough capital to stay afloat, but they fell behind in their capital ratio. For example, by October 2008, within only six months, Citigroup had $40 billion in losses. See Figure 4.3

IMPACT OF THE FINANCIAL CRISIS/ECONOMIC RECESSION ON INVESTORS

The financial markets hit many categories of investors hard: large, medium-size, and small. Many investors lost a big portion of their investment portfolio in the stock market, and others lost huge sums of money in their real estate investments. Even Warren Buffet, one of the most successful investors in the world, lost $25 billion in twelve months during the 2008/2009 financial crisis.

IMPACT OF THE FINANCIAL CRISIS/ECONOMIC RECESSION ON INVESTMENTS IN EQUITY

It was generally a bull stock market in the U.S. from 2002 to September 2007, and it is not surprising that the S&P 500 Index achieved the value of 1565.15, the highest of the decade. The roaring stock market and huge increases in stock prices encouraged many to shift more and more of their investment portfolios, including retirement portfolios such as their 401ks, into investments in the stock market. Many baby boomers and mutual funds did the same, and many educational institutions invested their excess funds in the stock markets.

When the stock markets declined in 2008, most investors were taken by surprise. By March 9, 2009, the value of the S&P 500 had declined to 676.53, representing a 57 percent decline. The S&P 500 is a very representative index, because it includes 500 stocks of large, public companies. These companies are traded on the NYSE Euronext, American stock market companies, and NASDAQ OMX. See Figure 4.3 for the steady increases in the value of the S&P 500 between 2002 and 2007 and the precipitous decline in 2008 and 2009.

Figure 4.3 S&P 500 Daily Index price, 1998 to 2009

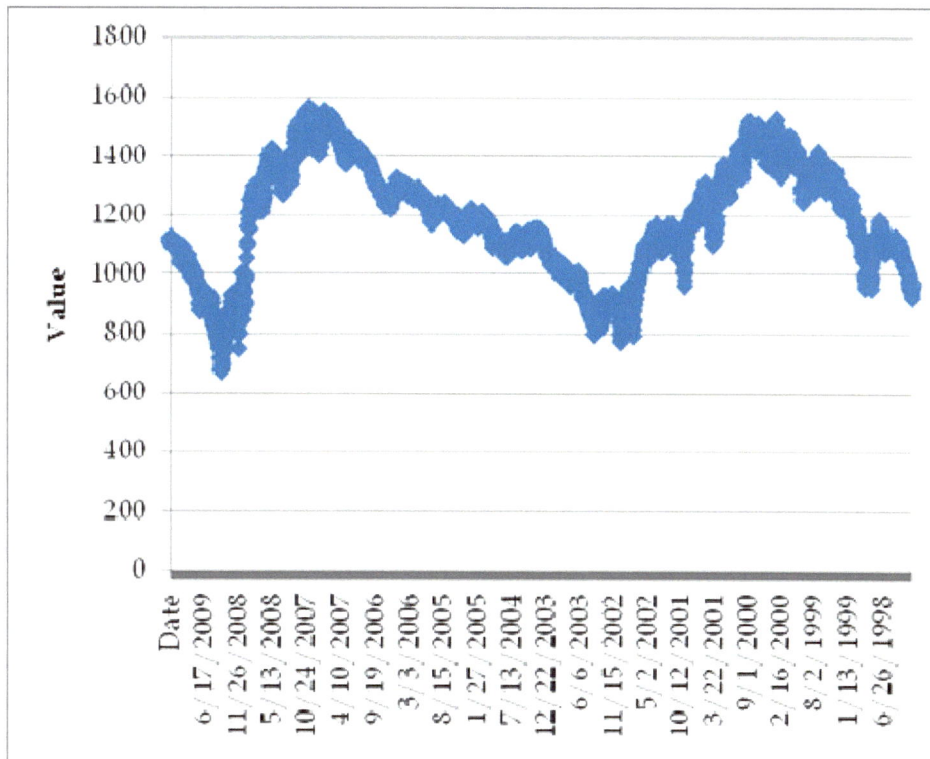

IMPACT ON INVESTORS

To gain an insight into the impact of the financial crisis and economic recession on investors, in April 2010, two years after the crisis began, we distributed questionnaires to one hundred investors in Connecticut. Some of the questions were open-ended and others were multiple choice.

The results indicated only 42 percent of the respondents owned stock. Fifty percent of the respondents consider their investment strategy conservative, 37 percent risky, and 13 percent moderate. Forty-seven percent of the respondents indicated that they suffered losses in their investments because of the financial crisis/economic recession. More than two-thirds of the respondents were worried about their investments, especially investments in stock losing their value in the future.

The investors that suffered immensely from this recession were investors who had invested a lot of their 401k in the stock market. In a 401k plan, an employee makes periodic monetary contributions from gross income before taxes. This value is usually matched by a certain amount of employer contributions. Both contributions are tax deferred and are normally transferred to a special account where the funds may be invested. For 2009, the maximum allowed elective deferred fund contribution for an employee per year was $16,500 for employees under the age of fifty and $22,000 for employees over the age of fifty. The fund is transferable if an employee changes employers, and the employee can begin to receive "qualified distributions" from the funds in the account when the account owner reaches the age of fifty-nine and a half. As employees start cashing out their 401k plans, they earn income that is subject to taxes.

Many employed investors with a 401k were nearing retirement when this huge stock market decline hit them. According to CBS,[23] sixty-year-old Alan Weir lost nearly half of his life savings, $140,000, in a matter of months. Alan planned to retire at the age of sixty-two but was not able to and has postponed his retirement until the age of seventy. Another person interviewed was fifty-nine-year-old Iris Hontz who lost her job as an accountant and half the value of her 401k.

An article in the *New York Times* recorded the experiences of some people's losses as a result of the diminished value of their portfolios.[24] Cindy and Eric Canup's portfolio values were off by 25 percent. Now, they are very careful with spending and have delayed by five to ten years their dream of buying land in Northern California or Oregon. In spite of this experience, they decided to stick with the stock market and took on riskier investments in mutual funds. In the case of Linda Blay, her portfolio lost 30 percent of its value. She still believes in the stock market, and that it outperforms any investment. According to Hewitt Associates, many people moved money from 401k plans to cash or bonds for safety in the first half of 2009.[25]

PSCA is a non-profit association of 1,200 companies that sponsor defined contribution plans for five million employees. PSCA offers unbiased best practices information, research, and technical assistance. According to a PSCA survey of 406 companies that offered a matching contribution on December 31, 2007, 14.8 percent of those companies suspended their matching contributions, 3.8 percent reduced them, 4.7 increased them, and 76.8 percent made no changes relative to matching.[26] Of the 264 companies that offered a non-matching company contribution, 26.8 percent suspended or reduced their contribution, and 73.2 percent made no changes relative to contributions. The survey revealed that large companies were more likely to suspend matching than smaller companies; 54.3 percent of all companies increased plan education efforts, and 9.6 percent of companies added investment advice. The bulk of the respondent companies were in the services, financial, wholesale, retail trade, and durable goods manufacturing industries. Many of these companies were responding to the financial crisis and economic recession. The suspension and reduction of matching contributions resulted in a decrease in savings for the workers in a situation where most of them had lost a significant amount of their 401k retirement funds in the stock market.

---

[23] See CBS, April 19, 2009, http://www.cbsnews.com/stories/2009/04/17/60minutes/main4951968.shtml.
[24] See Jack Healy, September 10, 2009, http://www.nytimes.com/2009/09/11/business/11investors.html
[25] Ibid
[26] See PSCA, "Impact of Economic Conditions on 401(k) and Profit Sharing Plans©," 2009,
http://www.psca.org/Portals/0/401k%20Economic%20Impact%20Survey%20Final.pdf.

IMPACT OF THE FINANCIAL CRISIS/ECONOMIC RECESSION ON SAVERS

According to the U.S. Department of Commerce, Bureau of Economic Analysis,[27] the U.S. personal saving rate was 14.6 percent in May 1975 and 12.2 percent in November 1981, the highest personal saving rates experienced since 1959. See Figure 4.4.

Figure 4.4 U.S. Personal Savings Rate, 1980 to 2010

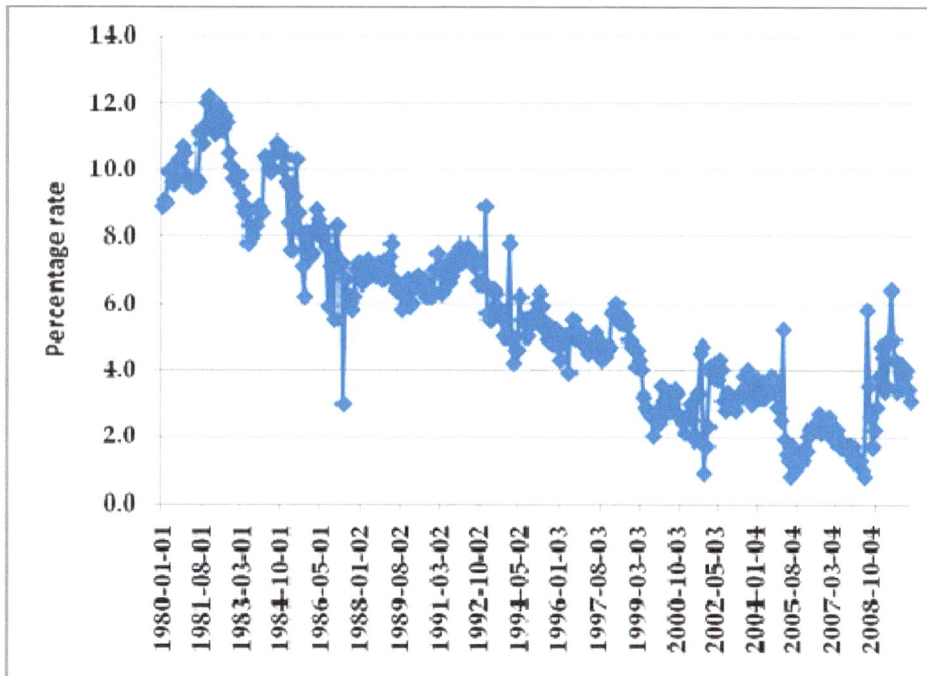

The 1970s was a period of great personal savings. The U.S. recorded an average personal saving rate of 9.6 percent. The average personal saving rate declined to 8.6 percent in the 1980s, to 5.5 percent in the 1990's, and to an abysmal 2.7 percent between 2000 and 2008. See Table 4.2.

Table 4.2 Average Saving Rates in Percent

Period	Average Saving Rates in percent
1950s and 1960s	8.2
1970s	9.6
1980's	8.6
1990s	5.5
2000-2008	2.7

Source: Constructed from data on Department of Commerce, Bureau of Economic Analysis, http://research.stlouisfed.org/fred2/series/PSAVERT?rid=54&soid=18.

---

[27] Economic Research, Federal Reserve Bank of St. Louis, December 29, 2010, http://research.stlouisfed.org/fred2/series/PSAVERT?rid=54&soid=18

In fact, in April 2008, the average personal saving rate was 0.8 percent. According to Kirsanova and Sefton,[28] averaged over the 1990s, the Italians saved a net of depreciation just below 20 percent of their disposable income; the British saved just under 8 percent, and the Americans just above 0 percent. The authors believe that the Italian saving rate is high, predominantly because Italians are unable to borrow much, particularly when they are young.

China's personal saving rate is said to be the highest in the world. China's personal saving rate is about 25 percent.[29] The reason for this very high personal saving rate is due mainly to uncertainty about the future. In addition, the 1978 economic reform ended financial dependence on the Government.[30]

The impact of the economic crisis on savers was conflicted. Initially, many people lost their homes or the equity in their homes and lost their jobs. They were not able to save more but instead dipped into their accumulated savings to get them through the difficult times. As the crisis progressed and the difficult economic situation was being compared to the Great Depression, many people became uncertain about the future and started to save more. According to the Christian Science Monitor,[31] Courtney Davis acknowledged that she was a spender, but she decided to have 20 percent of her pay directly deposited into a savings and investment account. Only 41 percent of Americans save regularly, and three-quarters of American households carry debt. The reasons for the lack of savings include higher housing prices, healthcare, and education costs that are changing the definition of need and want. People are banking on future earnings and not savings.

IMPACT OF THE FINANCIAL CRISIS/ECONOMIC RECESSION ON BUSINESSES

Assuming efficient management and good economic conditions, the success or failure of a business depends on the presence of demand for the goods or services produced as well as the ability of the business to deliver those goods or services at a reasonable or low cost. A decline in demand for the products or services generally leads to lower profits; a drastic decline will dissipate the profits. The presence of any factor or factors that seriously affect the demand of products or service diminishes the production level of businesses and profits plummet. Equally devastating to business survival is huge increases in operating or overall costs.

As the financial crisis progressed, demand for houses plummeted, and companies operating in the real estate industry were affected. These included mortgage brokers and real estate companies. The financial crisis negatively affected financial institutions, especially those that lent significantly to subprime borrowers or had inefficient operations. The impact of the financial crisis and economic recession on financial institutions is discussed earlier in this chapter. In this section, we focus on the impact of the financial crisis and economic recession on small businesses.

HOW IMPORTANT ARE SMALL BUSINESSES TO THE U.S. ECONOMY?

The Office of Advocacy of the Small Business Administration defines a small business, for research purposes, as an independent business having fewer than 500 employees. According to Kobe,[32] small

[28] See Tatiana Kirsanova and James Sefton, 2002, http://www.nes.ru/NES10/cd/materials/Kirsanova-savingNES.pdf.
[29] See Federal Reserve Bank of St Louis, August 2008, http://research.stlouisfed.org/publications/iet/20080801/cover.pdf.
[30] Federal Reserve Bank of St Louis, Why Do Chinese Households Save So Much? International Economic Trends, August 2008, http://research.stlouisfed.org/publications/iet/20080801/cover.pdf.
[31] Christian Science Monitor, March 1, 2010, http://moneycentral.msn.com/content/savinganddebt/savemoney/p145775.asp.
[32] http://www/advo/research/rs299tot.pdf [incomplete cite—this is no longer a valid web site]

firms represent 99.7 percent of all employer firms, and employ just over half of all private sector employees. Small businesses pay 44 percent of total U.S. private payroll. They generated 64 percent of net new jobs over the past fifteen years and create more than half of the non-farm private GDP. They hire 40 percent of high technology workers, such as scientists, engineers, and computer programmers. Fifty-two percent of small firms in the U.S. are home based and 2 percent are franchises. Small firms made up 97.3 percent of all identified exporters and produced 30.2 percent of known export value in the 2007 financial year. Small firms produce thirteen times more patents per employee than large patenting firms.

Despite the importance of small businesses in the U.S., the mortality rate of small businesses is very high. For example, a comparison of the number of small business births and closures from 2004 to 2008 indicates that, as a percentage of small business births, the closures constitute 86 percent in 2004, 88 percent in 2005, 89 percent in 2006, 86 percent in 2007 and 95 percent in 2008. See Table 4.3. The number of bankruptcies declined from 34,317 cases in 2004 to 19,695 cases in 2006. Unfortunately, the number of bankruptcies increased from 19,695 in 2006 to 43,546 in 2008, an increase of about 121 percent. It more than doubled in two years. See Table 4.3 and Figure 4.5.

Table 4.3 Starts and Closures of Employer Firms, 2004–2008

Year	Births	Closures	Closure rates in % of births	Bankruptcies
2004	628,917	541,047	86	34,317
2005	644,122	565,745	88	39,201
2006	670,058	599,333	89	19,695
2007	663,100	571,300	86	28,322
2008	627,200	595,600	95	43,546

Source: SBA (www.sba.gov), U.S. Department of Commerce (www.commerce.gov), Bureau of Census (www.census.gov,), Administrative Office of the U.S. Department of Labor (www.oalj.dol.gov), Employment and Training Association (http://www.eata.org)

Figure 4.5 Starts and Closures of Employer Firms, 2004–2008

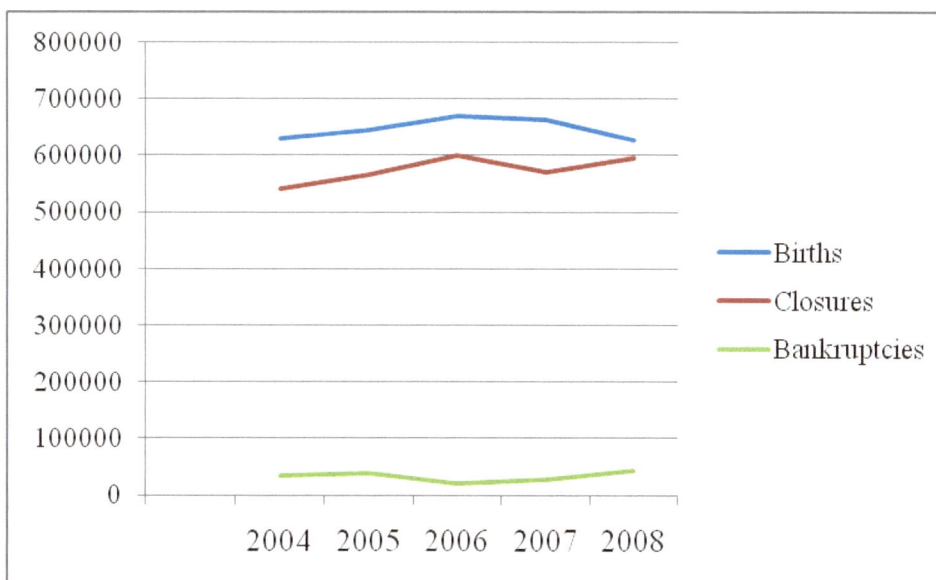

Although there is no consensus as to whether small businesses thrive in a recession or are hurt by it, the increased rate of small business closures and bankruptcies in 2008 must be due to the financial crisis and economic recession. Some of the factors that could lead to the vulnerability of small businesses in a financial crisis and recession include a low capital base, dependence on credit cards, and poor sales due to reduced demand for goods and services. As incomes decline and unemployment increases, mortgage problems for small businesses generally increase the cost of utilities and other factor inputs such as gas and so on. It is generally believed that the small businesses' worst problem was the credit crunch and their inability to borrow. However, in the April 2010 report of the National Federation of Independent Business, the NFIB reported that small businesses overwhelmingly continued to cite "Poor Sales" as their number one problem.

Small businesses' poor sales or decline in sales was illustrated by various CBS reports. One such report relates to Jerry Natkin, who owns a jewelry store in lower Manhattan, which caters to the Wall Street sector. "Customers were not buying like the good old days," said Jerry[33]. So he introduced a new inventory line. He stocked $450 watches for customers who used to easily spend ten times that amount of money. "So rather than lose this customer, we brought this product line in,"[34] Jerry explains. Even with the new line, store revenue was down about $1 million. Natkin cut salaries across the board by 10 percent and had to cut his workforce reducing it from twenty-four employees to eighteen.

In another CBS report regarding a one-time-popular house wine, Fetzer Vineyards in California, the Winery Director, Mike Haering, admits falling restaurant sales has affected its winery business. However, in Fetzer's warehouse, unsold cases are already growing into a mountain. The decli restaurant sales has been partially offset by people buying wine to drink at home. "We're down 6 p of what [we] expected to do for our plans,"[35] Haering said. "That's the equivalent of 2.5 million bo Two and a half million fewer bottles sold means less of everything. "It impacts what glass, what we need, how much fruit,"[36] Haering said.[37]

The CBS report emphasized the interconnection of many small businesses. The drop in demand for wine at restaurants also affected Butch Cameron's fleet of fifty trucks that move wine for Fetzer and other California wineries. "Our revenues are down 40 percent this year," Cameron said. "For us, that is into the millions." In 2009, revenue dropped by about $2 million, and he slashed his workforce from sixty to twenty-five.[38]

In another report, the president of Composites One, a supplier of fiberglass for boat hulls, talks about his business as being left high and dry and admits that it is a very scary time for a lot of people. Leon Garoufalis says, "It's a very challenging time, without question."[39] For the first time in the company's seventy-year history, it has been forced to lay off employees, one-hundred over the last six months. It is not just about slumping boat sales, manufacturers of RVs, big rigs and automobiles are buying reduced quantities of fiber glass these days. The suburban Chicago headquarters expects to see its 2009 sales total at least $150 million less than last year.[40]

---

[33] See Jim Axelrod, June 10, 2009,
http://www.cbsnews.com/stories/2009/06/10/eveningnews/main5078884.shtml?source=related_story.
[34] Ibid.
[35] John Blackstone, May 26, 2009, http://www.cbsnews.com/stories/2009/05/27/eveningnews/main5044560.shtml
[36] Ibid.
[37] Ibid.
[38] Ibid.
[39] Ibid
[40] John Blackstone, May 26, 2009, http://www.cbsnews.com/stories/2009/05/27/eveningnews/main5044560.shtml

IMPLICATIONS OF THE FINANCIAL CRISIS/ECONOMIC RECESSION ON SMALL BUSINESSES IN THE STATE OF CONNECTICUT

We distributed fifty questionnaires to small business owners in Hebron, Marlborough, and the Colchester regions in the State of Connecticut to ascertain the impact of the financial crisis/economic recession on their business. The questionnaires were distributed mainly to businesses in the service sector: restaurants, package stores, lumber yards, convenience stores, auto body repair shops, psychotherapists, and construction companies. These questionnaires were personally administered with a 100 percent response rate.

According to the feedback from these questionnaires, all the businesses were impacted by the financial crisis/economic recession. Thirty-eight percent of the respondents indicated that they suffered a decrease in customer demand. The same proportion of respondents indicated price inflation in needed goods. Twelve percent of the respondents experienced difficulty in obtaining bank credit. Prior to the financial crisis/economic recession, 62 percent of these small businesses obtained credit from commercial banks. Another 12 percent said that they lost some customers because they now preferred buying cheaper goods.

Seventy-five percent of the respondents experienced a loss in revenue with about 10 percent experiencing as much a 50 percent loss. It is interesting to note that 10 percent experienced an increase in profits. Package stores experienced increased sales from the recession, commenting that sales remained constant but customers were buying cheaper inventory. A private practice therapist indicated that he had more clients from the recession because of the heightened level of stress. An auto body repair shop indicated that customers were resorting to repairing their old cars instead of buying new ones. The auto body repair shops experienced an increase in revenues and customers during the recessionary period.

On the other hand, restaurants exhibited the largest negative impact from the financial crisis/recession. The restaurant business needs a constant flow of customers, and during this economic recession, people needed to make smart financial choices and eating out can be one less expense for them.

To adapt to the situation, 50 percent of the respondents decreased purchases of inventory, 20 percent engaged in pay cuts, 20 percent changed supplies, and only 10 percent reduced the number of employees by retrenching workers.

IMPACT ON THE UNEMPLOYED

In the first quarter of 2010, we administered an online survey on the impact of the financial crisis/economic recession on unemployed workers. The survey consisted of ten questions designed to solicit information regarding the effects of the recent financial crisis and recession on the unemployed population. Nine individuals completed the survey, and, in reviewing the results, the responses from two respondents who were retired were excluded. Even though the sample is small, the feedback from this questionnaire administration was insightful.

The respondents have been unemployed between one month and one year. Seventy-one percent of the respondents believed that the economic recession was responsible for their prolonged unemployment. Seventy-one percent were receiving unemployment benefits; however, only 29 percent needed to seek additional public assistance, such as food stamps. Fourteen percent indicated that they had lost personal property, such as a home or a car, as a result of their unemployment. The most significant impact was seen in the loss of savings. Eighty-six percent indicated that they needed to use a significant amount of their savings to support themselves. All the respondents were actively seeking employment, but some felt that they were rejected because of their age or qualifications or simply because companies were not hiring.

Even though the research findings indicated that plummeting sales had done the most harm to small businesses during the financial crisis and recession, the overwhelming use of credit as a source of financing by small businesses and the ensuing credit squeeze was a very important factor in this difficult time. Small businesses normally do not have as much cushion in terms of capital as big businesses. Therefore, in difficult economic times, such as a recession when sales generally decline, their profits decline as well. To stay in business, many small businesses rely on credit. The banks were not as forthcoming with credit availability as they used to be, because the economic recession was accompanied by a financial crisis. In 2009, 45 percent of small employers did not even try to borrow. Of the 55 percent of small employers that borrowed, only 40 percent had all their needs met. See Table 4.4.

Table 4.4 Small business employers, in percent

Small Business Employers	Percent
Small business employers attempted to borrow in 2009	55
Small business employers that did not attempt to borrow in 2009	45
Small business employers attempted to borrow in 2009 and had all their credit needs met	40
Small business employers attempted to borrow in 2009 and had most of their credit needs met	10
Small business employers attempted to borrow in 2009 and had some of their credit needs met	21
Small business employers attempted to borrow in 2009 and had none of their credit needs met	23

Source: NFIB Research Foundation

Prior to the financial crisis, about 90 percent of small employers that applied for credit had all their credit needs met. The lack of availability of loanable funds contributed significantly to the increase in small business bankruptcies in 2009. The fact that many small business operators were also struggling with the burden of the collapse of real estate prices in their personal capacities or because the businesses also held mortgages seriously worsened their financial condition. The lack of sufficient assets for collateral, poor credit scores, second mortgages, and lack of adequate capital made many small businesses unattractive to banks for lending purposes.

The National Association of Independent Business (NFIB) also reported that, unfortunately for small businesses, their larger counterparts enjoyed (at least) three distinct benefits that small businesses did not, including international sales, stronger balance sheets, and easier access to credit. The NFIB is the voice of small business in the U.S.

Believe it or not, some small businesses achieved improved business performance during the financial and economic recession according to the *New York Times*.[41] In a survey conducted by Sure Payroll, a payroll service in Chicago, of 300 small businesses, 30 percent reported increased sales over the last year. One example was a clothing company, the Brownstone (NY City Clothing & Accessories Boutique) that catered for 40 years to women with an unusual fashion sense. The strategy was designing bolder fashion lines, organizing a fashion show, and renting four times as many booths at business fairs to attract customers. The result was that profits went up 10 percent or $350,000.[42]

---

[41] Field Anne "November 24, 2009,
http://www.nytimes.com/2009/11/25/business/smallbusiness/25growth.html?_r=1&partner=rss&emc=rss.
[42] Ibid.

Another example of a small business that performed very well during this financial crisis and recession was CellGuru.com. The company reduced its marketing costs by eliminating paid advertising on the Internet. In addition, it opted for pay-per-click sites (shop by comparing prices) and reduced sales prices by two to three dollars per item. All these changes led to a 200 percent traffic increase throughout the store.[43]

Small businesses have certain advantages over big businesses. Being small in size allows them to respond more easily to customers' needs. Small business owners are often in touch with the customers on a day-to-day basis. They meet the needs of their customers with respect to the price, quality, and even affordability of the products and service. A small business that is sensitive to its customers' needs may be able to customize their products or services to meet the needs of their customers.

IMPACT OF THE FINANCIAL CRISIS/ECONOMIC RECESSION ON U.S. GOVERNMENT

The impact of the financial crisis and economic recession was very severe on the various tiers of the U.S. Government, especially the states and local governments. According to the Bureau of Economic Analysis (BEA), twelve states experienced declines in real GDP in 2008. The states included Connecticut, Rhode Island, Delaware, Indiana, Michigan, Ohio, Florida, Georgia, Kentucky, Arizona, Alaska, and Nevada. Interestingly, most of the states that suffered negative GDP growth rates, except for Arizona, Alaska, and Nevada, were located in the eastern part of the U.S. See Figure 4.6.

Figure 4.6 Map of the U.S

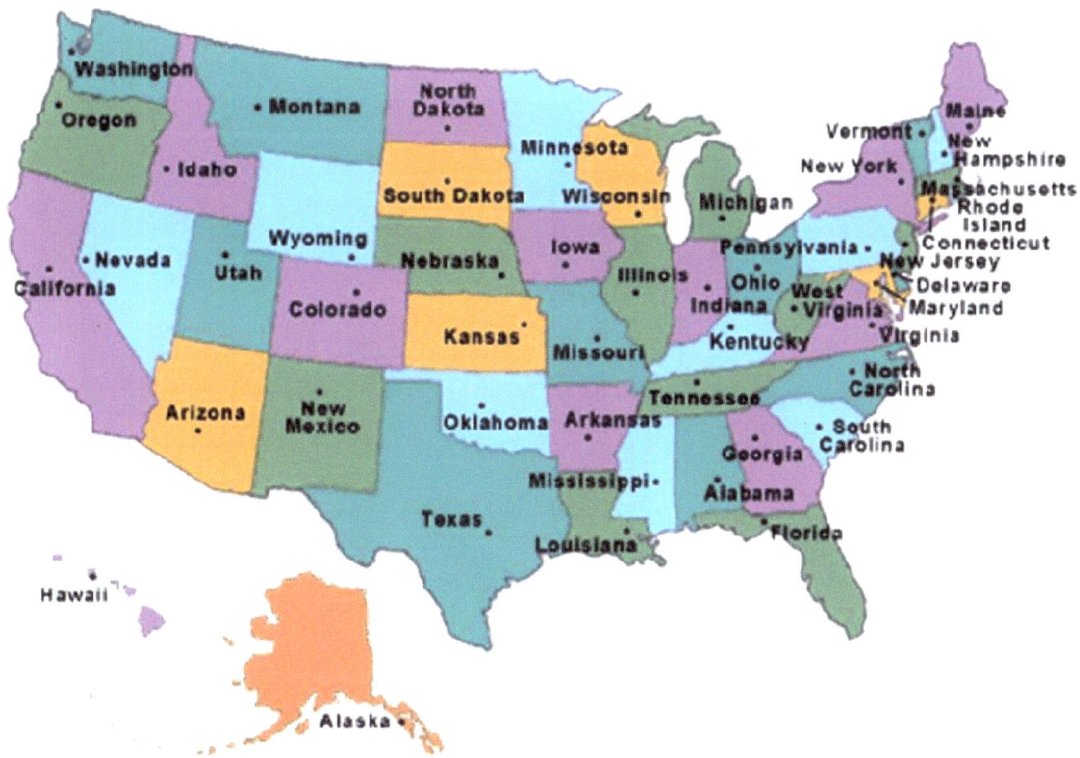

Source: Info please, http://www.infoplease.com/states.html

---

[43] Ibid.

Of these twelve states that experienced declines in GDP in 2008, only two of them, Rhode Island and Indiana, had negative GDP growth in 2005. See Figures 4.7 and 4.8. Perhaps the GDP decline did not have much to do with location. Naturally, the states that experienced huge increases in housing prices during the real estate bubble were more adversely affected by the negative change in the housing market. Also states that had a significant presence of insurance companies and banks that supported the subprime lending, which gave momentum to the boom also suffered severely when the housing prices plummeted.

Figure 4.7 GDP Percentage Change for Some States in the U.S. in 2005

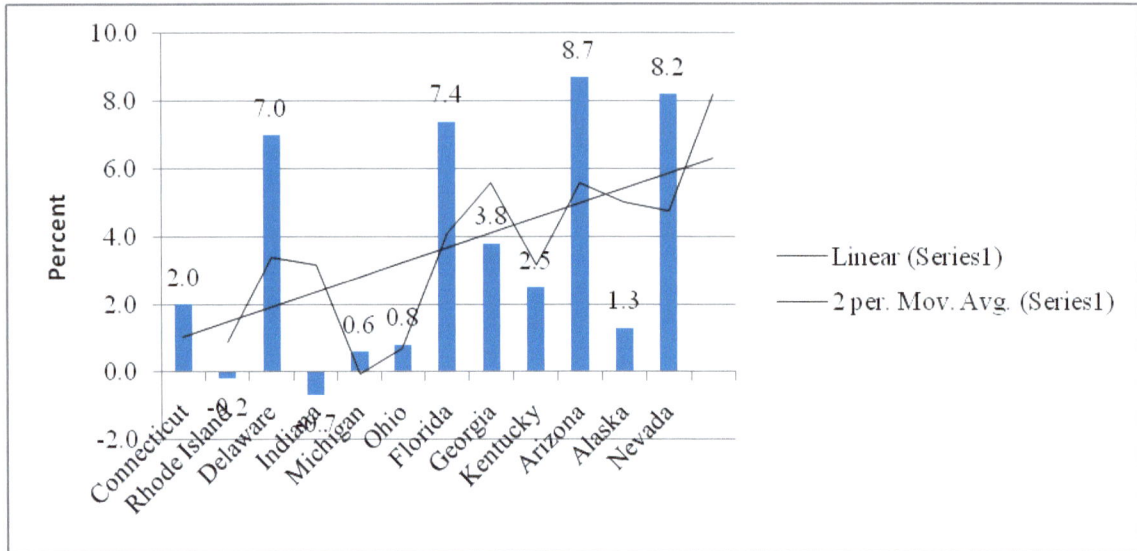

Figure 4.8 GDP Percentage Change for Some States in the U.S. in 2008

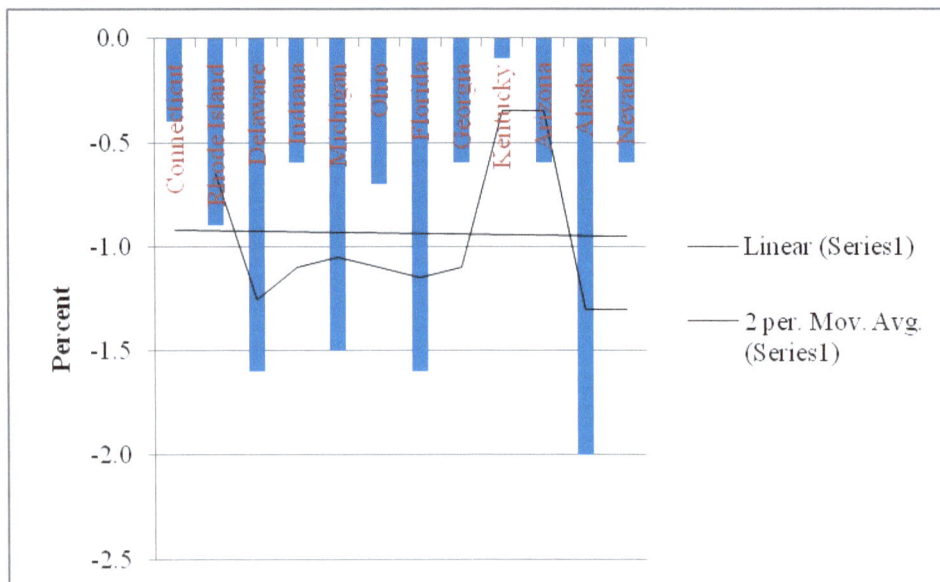

The BEA believes that weakness in the real estate market contributed to the relative poor GDP performance of Delaware, Rhode Island, Georgia, and Connecticut. Many states were struggling with different economic issues even before the financial crisis and economic recession. The decline in the manufacturing base in Michigan, Ohio, and Indiana due to U.S. manufacturing companies relocating overseas to take advantage of cheaper costs of production and the consequent decline in durable goods manufacturing were more responsible for the GDP declines. Be that as it may, Indiana and Ohio had positive GDP growth rates in 2007, 1.3 percent and 2 percent, respectively. In fact, out the twelve states that registered negative GDPs in 2008, only Michigan and Alaska had negative GDPs in 2007. The BEA believes that the decline in petroleum extraction contributed to the GDP decline in Alaska in 2008. Let us recall that economic recession generally leads to high unemployment, loss of income, and generally lower business activities resulting from declines in demand. Since the economic recession in the U.S. started in December 2007, coupled with the incidence of financial crisis, it is not surprising, therefore, that most states experienced a decline in economic activities in 2008 and 2009.

This was not the case with all the states. New Hampshire, North Dakota, Mississippi, Oklahoma, Colorado, and Wyoming recorded increases in their GDPs in 2008. North Dakota's GDP grew by 7.3 percent in 2008, the fastest economic growth in the U.S. Equally impressive is the GDP growth rate, in real terms, of Wyoming which increased by 4.4 percent between 2007 and 2008. Wyoming achieved the highest acceleration of economic activities in 2008. In 1998, the Wyoming Business Council dramatically changed Wyoming's approach to economic development.[44] Unlike the state's previous economic development efforts, this new organization was more of a corporate structure as it incorporated private business practices in order to drive programs and instituted regional offices throughout the state. The State of Wyoming created the Wyoming Business Council to focus public and private efforts to build a strong job creation base in the new economy with manufacturing and technology as core competencies, while strengthening the existing business and industry groups under energy, agriculture, tourism, and travel. In 2006, Wyoming's GDP growth rate was 7 percent.

All the fifty states suffered a decline in personal income in the third quarter of 2008 or the first quarter of 2009, and some in the third quarter of 2009. California and New York were negatively affected the most. The personal income for the fifty states is contained in Table 4.5 and the trend in their personal income from 2005 to 2009 is demonstrated in Figure 4.9.

---

[44] Wyoming Business Council, http://www.wyomingbusiness.org/about/aboutus.aspx.

Table 4.5 Personal income of U.S. states from 2005 to 2009

States	Personal Income 2005	Personal Income 2006	Personal Income 2007	Personal Income 2008	Personal Income 2009
Alabama	542468	577747	608545	629688	624625
Alaska	98453	105226	112119	120894	119079
Arizona	752613	827830	874558	892738	870971
Arkansas	309911	331717	358306	370021	369283
California	5550730	5982240	6289082	6416450	6265813
Colorado	718792	777573	822191	849282	831560
Connecticut	674663	735279	776274	788095	767762
Delaware	124309	133228	138147	141509	140936
District of Columbia	128676	140689	150214	156524	154527
Florida	2532793	2761092	2853960	2878831	2807873
Georgia	1170445	124708	1319933	1351843	1330499
Hawaii	181328	196494	209012	216700	217901
Idaho	168858	185091	196922	201595	196143
Illinois	1888739	2018512	2132647	2185378	2143022
Indiana	782360	827838	855499	882680	870367
Iowa	381435	401800	426016	449210	446558
Kansas	363400	394218	415379	435115	428768
Kentucky	475873	506100	528791	547760	540096
Louisiana	541267	572889	618608	642635	637570
Maine	167931	177225	184568	191976	193471
Maryland	950088	1011123	1057470	1090168	1110026
Massachusetts	1129787	1219881	1290608	1332186	1317107
Michigan	1302656	1339078	1374340	1398449	1361045
Minnesota	775751	823213	865745	898682	879939
Mississippi	311108	324545	345257	357325	355649
Missouri	746927	794733	830210	866187	855970
Montana	112715	121787	129901	134062	132755
Nebraska	240465	251482	268311	279284	275210
Nevada	367270	391271	420397	428317	409009
New Hampshire	199826	214643	224820	229596	227249
New Jersey	1519504	1646983	1739793	1783713	175535
New Mexico	221370	237097	252728	265349	265632
New York	3146284	3406537	3700252	3800838	3769076
North Carolina	1110917	1190234	1264092	1303816	1297142
North Dakota	82206	85544	93631	102303	102249
Ohio	1488531	1562581	1620945	1654928	1638294
Oklahoma	430564	474987	495555	524281	519900
Oregon	470684	509791	533621	550279	547967
Pennsylvania	1728161	1849606	1940410	1998677	2000676
Rhode Island	154270	162629	169423	173875	172839
South Carolina	497515	536816	546974	585340	580881
South Dakota	103338	106350	116137	124363	120815
Tennessee	750530	800675	843350	869492	869221
Texas	3026744	3297125	3512554	3675684	3621924
Utah	286133	315529	338837	349645	344816
Vermont	82776	89360	93651	96138	95862
Virginia	1176693	1262261	1332667	1374321	1380100
Washington	920007	1008093	1084032	1122710	115280
West Virginia	192556	207574	218222	229644	235134
Wisconsin	746379	794395	828805	850214	836631
Wyoming	79876	91649	97829	103568	99704

Source: Regional Economic Information System, Bureau of Economic Analysis, U.S. Department of Commerce
http://www.bea.gov/regional/sqpi/drill.cfm

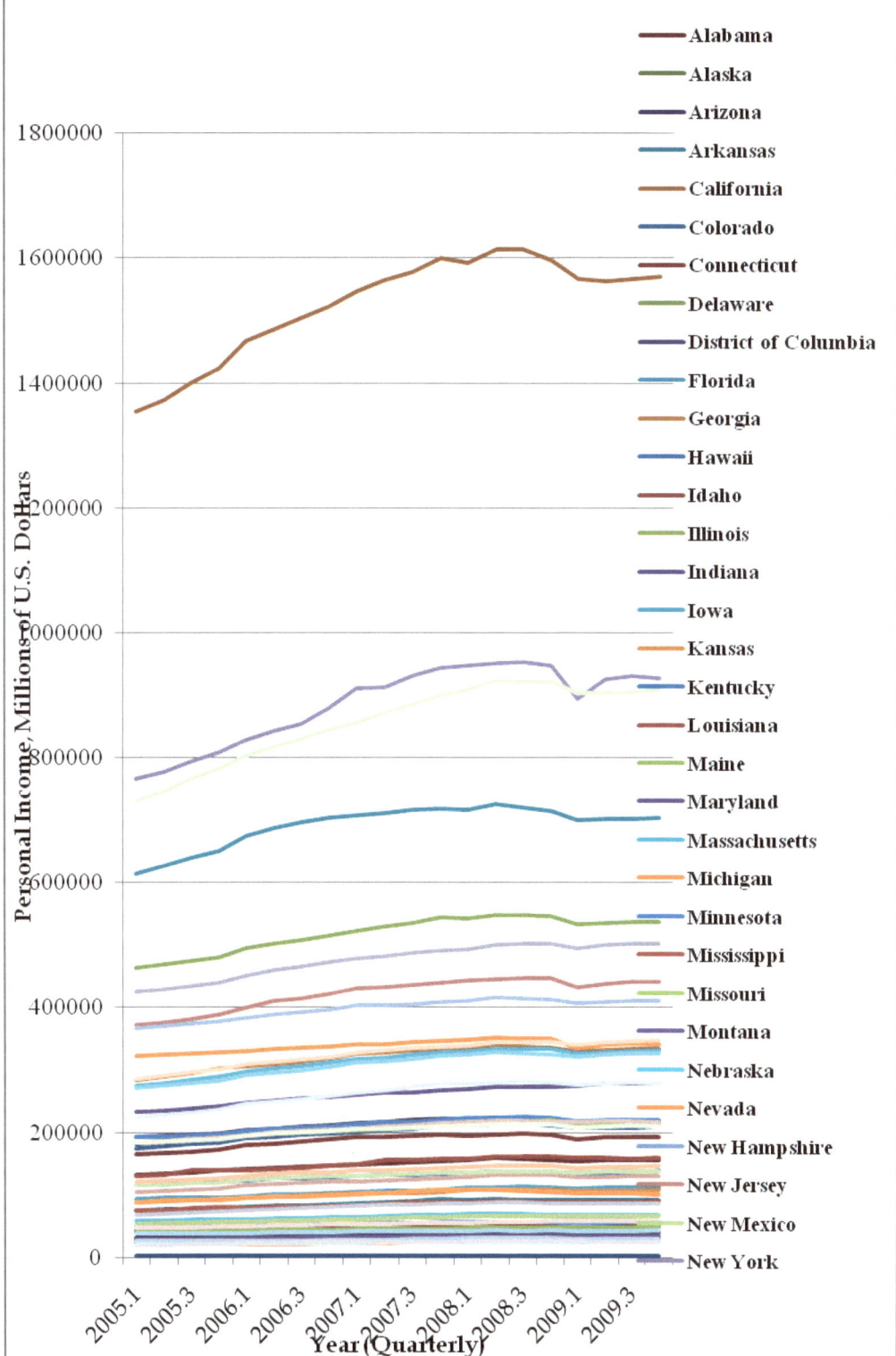

Figure 4.9 Personal Income Trends of 50 States of the U.S. between 2005 and 2009 (in millions of U.S. Dollars)

CONCLUSION

The combined effect of the financial crisis and economic recession led to many bank failures. A credit squeeze by banks on consumers and on the private sector resulted. Many investors lost a large portion of their investment portfolio in stock. Many lost huge sums of money in their real estate investments. The combined effect of these led to reduced demand. A decline in demand for products or services generally leads to lower profits; in fact, a drastic decline will dissipate the profits. Unemployment was a natural consequence of reduced demand and businesses cutting their work force. Many states experienced declines in real GDP in 2008. Another significant development was the loss of savings.

BIBLIOGRAPHY

"Assessing the Impact of the Current Economic Crisis on Health Care." *Managed Care Outlook*, no. 21, 9-10, November 2008.

Associated Press. "Treasury unveils plans to buy troubled assets." March 23, 2009. http://www.msnbc.msn.com/id/29817617/(accessed March 2010).

Auer, Peter, Raphael Auer, and Simon Wehrmüller. "Assessing the Impact of the Financial Crisis on the US Labour Market."November 21, 2008. http://www.voxeu.org/index.php?q=node/2603 (accessed March 2010).

Axelrod, Jim. "The Recession's Far Reach How Poor Attendance at a Vegas Convention Can Affect People in New York and Iowa." http://www.cbsnews.com/stories/2009/06/10/eveningnews/main5078884.shtml?source=related_story (accessed June 2010).

Bank for International Settlement. http://ddpext.worldbank.org/ext/DDPQQ/member.do?method=getMembers&userid=1&queryId=231(accessed March 2010).

BBC News. "Banks Reveal US Mortgage Losses." October, 1 2007. http://news.bbc.co.uk/2/hi/business/7021529.stm.

Blackstone, John. "The Recession's Six Degrees of Separation." cbsnews.com, May 26, 2009. http://www.cbsnews.com/stories/2009/05/27/eveningnews/main5044560.shtml?tag=related;wc5059741.

Bowers, Cynthia. "Connecting The Dots of The Recession, How Falling Boat Sales in Florida Leads to a Drop at sWisconsin Restaurant." May 13, 2009. http://www.cbsnews.com/stories/2009/05/13/eveningnews/main5012255.shtml?tag=related;wc5059741 (accessed March 2010).

Braun, Matias, and Borja Larrain. "Finance and the Business Cycle: International, Inter-Industry Evidence." *Journal of Finance* 60 (3), 2004, 1097-1128.

Buzzle.com. "Recession Costs 7 Million Jobs." http://www.buzzle.com/articles/recession-cost-7million-jobs.html (accessed March 2010).
———. "US Economic Crisis: Impact on Automobile Industry." http://www.buzzle.com/articles/us-economic-crisis-impact-on-automobile-industry.html (accessed March 2010).

CBS. "Retirement Dreams Disappear with 401(k)s." http://www.cbsnews.com/stories/2009/04/17/60minutes/main4951968.shtml (accessed March 2010).

Christian Science Monitor. "Why can't Americans save a dime?" MSN Money. http://moneycentral.msn.com/content/savinganddebt/savemoney/p145775.asp (accessed March 2010).

Dell'Ariccia, Giovanni, Enrica Detragiache, and Raghuram Rajan. "The Real Effect of Banking Crises." Mimeo, International Monetary Fund, October 2004.http://www.imf.org/External/Pubs/FT/staffp/2004/00-00/detrag.pdf.

Federal Reserve Bank of St. Louis. "Personal Saving Rate (PSAVERT)."December 29, 2010. http://research.stlouisfed.org/fred2/series/PSAVERT?rid=54&soid=18.

Federal Reserve Bank of St Louis. "Why Do Chinese Households Save So Much? International Economic Trends."August 2008. http://research.stlouisfed.org/publications/iet/20080801/cover.pdf (accessed December 29, 2010).

Field Anne. "Even in Recession, Some Small Businesses Grow." *New York Times,* November 24, 2009. http://www.nytimes.com/2009/11/25/business/smallbusiness/25growth.html?_r=1&partner=rss&emc=rss (accessed March 2010).

Financial Time Canada. "Financial job losses." January 2, 2011. http://www.ft.com/indepth/financejobcuts.

Healy, Jack. "Cautiously, Small Investors Edge Back Into Stocks." *New York Times*, September 10, 2009. http://www.nytimes.com/2009/09/11/business/11investors.html.

International Labour Organization. "Impact of the Financial Crisis on Finance Sector Workers." Issues paper for discussion at the Global Dialogue Forum on the Impact of the Financial Crisis on Finance Sector Workers Geneva, 24-25 February 2009. http://www.ilo.org/wcmsp5/groups/public/---dgreports/---dcomm/documents/meetingdocument/wcms_103263.pdf.

Kirsanova, Tatiana, and James Sefton. "A Comparison of Personal Sector Saving Rates in the UK, US, and Italy" November 18, 2002. http://www.nes.ru/NES10/cd/materials/Kirsanova-savingNES.pdf.

Klingebiel, Daniela, Randall S. Kroszner, and Luc A. Laeven."Financial Crises, Financial Dependence, and Industry Growth." World Bank Policy Research Working Paper No. 2855, June 2002.

Kobe Kathryn. "How Important Are Small Businesses to the U.S. Economy?" Department of Commerce, Bureau of the Census and International Trade Administration. 2007.

National Federation of Independent Business (NFIB), Small Business Economic Trends (SBET) Survey. http://www.nfib.com (accessed April 2010).

PSCA. "Impact of Economic Conditions on 401(k) and Profit Sharing Plans." 2009. http://www.psca.org/Portals/0/401k%20Economic%20Impact%20Survey%20Final.pdf.

Rajan, Raghuram G., and Luigi Zingales. "Financial Dependence and Growth." *American Economic Review* 88 (3), 1998, 559–596

"SBA, Frequently Asked Questions, Office of Advocacy." http://web.sba.gov/faqs/faqIndexAll.cfm?areaid=24

Shimek, Luke M., and Yi Wen. "Why Do Chinese Households Save So Much?" *International Economic Trends*, August 2008. http://research.stlouisfed.org/publications/iet/20080801/cover.pdf.

Starr, Stephen. "Economic Crisis Hits Restaurants." October 11, 2008. http://www.newyorkbankruptcylawyerblog.com/2008/10/new_york_financial_crisis_affe.html (accessed March 2010).

Stewart, Heather. "IMF says US crisis is 'largest financial shock since Great Depression." April 9, 2008. http://www.google.com/search?hl=en&source=hp&q=imf+and+us+credit+crunch&aq=f&aqi=&aql=&oq=&gs_rfai.

The Nation, "Tell 'the Nation': Recession Stories." December 7, 2009. http://www.thenation.com/doc/20091207/recession_stories.

U.S. Department of Labor, Bureau of Labor Statistics. CHI Research, 2003 (www.sba.gov/advo/research/rs225tot.pdf).

CHAPTER 5

IMPACT OF THE U.S. FINANCIAL CRISIS AND ECONOMIC RECESSION ON THE GLOBAL FINANCIAL MARKETS AND ECONOMIES

INTRODUCTION

The financial crisis that started in the United States in 2008 turned into a recession, which became a global phenomenon. Even though the negative financial and economic developments climaxed in 2008, the effects still reverberate globally.

Global financial flows have slowed significantly. In 2009, Hungary recorded a negative growth rate in Foreign Direct Investment (FDI) flows of -165.2 percent, the United Kingdom -92.7 percent, and Malaysia -66.6 percent. It is interesting to note that amidst the abysmal worldwide evidence in FDI flows, some countries recorded an impressive growth rate in FDI flows. For example, Italy recorded a growth rate of 75.5 percent in 2009.

Many countries experienced, and some are still experiencing, exchange rate depreciation. For example, the South African Rand lost 47.42 percent in 2008. Major capital markets suffered astronomical losses, whereas many big businesses failed and some were bailed out by their governments. Some of these businesses include well-known names like Toyota and General Motors. Bank failures have also been rampant. As banks struggle to contain their losses and achieve a strong balance sheet, credit for individual consumption and investments has become very tight.

Some people wonder why a financial crisis and economic recession that started in the United States would impact the economies of countries so far away. This occurred because many countries adopted the U.S. financial system and, more importantly because of the high proportion of the U.S. share of world imports. This share was 19.4 percent in 2000, 16.1 percent in 2005, and 12.9 percent in 2009. In 2009, U.S. imports fell by $700 billion. Figure 5.1 shows the global share of U.S. imports in 2008 and 2009.

Figure 5. 1 Global Share of U.S. Imports 2008 and 2009 (in millions of dollars)

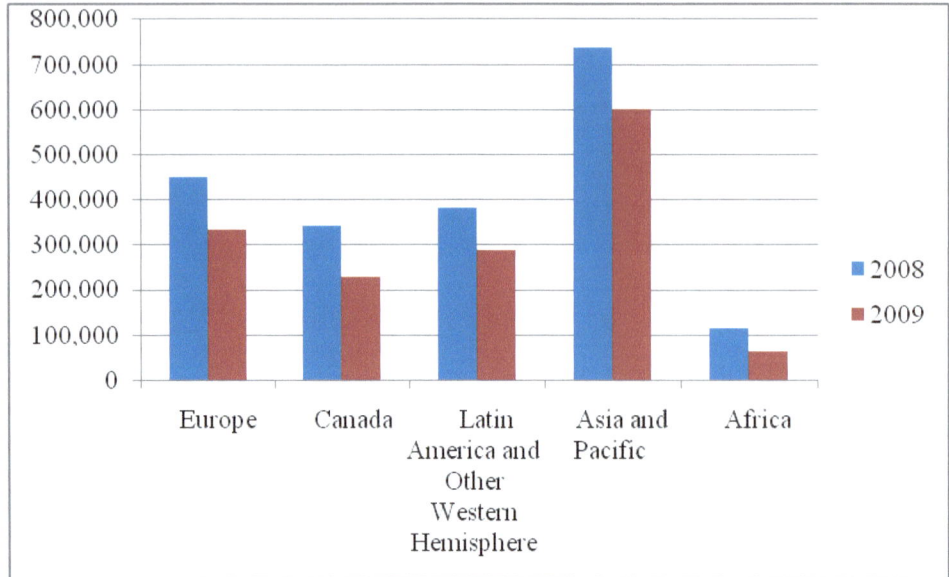

Source: Constructed with data from the Bureau of Economic Statistics

Figure 5.2 Global Distribution of U.S. Imports in 2009

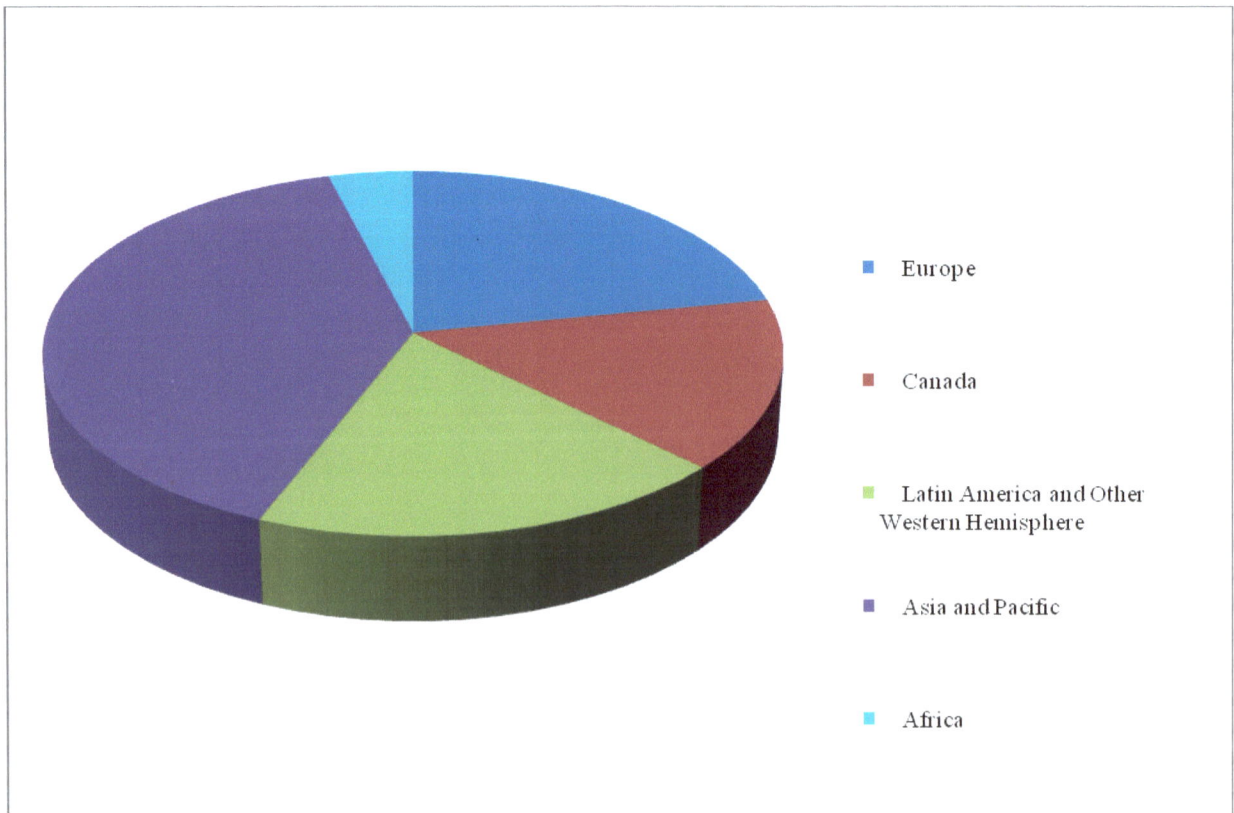

Source: Constructed with data from the Bureau of Economic Statistics

The Asia-Pacific region has the greatest share of U.S. imports for both 2008 and 2009, but all regions suffered declines in the amount of goods and services imported from them to the U.S. The value of goods and services imported into the U.S. from Africa in 2008 was $113.8 billion. This is a paltry amount when compared to other regions, and it declined by 44 percent in 2009. See Figure 5.2.

This chapter examines the impact of the financial crisis and economic recession on Africa, the Asia/Pacific region, Europe, and Latin America.

IMPACT ON CAPITAL MARKETS

Most of the African stock markets suffered huge losses in 2008. The African stock markets of Malawi, Ghana, Tanzania, and Tunisia were the few markets that recorded positive yields, both in local currency and in U.S. dollars in 2008. This performance was evidenced in their respective performance indexes. The Domestic index of Malawi achieved the yield of 24.07 percent, the DSI index of Ghana 11.28 percent, the DSEI index of Tanzania 7.23 percent, and the TUNINDEX index of Tunisia 2.96 percent.

The indexes that recorded the worst performances were the Overall index of Namibia with the worst loss of -57.4 percent, the Case 30 index of Egypt -56.82 percent, and the All Share index of Nigeria -54.6 percent. Generally this poor performance was attributed to the global financial crisis that exacerbated the credit crunch and diminished capital flows and induced capital flights in some cases. Decline in demand for primary products also contributed, in part, to the contraction of the stock market. See Table 5.1 for the performance of the indexes of the following countries and the Bourse Régionale des Valeurs Mobilières (BRVM) Composite in 2008 with regard to yield in local currency and in U.S. dollars:[45] Malawi, Ghana, Tanzania, Tunisia, BRVM, Morocco, Botswana, Uganda, Zambia, Mauritius, South Africa, Kenya, Nigeria, Egypt, and Namibia.

Table 5.1 Performance of the African Stock Markets, 2008

Country	YTD (LC)	YTD (USD)
Malawi (Domestic)	25.92%	24.07
Ghana (DSI)	40.68%	11.28
Tanzania (DSEI)	21.26%	7.23
Tunisia (TUNINDEX)	10.65%	2.96
Bourse Régionale des Valeurs Mobilières (BRVM)	-10.67%	-14.11
Morocco (MASI)	-13.48%	-17.59
Botswana (DCI)	-16.51%	-32.41
Uganda (ALSI)	-21.38%	-32.85
Zambia (All Share)	-28.14%	-43.84
Mauritius (SEMDEX)	-36.14%	-45.8
South Africa (JSE All Share)	-25.72%	-46.21
Kenya (NSE 20)	-35.33%	-48.47
Nigeria (All Share)	-45.77%	-54.6
Egypt (Case 30)	-56.43%	-56.81
Namibia (Overall)	-40.15%	-57.4

Source: Databank Research, http://emerging-africa.com/stockmarketsreview.html

See also Figure 5.3 for the graphical illustration of the African stock markets performance in 2008.

---

[45] Bourse Régionale des Valeurs Mobilières, a regional stock exchange located in Abidjan, Cote d'Ivoire, that serves Benin, Burkina Faso, Guinea Bissau, Cote d'Ivoire, Mali, Niger, Senegal, and Togo. Formed in 1996, it started operations in 1998.

Figure 5.3 Performance of African Stock Markets: Percentage Yield in U.S. in 2008

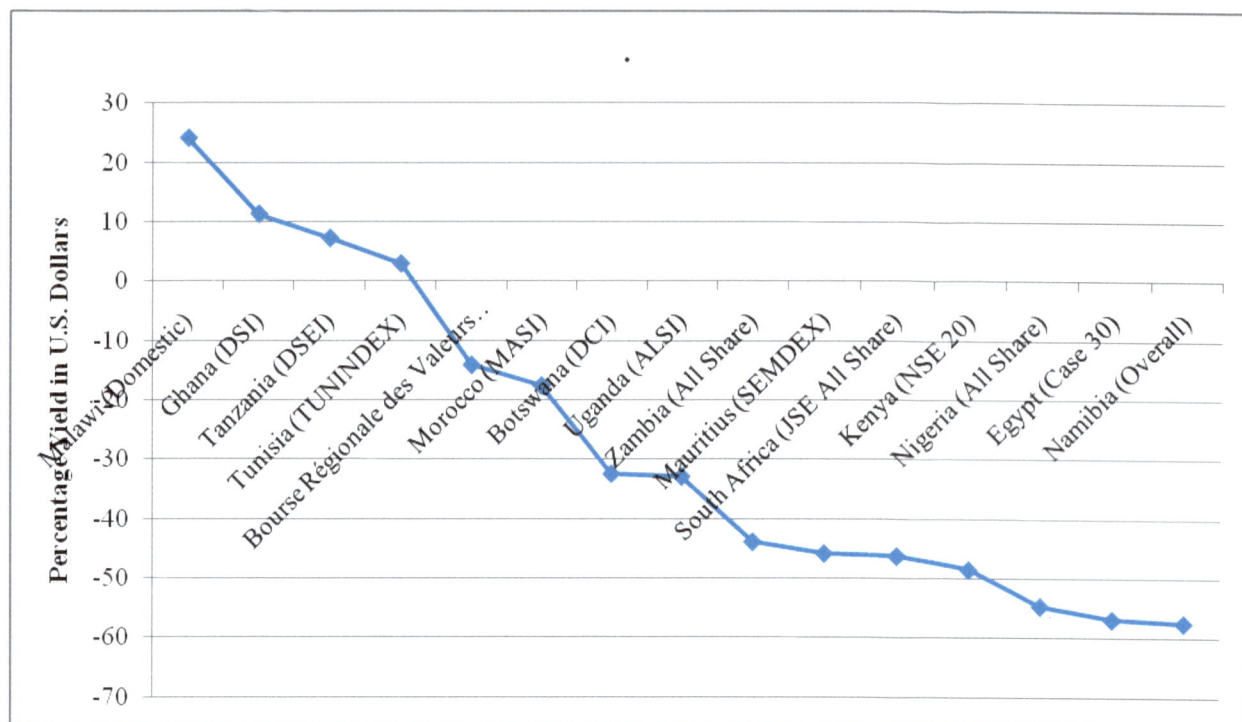

The financial crisis was an unfortunate development for African stock markets. After decades of low activity and of being riddled with problems such as illiquidity, lack of depth, transparency, operational inefficiencies, high political risk, occasional abrupt and negative changes in government policies, extreme currency fluctuation, and the general international perception of Africa as a high risk region, African stock markets made significant progress in the last decade. This was due to the fact that many governments in Africa undertook several macroeconomic, political, and institutional reforms to reduce specific country risk and to maintain some stability in policy. Stock exchanges made significant reforms as well, to improve the liquidity and the market, in an effort to achieve greater functional efficiency. The reform efforts also achieved greater operational efficiency in trading systems. Regional stock exchange integration also improved the operational efficiency. In addition, the high investment returns from the late 1990s turned the risk-return trade-off in value of greater investments in African stock markets. The high returns from investments in Africa led to greater investment flows to Africa. Most African stock markets experienced a boom between the 1990s and 2007. The Zimbabwe Industrial Index increased by 12,161 percent between 1997 and 2004. This was so despite the controversy surrounding the 1997 land reform designed to seize 1,500 commercial farms, mostly owned by white people and the generally high inflation in that country. The Ghana All Share Index increased by 4,205 percent between 1994 and 2004. See Table 5.2 for more African indexes that grew significantly during similar periods.

Table 5.2 Past/Recent Performance of African Stock Indexes

Index	Date	Index Values	Percentage Increase
Botswana Domestic Companies Index	1/7/1994	279.76	
	5/17/2004	2,820.85	908
Egypt Case 30 Index	1/3/1994	305.3119555	
	12/30/2004	2,567.99	741
Ghana All Share Index	1/4/1994	170.87	
	8/6/2004	7,356.68	4205
Kenya 20 Index	1/3/1994	2,533.89	
	12/31/2004	2945.58	16
Malawi Domestic Companies Index	1/2/1997	137.57	
	12/22/2004	426.03	210
Mauritius Semdex Index	1/10/1994	307.33	
	12/31/2004	710.77	131
Morocco All Share Index	1/3/1994	1,504.91	
	12/31/2004	4,521.98	200
Namibia Overall index	1/7/1994	133.49	
	11/30/2004	420.17	215
Nigeria All Share Index	2/14/1997	7,364.24	
	12/31/2004	31,156.69	323
South Africa All Share Index	6/30/1995	4,865.90	
	12/31/2004	12,656.86	160
Tunisia BVMT Index	1/2/1997	559.39	
	12/31/2004	974.82	74
Zimbabwe Industrial Index	1/6/1997	8,951	
	12/31/2004	1,097,492.53	12,161

Source: African Financial Markets, http://www.africanfinancialmarkets.com

It is important to note that foreign risk, as exemplified by the incidence of the financial crisis, is an important risk factor for African stock markets.

IMPACT OF THE U.S. FINANCIAL CRISIS AND ECONOMIC RECESSION ON EXCHANGE RATES IN AFRICA

It is true that a low exchange rate for a currency can make goods and services produced in that country more competitive in the international foreign exchange market. It is also true that a drastic reduction in the value of a country's currency can greatly impair the country's ability to engage in the purchase of goods and services from other countries. This is more so for most African countries that operate with a paucity of capital and sometimes with limited reserves.

Following the financial crisis, many African countries experienced significant exchange rate deterioration. Some of the countries most affected were Namibia, Ghana, Botswana, South Africa, and Nigeria. By the end of 2008, the Namibian Dollar had lost 28.8 percent of its value; South African Rand 27.8 percent; Botswana Pula 21.4 percent; Ghanaian New Cedi 22.6 percent; and Nigerian Naira 18.2 percent. Foreign currency volatility has continued even as recently as 2010. For example, the Nigerian Naira has deteriorated further in 2010. See Figure 5.4. It is true that exchange rates fluctuate in all economic conditions, but the incidence of the global financial crisis and economic recession unduly exacerbated the situation in Africa.

Figure 5.4 Nigerian Naira Exchange Rates: 2000-2010

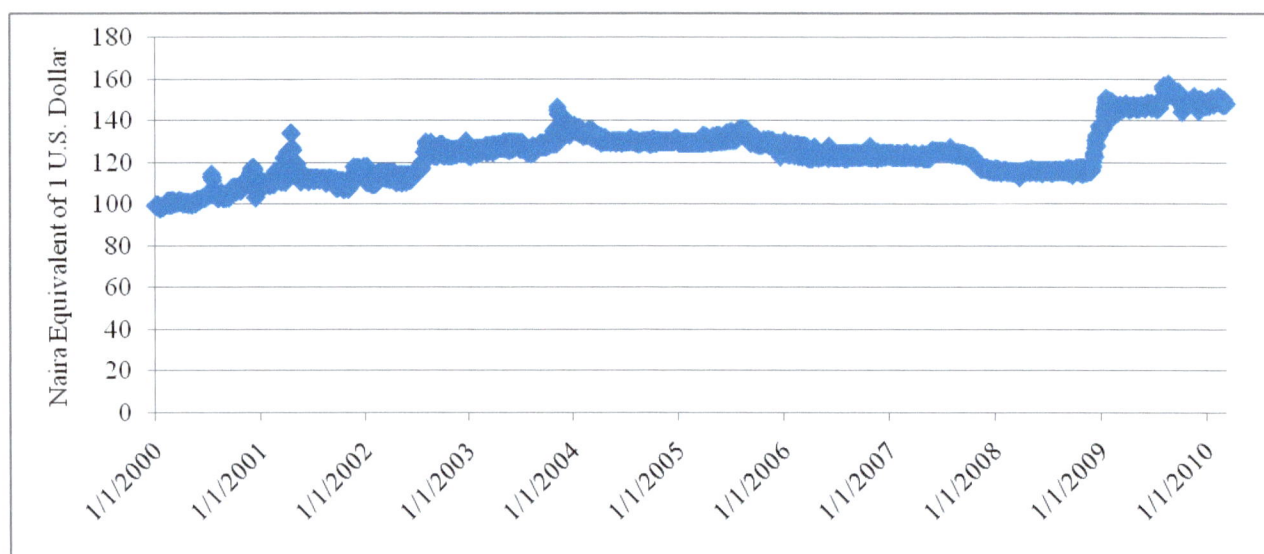

Source: Constructed from data on Source: http://www.oanda.com/currency/historical-rates

IMPACT OF THE U.S. FINANCIAL CRISIS AND ECONOMIC RECESSION ON FDI FLOWS TO AFRICA

In the pursuit of the wealth maximization objective, firms engage in foreign direct investment (FDI), in addition to domestic investment and international trade in an attempt to create more value for their shareholders than is available in their domestic markets. The benefits to be derived by host countries are not a major consideration of the firms engaging in FDI, except when these are requirements in any pre-investment dialogue or negotiation with a host government. Conditions such as trade barriers, access to markets, cost considerations, political considerations and other yet unexplained variables make FDI investments in certain locations of the world more attractive than in others. The flow of FDI into a country increases the level of domestic investment in that country in excess of the country's level of savings. The achieved increase in capital investment precipitates economic growth in that country without a significant decrease in current consumption. There is a simultaneous increase in employment, general increase in income levels, and possible transfer of technological know-how. These in turn generate entrepreneurial activities in the host country, especially in emerging economies.

Africa was the second largest recipient of FDI flows in the early 1970s. Africa's share eroded such that, by the 1990s, FDI flow to Africa was abysmal. For example, from 1993 to 1998, the African region's share of FDI was 4.7 percent of the total FDI flows to developing regions in comparison to 33 percent to Latin America and the Caribbean countries, and 53 percent for Asia and the Pacific. For example, the whole continent of Africa received only $5 billion in FDI in 1997. [46] This situation with regard to Africa's attraction of FDI flows improved significantly in the last decade. According to the Organization for Economic Cooperation and Development statistics, the FDI flow to Africa was $9.7 billion in 2002. It increased to $87.6 billion in 2008 representing an increase of about 800 percent in less than a decade. A more favorable political climate and economic progress were said to be responsible for this growth.

However, in 2009, the FDI flow to Africa slumped to $55.9 billion, a decline of 36.2 percent. Table 5.3 contains the FDI flows to Africa from 2000 to 2009 and Figure 5.5 depicts the trend.

Table 5.3 FDI Flows to Africa (in billions)

Year	Amount
2000	9.737
2001	19.982
2002	16.053
2003	20.907
2004	22.125
2005	38.222
2006	57.058
2007	69.17
2008	87.647
2009	55.9

Source: http://stats.oecd.org/Index.aspx?

---

[46] See Charles W. L. Hill, *International Business: Competing in the Global Market Place*, Boston, MA: Irwin McGraw-Hill, 1999.

Figure 5.5 FDI Flow to Africa 2000-2009

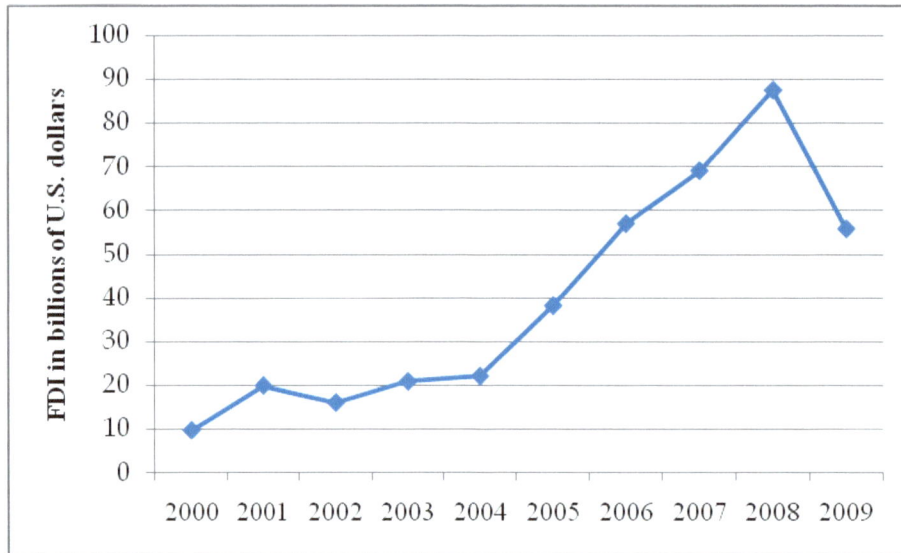

Source: Constructed with data from OECD, http://stats.oecd.org/Index.aspx

The amount of U.S. imports from Africa declined in the third quarter of 2008 until the second quarter of 2009. See Figure 5.6.

Figure 5.6 Africa's Share of U.S. Imports Quarterly Data 2008 to 2010

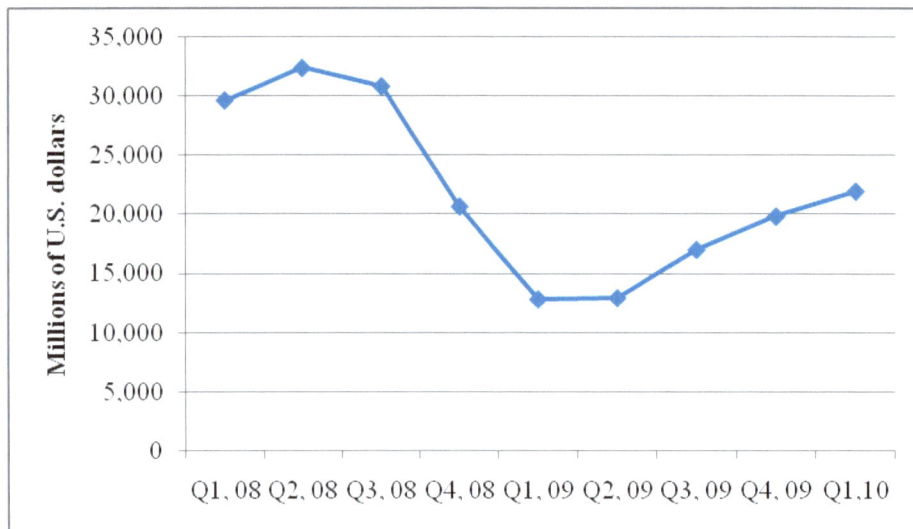

Source: Constructed with data from Bureau of Economic Analysis

The impact of the U.S. financial crisis and economic recession on some other foreign programs beneficial to Africa may yet unfold. For example, in May 2000, the U.S. Congress, during the Presidency of Bill Clinton, approved legislation known as the African Growth and Opportunity Act (AGOA) for the purpose of assisting the economies of sub-Saharan Africa. The purpose was to improve economic relations between the United States and the region. Under the Generalized System of Preferences of the United Nations (UN), many sub-Saharan African countries have been able to export apparel and certain textiles, cut flowers, horticultural products, automotive, and steel to the United States under the AGOA duty-free program. As of August 2009, there are forty-one AGOA eligible sub-

Saharan African countries. In fiscal year 2008, the United States exported $18,471.9 million in goods to the forty-one AGOA countries and imported $86,052.7 million for a balance of $67,580.8 million in favor of the AGOA countries. AGOA was described by Rosa Whitakeras, "...a powerful engine for growth with its trade preferences."[47] In addition, it provides effective development programs and reforms that build the capacity for African businesses to succeed in international markets.

IMPACT OF THE U.S. FINANCIAL CRISIS AND ECONOMIC RECESSION ON CAPITAL MARKETS IN ASIA AND PACIFIC

Following the U.S. financial crisis that began in October 2008, the Asia Pacific stock indexes plummeted. The hardest hit was the China SSE Composite which lost 67.56 percent of its beginning-of-year value on November 4, 2008. Between January 2008 and March 2009, the highest decline in the stock indexes of Australia, China, Hong Kong, India, Indonesia, Japan, Malaysia, New Zealand, Singapore, South Korea, and Taiwan ranged between 40 percent and 68 percent, the lowest decline occurring in New Zealand NZ 250. See Table 5.4 for these percentage declines.

Table 5.4 Asia-Pacific Post-Financial Crisis Stock Index Performance

Index	Interval	Index Values	Percent Change
Australia All Ordinary	1/2/2008	6434.1	
	3/6/2009	3111.7	-51.64
China SSE Composite	1/1/2008	5261.56	
	11/4/2008	1706.7	-67.56
Hong Kong Hang Sang	1/2/2008	27560.52	
	10/27/2008	11015.84	-60.03
India BSE SENSEX	1/2/2008	20465.3	
	3/9/2009	8160.4	-60.13
Indonesia JKSE	1/2/2008	2731.51	
	10/28/2008	1111.39	-59.31
Japan Nikkei 225	1/4/2008	14691.41	
	3/10/2009	7054.98	-51.98
Malaysia KJSE	1/2/2008	1435.68	
	10/29/2008	829.41	-42.23
New Zealand NZ 250	1/3/2008	4033.93	
	3/3/2009	2417.95	-40.06
Singapore Strait Times	1/2/2008	3461.22	
	3/9/2009	1456.95	-57.91
South Korea Composite KOSPI	1/2/2008	1853.45	
	10/24/2008	938.75	-49.35
Taiwan TWII	1/2/2008	8323.05	
	11/20/2008	4089.93	-50.86

Source: Calculated from data on Yahoo Finance, http://finance.yahoo.com/intlindices?e=asia

---

[47] Rosa Whitaker is a former Assistant U.S. Trade Representative (USTR) for Africa.

It is interesting to note that most of the Asia-Pacific indexes, unlike the African stock indexes, experienced a quick rebound.

IMPACT OF THE U.S. FINANCIAL CRISIS AND ECONOMIC RECESSION ON FDI IN ASIA AND PACIFIC

The Asia-Pacific region has been very successful in attracting FDI in recent decades. For example, the Asia-Pacific region's share of FDI flows to developing countries from 1993 to 1998 was 53 percent, in comparison to Africa's share of 4.7 percent and Latin America and Caribbean shares of 33 percent.[48] This trend continued such that by the end of 2008 the developing economies of South, East, and Southeast Asia attracted $297.6 billion. Similar countries in Latin America and Africa attracted $144 billion and $87 billion, respectively. This growth in FDI flows to Asia suffered declines in 2009. There was a decline in FDI flows of 2.6 percent to China, 42.8 percent to Hong Kong-China, 19 percent to India, 36 percent to Indonesia, 19.5 percent to Singapore, 54.3 percent to Thailand, and 66 percent to Malaysia.

Some countries in Asia have been particularly successful in attracting FDI, China especially, and more recently India. In the past thirty years, China's GDP growth rate has ranged between 8 and 9 percent. With a human population of over 1.3 billion, according to the International Monetary Fund's (IMF) 2003 mid-year estimate, and just emerging from a socialist economy, it is not surprising that this achievement stands out globally. It has been suggested that FDI growth is the most important factor driving this economic growth. Between 2000 and 2009, FDI inflows to China grew on average by 8.69 percent. In 2001, they grew by 15.1 percent and by 18.6 percent in 2007. During this period, it only declined in 2005 and 2009. Figure 5.7 depicts this trend in FDI flows to China.

Figure 5.7 Non-financial FDI Inflows to China 2000-2009

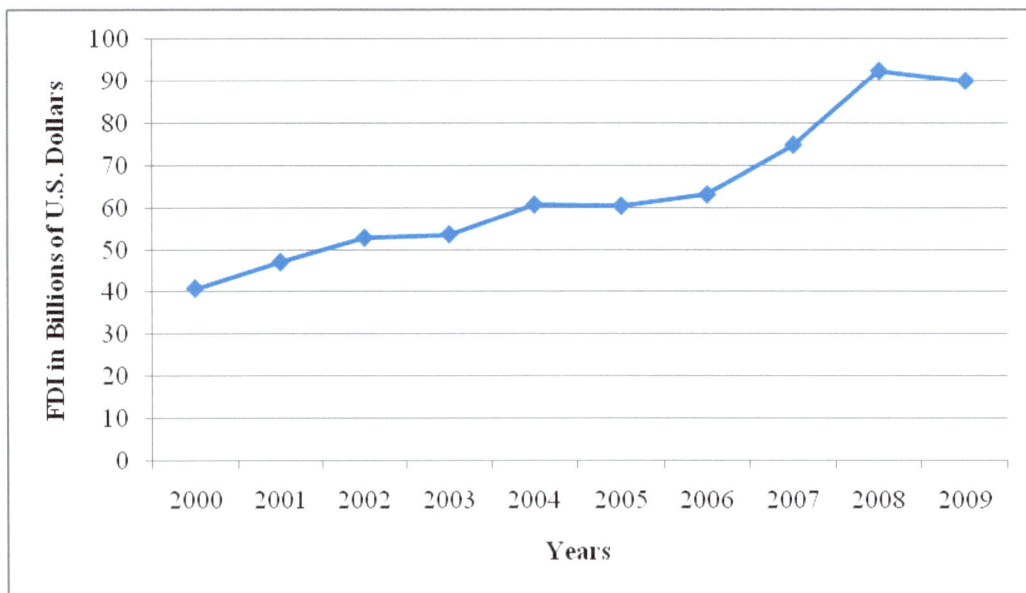

Source: Constructed with data from the US-China Business Council,
           http://www.uschina.org/statistics/fdi_cumulative.html

---

[48] Nomathemba Mhlanga and Ralph D. Christy, Capital Flows to Africa: an Analysis of the Structure of Official and Private Capital Flows, Working Paper, Cornell University, 2006.

The top ten origination locations of non-financial flows to China in 2008 and 2009 were Hong Kong, Taiwan, Japan, Singapore, United States, South Korea, United Kingdom, Germany, Macao, and Canada. Even though the total global FDI to China declined in 2009; the FDI flows from most of these countries increased in 2009, namely, Hong Kong, Taiwan, Japan, United States, United Kingdom, Germany, Macao, and Canada. See Table 5.5.

Table 5.5 Top Origins of Non-financial Flows to China in 2008 and 2009 (billions of dollars)

Country	2008	2009
Hong Kong	41	54
Taiwan	1.9	6.6
Japan	3.7	4.1
Singapore	4.4	3.9
United States	2.9	3.6
South Korea	3.1	2.7
United Kingdom	0.9	1.5
Germany	0.9	1.2
Macao	0.6	1
Canada	0.5	1
Total	59.9	76.6

Source: US-China Business Council, http://www.uschina.org/statistics/fdi_cumulative.html

Because FDI is so important for developmental purposes, some existing literature on factors that attract FDI to a particular country, such as those responsible for the huge FDI flows to China in recent years, and the link between FDI and economic growth will be reviewed here. It has been suggested that institutional factors contribute significantly to the direction of FDI flows. In studies done by James Hines and Shang-Jin Wei, each examined the impact of institutional factors on the direction of FDI flows.[49] Using OECD direct investment data and employing cross-sectional examinations, Wei showed that corruption and high tax rates have negative effects on FDI flows. By employing a corruption index, Hines was able to demonstrate that FDI grew faster in less corrupt economies.

There is evidence that multiple factors contribute to increased FDI flows. For example, market size, labor costs, tax rates, and institutional reforms are important for determining various sources of FDI into different provinces of China.[50] Other factors that contribute to increased FDI flows are policy reforms, expected growth rates, corporate tax rates, and the degree of openness.[51] Further research

---

[49] See James R. Hines, Jr., "Forbidden Payment: Foreign Bribery and American Business after 1977," NBER Working Paper. No. 3266, 1995; Shang-Jin Wei, "Why is corruption so much more taxing than tax? Arbitrariness Kill," NBER Working Paper No. 6255, 1997.

[50] See K. C. Fung, Alicia Garcia-Herrero, Hitomi Iizaka, and Alan Siu," Hard or Soft? Institutional Reforms and Infrastructure Spending as Determinants of Foreign Direct Investment in China," *Japan Economic Review*, 2005; K. C. Fung, Hitomi Iizaka, and Alan Siu, "Japanese Direct Investment in China," *China Economic Review* 14, (2003): 304-315; K. C. Fung, Hitomi Iizaka, and Stephen Parker, "Determinants of U.S. and Japanese Direct Investment in China," *Journal of Comparative Economics* 30 (2002): 567-578.

[51] See Victor M. Gastanaga, Jeffrey B. Nugent, and Biastra Pashamova, "Host Country Reforms and FDI flows, How much difference do they make?" *World Development* 26, no. 7, (1998): 1299-314.

results indicate the dynamics of FDI evolution are closely associated with the process of legal modernization and policy reforms via institutionalization that is required to move toward a market-oriented host country for global international capital. FDI absorption in China after World Trade Organization (WTO) will follow the market power of agglomeration economics.[52] Academic research seems to reinforce the importance of reforms; macroeconomics and political stability as a *sine qua non* for increased FDI flows. Corporate executives seemed to have a different view in 2004. According to A.T. Kearney Global Management Consultants, for the first time since 2000, in an FDI Confidence Index publication a sizable majority or 69 percent of leading executives were more optimistic about the global economy compared to only one in ten expressing more pessimism. Helping spur likely future FDI, corporate investors see macroeconomic and political risks as less threatening and perceive greater profit opportunities and reduced risk in the world's leading, emerging markets. A fundamental shift in investor outlook and risk perception is underway, which could presage the return to positive growth in global FDI flows. However, it is possible that a complicated mix of operational risks could undercut investors' renewed interest in venturing overseas.

In another recent study, using a panel cointegration framework, Basu, Chakraborty, and Reagle explored the two-way link between FDI and growth for a panel of twenty-three developing countries and the impact of liberalization on the dynamics of the FDI and GDP relationship.[53] They found a long-run, cointegrating relationship between FDI and GDP after allowing for heterogeneous country effects. The cointegrating vectors reveal a bidirectional causality between GDP and FDI. For more open economies and for relatively closed economies, long-run causality appears unidirectional and runs from GDP to FDI, implying that growth and FDI are not mutually reinforcing under restrictive trade and investment regimes.

According to the US-China Business Council, FDI poured into China at record levels in 2004, totaling more than $153 billion in new agreements. This represented a one-third increase over the level in 2003. Utilized FDI (the amount actually invested during the year) also surged to a record high of almost $61 billion, increasing 13.3 percent over 2003. Even though this is not a record high, the number of contracts in 2004 reached 43,664. This is equal to an increase of about 6.3 percent. The future direction of FDI in China seems impressive.

Facilitated by WTO-related market openings and increasingly comprehensive infrastructure and distribution systems, FDI in China will continue to move beyond the traditional investment locales and sectors. Similarly, although China will remain an important, low-end export manufacturing base in the near future, multinational corporations and Chinese companies are producing increasingly sophisticated goods in the information technology, high technology, pharmaceutical, and chemical sectors. China is also becoming a credible center for low-cost research and development (R&D) in certain industries, marking a shift away from pure production. FDI flows into the professional and financial service industries will also increase as China removes barriers to foreign competition to meet WTO obligations. Moreover, investments in entertainment and consumer goods will increase to meet increased demand due rising income levels.

Since China introduced its economic reform and initiated its "open-door" policy in 1978, FDI flows to China have grown dramatically. The dominant sources of these flows were Hong Kong, Taiwan, and Macau during the 1980s and early 1990s. Hong Kong basically moved all of its manufacturing to the mainland, as its own production costs rose, thus accounting for up to 68 percent of FDI in China. Even though this percentage has been reduced in recent years to about 58 percent, Hong Kong continues to be the leading source of FDI to China. Other important sources of FDI to China, (listed in descending order of magnitude of contribution) are the United States, Taiwan, Japan, Singapore, Virgin Islands, South Korea, United Kingdom, Germany, France, Macau, Netherlands, Canada, Malaysia, and Australia. The share of the United States' contribution of FDI to China was 4.6 percent in 1992, 10.8 percent in 2000, and 10.3 percent in 2002.[54]

---

[52] See Chyau Tuan, and Linda F. Y. Ng, "Manufacturing agglomeration as incentives to Asian FDI in China after WTO," *Journal of Asian Economics* 15, no. 2 (2004): 673-694.

[53] Basu, Chakraborty, and Reagle, March 2007, http://onlinelibrary.wiley.com/doi/10.1093/ei/cbg024/pdf.

[54] China Statistical Book---Insert complete cite.

It is important to note that the Asia-Pacific region is responsible for a higher proportion of FDI flows to the U.S. than Latin America and Africa. Europe is by far the greatest contributor with a contribution of $71 billion of FDI to the U.S. in 2008 followed by Asia-Pacific with a contribution of $16 billion. The regional contribution of FDI to the U.S. in 2008 is shown in Table 5.6 and depicted in Figure 5.8.

Table 5.6 Percentage of Total FDI Flows to the U.S. in 2008 (in billions of dollars)

Region/Country	Percentage Share
Europe	71
Asia/Pacific	16
Canada	10
Latin America	2
Middle East	1
Africa	0.01

Source: BEA, International Economic Accounts: Operations of Multinational Companies 2008, http://www.bea.gov.

Figure 5.8 Percentage of RegionalFDI Flows to the U.S. in 2008

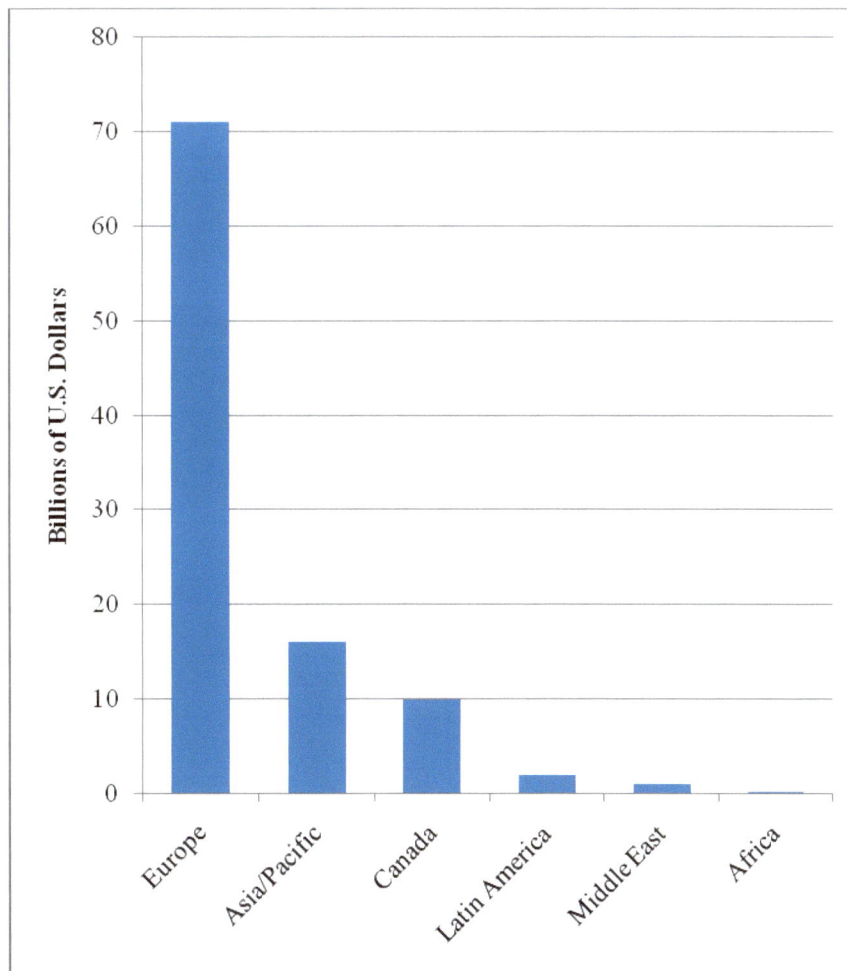

Source: Constructed with data from the Bureau of Economic Analysis, International Economic Accounts: Operations of Multinational Companies 2008, http://www.bea.gov.

IMPACT OF THE U.S. FINANCIAL CRISIS AND ECONOMIC RECESSION ON EXCHANGE RATES IN ASIA AND PACIFIC

The currencies of most of the Asia-Pacific countries depreciated in value. Most of these currencies experienced the greatest decline in value in March 2009. The Korean Won and the New Zealand Dollar experienced declines on January 1, 2008 values of 40.86 percent and 35.59 percent respectively. The Australian Dollar's huge decline occurred earlier in October 2008. Other currencies that recorded declines in March 2009 were: Indian Rupee 24.87 percent, Thai Baht 18.23 percent, Indonesia Rupiah 18.07 percent, Japanese Yen 14.76 percent, Malaysian Ringgit 11.84 percent, and Singapore Dollar 7.27 percent.

These are huge declines but do not compare with the currency declines that some Asian countries experienced during the Asian financial crisis in 1997. The crisis was perpetrated by the financial fragility of South Korean and Thai economies, which first led to the sudden collapse of their two currencies in the first two weeks of July 1997. Thereafter, the contagion of the currency decline spread to other neighboring trading partners, resulting in both political and economic changes of far-reaching magnitude. The South Korean Won depreciated by 88.40 percent, and the Thai Baht depreciated by 64 percent. With that magnitude of currency collapses in these and other countries, governments had to call on the IMF to restructure their economies with massive bailout loans. The IMF initially approved $35 billion in financial support for reform programs in Indonesia, South Korea, and Thailand. Later, the amount ballooned to $77 billion of additional financing. The GDP growth rates of Asian countries dropped from almost double digits to the negative. Singapore, South Korea, Thailand, and Taiwan registered negative growth rates in 1998. After the recovery, which was achieved through the IMF bailout, reforms, and restructuring, several Asian countries are now achieving very high GDP growth rates.

The U.S. imports from Asia and the Pacific region declined in the fourth quarter of 2008 until the third quarter of 2009. See Figure 5.9.

Figure 5.9 Asia-Pacific Region Share of U.S. Imports, Quarterly Data 2008 to 2010

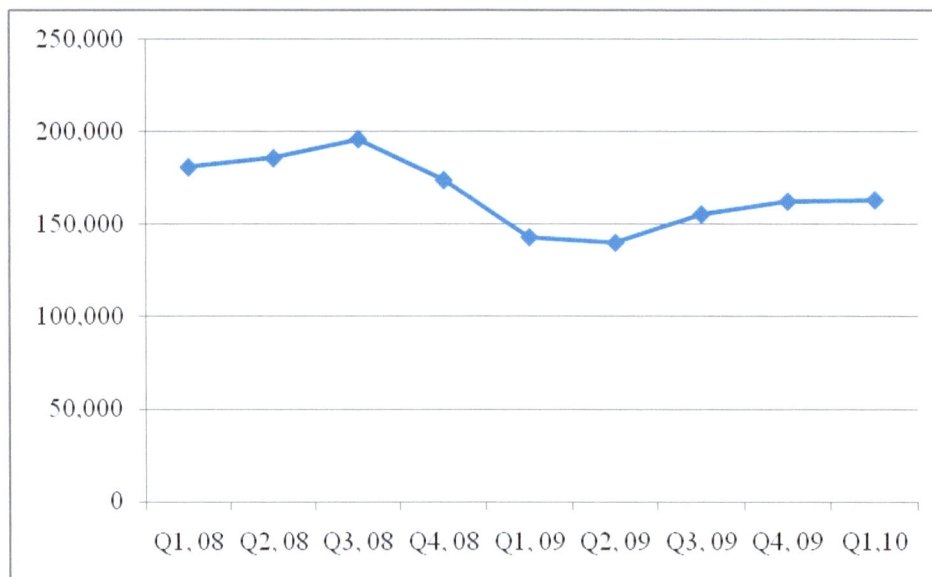

Source: Constructed with data from the Bureau of Economic Analysis, International Economic Accounts: Operations of Multinational Companies 2008, http://www.bea.gov.

IMPACT OF THE U.S. FINANCIAL CRISIS AND ECONOMIC RECESSION ON THE EUROPEAN FINANCIAL MARKETS AND ECONOMIES

The region most affected by the financial crisis outside the U.S. is probably Europe. This is because of the very close economic and political ties between the U.S. and Europe. It is also because of the similarity of their financial systems. The financial crisis started in the U.S., but in a very short period the capital markets of Europe suffered huge losses; the Euro lost significant value, and industrial output declined as U.S. imports from Europe declined. As the economic recession emerged and European countries increased spending to boost their economies against the background of fragile banking systems with huge debt exposures, sovereign debt crisis situations emerged in some European countries. Greece, Ireland, Spain, Portugal, and Italy were the most exposed.

At the end of 2009, the lowest ratios of the Euro area and EU Government debt to GDP were recorded as follows:[55] in Estonia 7.2 percent, Luxembourg 14.5 percent, Bulgaria 14.8 percent, Romania 23.7 percent, Lithuania 29.3 percent, and the Czech Republic 35.4 percent. Twelve Member States had government debt ratios higher than 60 percent of their GDP in 2009: Italy 115.8 percent, Greece 115.1 percent, Belgium 96.7 percent, Hungary 78.3 percent, France 77.6 percent, Portugal 76.8 percent, Germany 73.2 percent, Malta 69.1 percent, the United Kingdom 68.1 percent, Austria 66.5 percent, Ireland 64.0 percent, and the Netherlands 60.9 percent.

Following the request of the Greek Government on April 23, 2010, for the EU/IMF emergency loans/bailout package, the Standard & Poor's rating agency downgraded the Greek two-year bonds to BB+, a junk bond status. The rating indicated possible default and estimated that in the event of default, investors would lose 30–50 percent of their money. With great difficulty, the German Government backed the €110 billion EU bailout package for Greece. This package included the expectation of a reduction in deficit, cut in wages, increased taxes, and increase in retirement age among others.

Between the second quarter of 2008 and the second quarter of 2009, U.S. imports from Europe declined from $121.8 billion to $80.3 billion, a decline of 34 percent. See Figure 5.10.

Figure 5.10 Europe's Share of U.S. Imports Quarterly Data 2008 to 2010

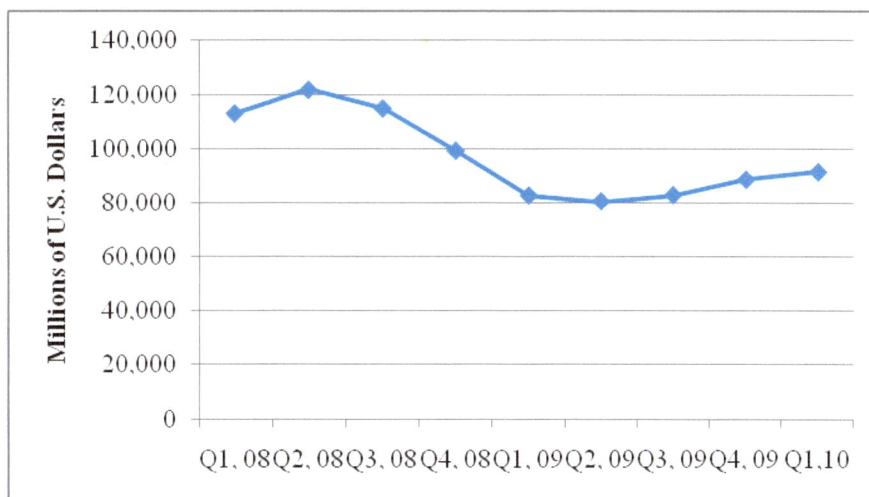

Source: Constructed with data from the Bureau of Economic Analysis, International Economic Accounts: Operations of Multinational Companies 2008, http://www.bea.gov.

[55] Eurostat News Release, April, 22, 2010.

In the wake of the U.S. financial crisis, on October 29, 2008, the Euro depreciated by 14.4 percent to a value of 1.25 against the U.S. Dollar. It rebounded and continued to fluctuate. With the emergence of the national debt crisis in Greece and evidence of the excessive debt burden on many European countries participating in the Euro, such as Portugal, Italy, Spain, and the United Kingdom, the Euro deteriorated further. By June 2010, it had lost about 18 percent of its value against the U.S. Dollar. See Figure5.11.

Figure 5.11 Value of the Euro against the U.S. Dollar 2008 to 2010

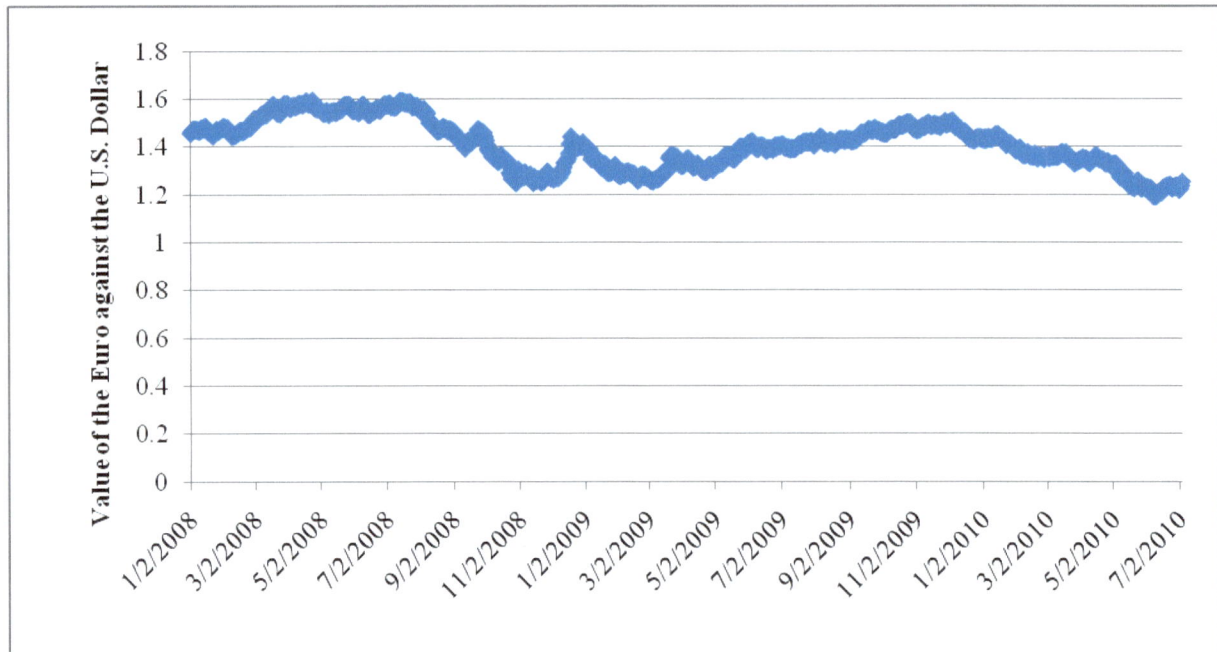

Source: Constructed from data on Source: http://www.oanda.com/currency/historical-rates

IMPACT OF THE U.S. FINANCIAL CRISIS AND ECONOMIC RECESSION ON EUROPEAN CAPITAL MARKETS

The stock markets usually react immediately to negative developments. The reaction of the European stock markets during the U.S. financial crisis in October 2008 was swift. By March 2009, the Austrian ATX plummeted from an index value of 4509.24 on January 2, 2008, to 1411.95, representing a loss of almost 69 percent. In a similar period, the German DAX lost about 54 percent of its value. By February 2009, the U.K. FTSE had lost about 45 percent of its value. By the end of the first quarter of 2009, all the European stock indexes recorded a similar trend albeit in different degrees. The recovery of the European stock markets was decelerated by the European debt crisis. See Figure5.12.

Figure 5.12 European Daily Stock Index Performances Trend from 2008 to 2010

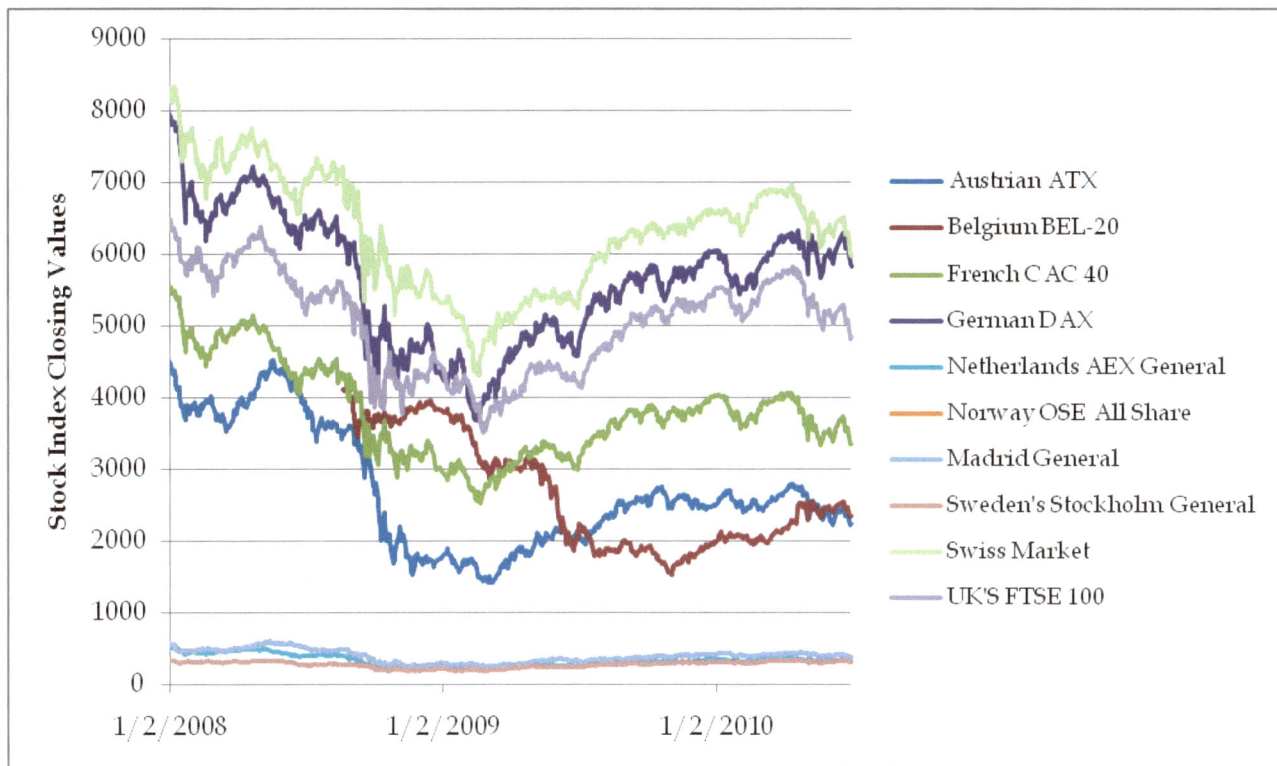

Source: Constructed from data on Yahoo Finance, http://www.oanda.com/currency/historical-rates

IMPACT OF THE U.S. FINANCIAL CRISIS AND ECONOMIC RECESSION ON THE LATIN AND NORTH AMERICAN REGIONS

According to José Rivera,[56] the U.S. FDI in Latin America and the Caribbean totals $50 billion a year, and remittances sent home by Latin Americans living in the United States amount to $45 billion dollars a year. In addition, the United States absorbs half of this region's exports, amounting to $375 billion a year.

Another important factor in the U.S.-Latin American relationship is that in 2008 about 19 percent of U.S. imports or $383 billion came from Latin America and other western hemisphere countries excluding Canada and Europe. It is therefore reasonable to expect that the financial crisis and economic recession that had a devastating effect on the U.S. economy would have severe negative repercussions on Latin America and the Caribbean.

Some people think differently, because they believe that some countries in that region are now much stronger than they were in the 1990s. For example, as a result of the structural change in Brazil's economy, a strong middle class is emerging, poverty is on the decline, and there is evidence of a boom in consumption. Many foreign companies are rushing in to position themselves to benefit from this positive economic development. Even as the financial crisis was unfolding in September 2008, Hyundai of South Korea, Suzuki of Japan, and Whirlpool and the Sheraton Hotels of the United States each announced new large-scale projects or expansions in Brazil. Chinese, Portuguese, and Scandinavian wood pulp manufacturers are all contemplating major factories in Brazil. In addition to Germany's ThyssenKrupp, two other international steel companies, Baosteel of China and Dongkuk of South Korea, are building multibillion-dollar steel plants in partnership with Brazilian iron ore producer, Vale.

---

[56] The permanent secretary for the Latin American Economic System (SELA)

They are investing to produce steel for export to Asian markets but also to supply Brazilian manufacturers struggling to meet an accelerating domestic demand for motor vehicles, appliances, housing, and public works.[57]

So how did the U.S. financial crisis and economic recession affect the Latin American, Caribbean, and the North American region's stock markets?

IMPACT OF THE U.S. FINANCIAL CRISIS AND ECONOMIC RECESSION ON STOCK MARKETS IN THE AMERICAS

Usually the stock markets react quickly to situations like this, and the region's stock indexes indeed reacted swiftly. In the months following the eruption of the U.S. financial crisis, the values of the Latin American and the Caribbean stock indexes plummeted. On October 22, 2008, trading on Brazil's stock market, the biggest in Latin America, was automatically suspended when the main Bovespa index plunged more than 10 percent.[58] By November 21, the Argentine MERV had lost 61 percent of its January 1, 2008, value. By October 14, 2008, the Mexican MXX had lost 41 percent of its beginning-of-year value. Even Canada, whose banks had not engaged in subprime lending and did not experience the mortgage crisis, was not immune. By February 20, 2009, the Canadian S&P/TST had lost 53 percent of its January 1, 2008, value. Canada is the Unites States' closest trading partner. The stock markets started recovering from this shock in the second quarter of 2009. See Figures5.13 and 5.14.

Figure 5.13 Daily Percentage Stock Index Stock Changes in Argentina, Canada, Mexico and the U.S. between 2008 and 2010

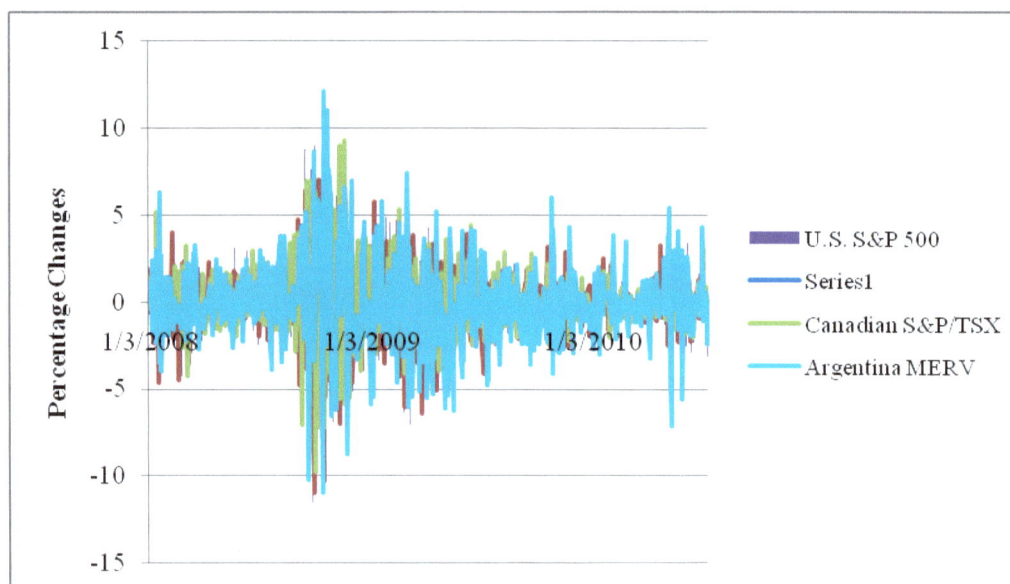

Source: Constructed from data on Yahoo Finance, http://www.oanda.com/currency/historical-rates

---

[57] Chris Kraul, "Brazil unfazed by U.S. market crisis," *Los Angeles Times*, September 22, 2008, http://articles.latimes.com/2008/sep/22/world/fg-brazil22 (accessed July 12, 2010).

[58] *Huffington Post*, "Brazilian Stock Market Halts trading as the Bovespa Index Plummets," November 22, 2008, http://www.huffingtonpost.com/2008/10/22/brazilian-stock-market-ha_n_136959.html (accessed July 12, 2010).

Figure 5.14 Daily Stock Index Stock Changes in Argentina, Canada, Mexico and the U.S. between 2008 and 2010

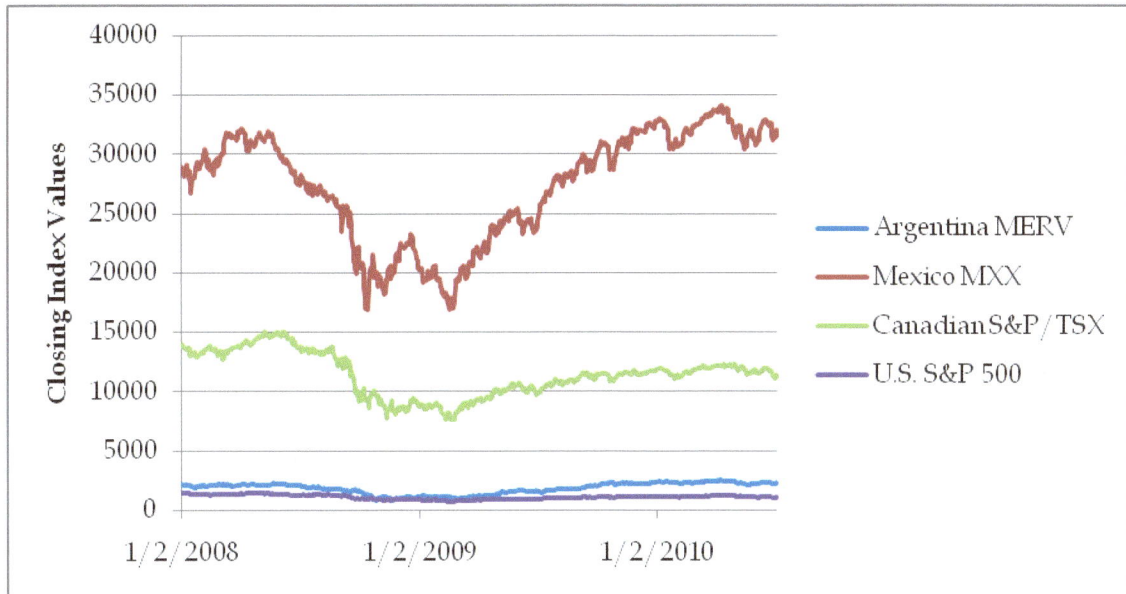

Source: Constructed from data on Yahoo Finance, http://www.oanda.com/currency/historical-rates

IMPACT OF THE U.S. FINANCIAL CRISIS AND ECONOMIC RECESSION ON REMITTANCES TO LATIN AMERICA AND THE CARIBBEAN COUNTRIES

Remittances from migrant workers constitute an important source of income for many Latin American and Caribbean countries. According to World Bank data for seven countries in Latin America and the Caribbean, remittances accounted for over 10 percent of GDP in 2007. For three of these countries (Guyana, Haiti, and Honduras) remittances accounted for over 20 percent of GDP. In El Salvador, the number is around 18 percent. In Mexico, though remittances as a percent of the GDP, was only 3 percent, the dollar amount is above $20 billion per year. See Table5.7

Table 5.7 Remittances as a Percent of GDP in Latin American Countries in 2007

Country	Percentage
Argentina	0.2
Belize	5.3
Bolivia	6.6
Brazil	0.3
Chile	0
Colombia	3
Costa Rica	2.3
Dominica	8

Country	Percentage
Dominican Republic	9.3
Ecuador	6.9
El Salvador	18.4
Guatemala	10.6
Guyana	23.5
Haiti	20
Honduras	24.5
Jamaica	19.4
Mexico	3
Nicaragua	12.1
Panama	0.8
Paraguay	3.2
Peru	1.9
St. Lucia	3.5
St. Vincent and the Grenadines	6.7
Uruguay	0.4
Venezuela,	0.1

Source: World Bank staff estimates based on the International; Monetary Fund's Balance of Payments Statistics Yearbook 2008

Overall, about 43 percent of the total remittances came from the U.S.[59] A reduction in remittances became noticeable early in 2008, and by the end of the year, the $69.6 billion that migrants sent home to the region barely increased by less than 1 percent over 2007. An overall 7 percent decline was projected for 2009 and an 11 percent decline in remittances from the U.S. to Latin American and Caribbean countries.

IMPACT OF THE U.S. FINANCIAL CRISIS AND ECONOMIC RECESSION ON EXCHANGE RATES

The reaction of this region's currencies to the U.S. financial crisis was interesting. It appears that only the Chilean currency lost substantial value in the early days of the crisis. On November 1, 2008, it had lost about 26 percent of its January 1, 2008, value. By the end of the first quarter of 2009, most of the currencies of the Latin American and Caribbean countries had lost substantial value on their January 2008 values. By the end of March 2009, the Brazilian Real had lost 32 percent, Mexican Peso 24 percent, and Colombian Peso and Jamaican Dollar 22 percent. Most of the currencies started appreciating in value in the second quarter of 2009. An interesting observation relates to the Panama

---

[59] Regional Bureau for Latin America and the Caribbean, "Crisis Update No. 4, The Decline of Remittances," March 30, 2009.

Balboa that experienced a little depreciation during the financial crisis and appreciated, albeit marginally, by 0.17 percent at the end of March 2009.

IMPACT ON FOREIGN DIRECT INVESTMENTS (FDI) FLOW TO LATIN AMERICA AND THE CARIBBEAN COUNTRIES

Due to the normal paucity of capital in developing economies in contrast to their monumental developmental needs, emerging economies always desperately need FDI. The flow of FDI to Latin America and the Caribbean in the past couple of decades has been very erratic. Between 1992 and 1998, FDI flows to the area increased significantly. These flows started declining by 2003; the FDI to Latin America and the Caribbean fell to 1996 levels.

Despite this drought in FDI flows to this region, some countries achieved increased FDI flows during this period, such as Mexico, Brazil, Argentina, Chile, Ecuador, Bolivia, Costa Rica, and Central America. Mexico benefitted from the *North American Free Trade Agreement* (NAFTA) of 1994. Many countries in the area engaged in extensive restructuring of their economies. There was an intensive diversification of the economic base and global international alliances. In the post-emerging market crises that occurred in Asia, Russia, Brazil, and Argentina, there was a surge of FDI flows to Latin America and the Caribbean. It is believed that the paucity of FDI flows to this region earlier in this decade reflected investor's pessimism towards emerging markets. In 2007, FDI flows to Latin America and the Caribbean was 52 percent. See Figure5.15.

Figure 5.15 FDI Flows to Latin America and the Caribbean, 1992-2008 (billions of dollars)

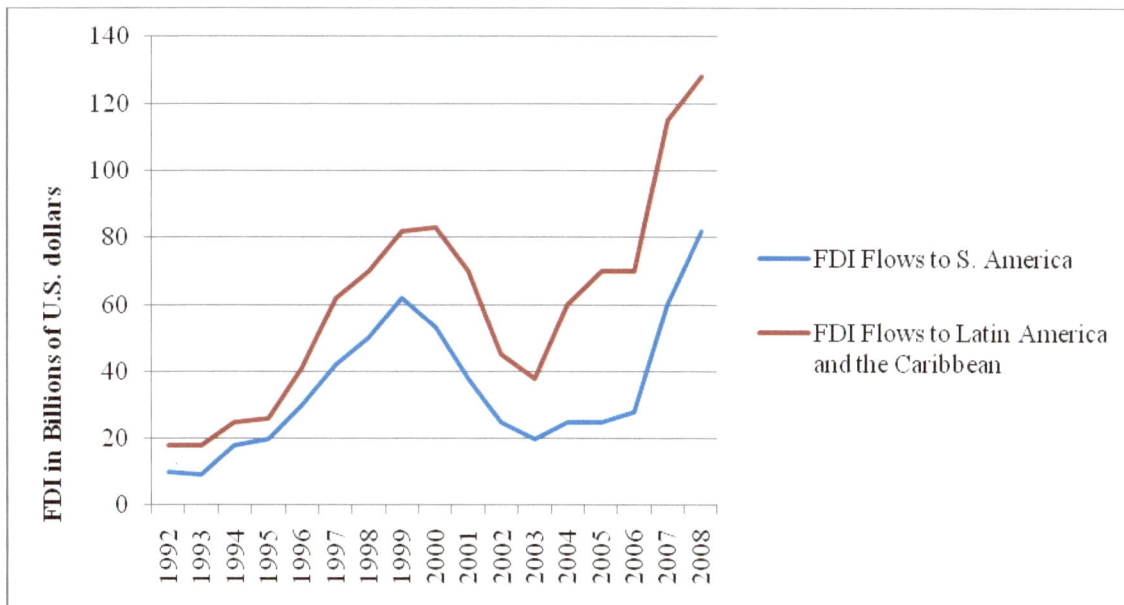

Source: Constructed with data from OECD,
           http://stats.oecd.org/Index.aspx?DataSetCode=AEO_OVERVIEWCHAPTER2FIG1

The financial crisis FDI flows to the region were 13 percent higher in 2008 than the previous year. This was an impressive performance considering there was a 15 percent contraction in global FDI flows. The region achieved growth in FDI flows despite the financial crisis because of already existing contracts. The prediction of FDI flows to the region was not optimistic as they were expected to decline between 35 percent and 45 percent during 2009.

CONCLUSION

The U.S. financial crisis led to a global financial crisis and eventually to a world recession. Even though almost all countries were negatively impacted, countries that had similar policies to the U.S., especially with regard to lending and subprime lending in particular, were more severely impacted. Many European countries fall under this category. It affected many countries in Asia, the Pacific region, and Latin American regions, but there was a quick rebound. It particularly affected countries in Africa, possibly because of the fragile economic recovery of many African countries in the last decade. The financial and economic dependence of many African countries on the U.S. and many countries in the western hemisphere perhaps also contributed to the severe impact.

Investors from all over the world who invested in many U.S. securities, especially the mortgage backed securities, were also negatively affected impacted because most of these securities turned out to be toxic.

BIBLIOGRAPHY

ATKearney. "2004 Foreign Direct Investment Confidence Index." *The Global Business Policy Council*, October 2004, Volume 7. http://www.atkearney.com/index.php/Publications/2004-foreign-direct-investment.html?q=2004+foreign+direct+investment+confidence+index (accessed July 12, 2010).

Basu, Parantap, Chandana *Chakraborty*, and Derrick *Reagle.* "Liberalization, FDI, and Growth in Developing Countries: A Panel Cointegration Approach." *Economic Enquiry* 41, no. 3: 510–516. *Business Pundit*. "10 countries least affected by the financial crisis." Filed in archive Economics, Finance, Government by Drea on October 8, 2008. http://www.businesspundit.com/10-countries-least-affected-by-the-us-financial-crisis/(accessed July 12, 1010).

Carter, Alexis R. "United States Commits to Strengthening Asia-Pacific Trade Partnership talks provide forum to integrate economic strategies." June 17, 2010. http://www.america.gov/st/business-english/2010/June/20100616174213frnedloh0.5610926.html (accessed July 12, 2010; site now discontinued).

Chukwuogor-Ndu, Chiaku. "Recent Trends in Global FDI Flows: Implication for the 21st Century." *International Journal of Banking and Finance*, Vol. 1, No 2, 2003, ISSN 1675-7227, pp. 49-67.

Chukwuogor-Ndu, Chiaku. "Day-of-the-week Effect and Volatility in Stock Returns: Evidence from East Asian Financial Markets." *International Journal of Banking and Finance*, Vol. 5, August-September, 2007, ISSN 1675-7227, pp. 153-164.

DLC, Trade & Global Markets. "U.S. imports fell by $700 billion last year," January 6, 2010. http://www.dlc.org/ndol_ci.cfm?contentid=255097&kaid=108&subid=900003.

Emerging Africa LMT. http://emerging-africa.com/stockmarketsreview.html (accessed July 12, 2010).

Eurostat News Release. "Provision of Deficit and Debt Data for 2009 - First Notification Euro Area and EU27 Government Deficit at 6.3% and 6.8% of GDP Respectively Government Debt at 78.7% and 73.6%," April 22, 2010. http://epp.eurostat.ec.europa.eu/cache/ITY_PUBLIC/2-22042010-BP/EN/2-22042010-BP-EN.PDF (accessed July 12, 2020).

Fernandez, Almudena, Luis F. Lopez-Calva, and Eduardo Ortiz. "Crisis Update No. 4, The Decline of Remittances." *Cluster for Poverty, Human Development, and MDGs, Regional Bureau for Latin America and the Caribbean*, March 30, 2009. http://economiccluster-lac.org/images/pdf/crisis-update/CrisisUpdateNo4.pdf (accessed July 12, 2010)

Fung, K. C., Alicia Garcia-Herrero, Hitomi Iizaka, and Alan Siu. "Hard or Soft? Institutional Reforms and Infrastructure Spending as Determinants of Foreign Direct Investment in China." *Japan Economic Review*, 2005.

Fung, K.C., Hitomi Iizaka, and Alan Siu. "Japanese Direct Investment in China." *China Economic Review* 14, (2003): 304-315.

Fung, K. C., Hitomi Iizaka, and Stephen Parker. "Determinants of U.S. and Japanese Direct Investment in China." *Journal of Comparative Economics* 30 (2002): 567-578.

Gastanaga, Victor M., Jeffrey B. Nugent, and Biastra Pashamova. "Host Country Reforms and FDI Flows, How Much Difference Do They Make?" *World Development* 26, no. 7, (1998): 1299-314.

Helsel, D. R., and R. M. Hirsch. "Statistical Methods in Water Resources." *Techniques of Water Resources Investigations*, Book 4, chapter A3. U.S. Geological Survey, 2002.

Hill, Charles W. L. *International Business: Competing in the Global Market Place*. Boston, MA: Irwin McGraw-Hill, 1999.

Hines, James R. Jr. "Forbidden Payment: Foreign Bribery and American Business after 1977." NBER Working Paper. No. 3266, 1995.

Huffington Post. "Brazilian Stock Market Halts trading as the Bovespa Index Plummets," November 22, 2008. http://www.huffingtonpost.com/2008/10/22/brazilian-stock-market-ha_n_136959.html (accessed July 12, 2010).

Irish Times. "Greece seeks activation of €45 billion aid package," December 22, 2010. http://www.irishtimes.com/newspaper/breaking/2010/0423/breaking28.html (accessed December 22, 2010).

Kraul, Chris. "Brazil unfazed by U.S. market crisis." *Los Angeles Times*, September 22, 2008. http://articles.latimes.com/2008/sep/22/world/fg-brazil22 (accessed July 12, 2010).

Márquez, Humberto. "Crisis Means Slower Growth Ahead." *IPS*, October 1, 2008. http://ipsnews.net/news.asp?idnews=44088 (accessed July 12, 2010).

Martin, Katie, and Terence Roth. "*Dow Jones Newswires." Wall Street Journal,* April 28, 2010.http://www.theaustralian.com.au/business/markets/sp-downgrades-greek-debt-to-junk/story-e6frg91o-1225859110788 (accessed July 12, 2010).

Mhlanga, Nomathemba, and Ralph D. Christy. "Capital Flows to Africa: an Analysis of the Structure of Official and Private Capital Flows." Working Paper, Cornell University, 2006. http://www.dyson.cornell.edu/research/researchpdf/wp/2006/Cornell_Dyson_wp0619.pdf (accessed December 31, 2010).

Moneyweb, Daily Indicators. http://www.moneyweb.co.za/mw/view/mw/en/page296405 (accessed July 12, 2010).

Stanimir, Alexandrov, Amelia Porges, and Meredith Moroney. "FDI Growth in Asia: The Potential for Treaty-Based Investment Protection." In *The Asia-Pacific Arbitration Review 2009* (Global Arbitration Review, 2009). http://www.globalarbitrationreview.com/reviews/12/sections/47/chapters/488/fdi-growth-asia-potential-treaty-based-investment-protection/(accessed July 12, 2010).

Tuan, Chyau, and Linda F. Y. Ng. "Manufacturing Agglomeration as Incentives to Asian FDI in China after WTO." *Journal of Asian Economics* 15, no. 2 (2004): 673-694.

United Nations. World Investment Report. New York and Geneva: United Nations, 1998.

US-China Business Council. "Foreign Investment in China," last updated March 14, 2005. http://www.uschina.org/statistics/2005foreigninvestment.html (accessed July 12, 2010).

U.S. Department of Commerce, International Trade Administration. "U.S.-African Trade Profile 2009." http://www.agoa.gov/resources/US_African_Trade_Profile_2009.pdf (accessed July 12, 2010).

U.S. House of Representatives. "Pursuing African Prosperity, The African Growth and Opportunity Act." http://www.house.gov/mcdermott/agoa/agoa_what.shtml (accessed July 12, 2010; site now discontinued).

Wei, Shang-Jin. "Why Is Corruption so Much More Taxing than Tax? Arbitrariness Kill." NBER Working Paper No. 6255, 1997.

Whitaker R. "U.S. market still open to Africa." http://thewhitakergroup.us/wordpress*(accessed July 12, 2010).*

Yahoo Finance, Major World Indices. http://finance.yahoo.com/intlindices?e=asia.

CHAPTER 6

ACTIONS TAKEN TO ADDRESS THE MALADIES OF THE FINANCIAL CRISIS/RECESSION, CREATE JOBS, AND PREVENT FUTURE FINANCIAL CRISES AND ECONOMIC RECESSIONS

INTRODUCTION

In an effort to curb the crisis, the U.S. Government enacted many bills after signs of the real estate mortgage crisis emerged in 2007. When the real estate mortgage crisis turned into a full-blown financial crisis and economic recession in 2008, the Government enacted more bills, and various federal agencies introduced additional regulations. The objectives of these actions were to check and control some of the negative developments in the real estate sector, the banking sector, and capital markets. The Government focused on injecting funds into the economy to mitigate the negative impact of the crisis on the middle class and the poor. Some of the actions focused on saving the financial system and the automobile industry, while others were aimed at preventing future financial and economic crises.

In particular, these bills addressed troubling developments associated with subprime lending, predatory lending, the size and activities of the nation's largest banks, losses in real estate investments, and abuses of credit card lending. The U.S. Government introduced other significant legislations and including the Emergency Economic Stabilization Act of 2008, Troubled Assets Relief Program (TARP), Economic Stimulus Act of 2008, American Recovery and Reinvestment Act of 2009, The Wall Street Reform and Consumer Protection Act, the Formation of Consumer Financial Protection Agency (CFPA), and the Financial Reform Act of 2010. This chapter reviews these various actions.

PREDATORY AND SUBPRIME MORTGAGE LENDING ISSUES

Predatory lending and the number of subprime mortgage loan originations reached unprecedented levels in 2005 and home foreclosures escalated. In reaction to these negative developments, on November 15, 2007, the U.S. Senate passed a law known as the Mortgage Reform and Anti-Predatory Lending Act of 2007 to address predatory and subprime mortgage lending issues.

This law mandates the registration of mortgage originators in an attempt to prevent abuses by requiring the originators to be part of a national registration system either through the states or through the Department of Housing and Urban Development, thereby establishing a national database of mortgage originators (much like securities brokers) and to meet minimum education and certification standards. This law also attempts to ensure responsible lending. Mortgage originators are required to provide full disclosure and to provide consumers with appropriate mortgages. The implication of this reform is that the originator is obligated to ensure that a consumer who receives a mortgage loan has a reasonable ability to repay the loan and to receive a net tangible benefit from the loan in the event of refinancing.

The Act also further sought to prevent abusive and discriminatory lending. Statistics have shown that many homeowners involved in the mortgage crisis had received large loans for which they were not qualified. This is often the result of a predatory practice known as "steering." This law prohibits the undisclosed and unfair compensation schemes that place some borrowers at a disadvantage, and requires regulations to prevent steering for subprime loans. Mortgage originators who engage in predatory practices and loan steering are subject to strict penalties. This law tried to make Wall Street firms that securitize mortgage loans accountable if they buy, sell, or securitize loans that consumers cannot pay. The Act also sought to enhance the protection to consumers against high cost loans. It extended the protections provided under the Home Owners Equity Protection Act by lowering points, fees, and interest rate triggers and generally prohibited practices that increase the risk of foreclosure, such as balloon payments that often encourage a borrower to default. It also required more pre-loan counseling. This buttresses the Home Owners Equity Protection Act, an amendment to the provisions in the Truth in Lending Act.

EMERGENCY ECONOMIC STABILIZATION ACT OF 2008 (EESA)

Chapter 1 of this book contains information on the tremendous financial upheaval and economic uncertainty that lead to the financial crisis, especially the several negative events in September 2008 that culminated in the financial crisis. Notable among these events were the filing for bankruptcy protection by Lehman Brothers, (a prominent securities firm), the agreement of Merrill Lynch to sell itself to Bank of America for about $50 billion, and the $40 billion bailout of the insurance giant American International Group (AIG) by the Federal Reserve. Earlier negative events included the Federal Government takeover of the troubled mortgage finance companies Fannie Mae and Freddie Mac, not to mention the failure of Bear Stearns and its forced merger with J.P. Morgan Chase. Recall that the root of the financial crisis was the subprime mortgage crisis. All these actions, among others, heightened investors' nervousness to extraordinary levels. The stock markets reflected this situation and stock values plummeted. This impending financial doom forced the Government to step in to rescue the financial system.

On October 3, 2008, the Emergency Economic Stabilization Act of 2008 (EESA) was signed into law. This act authorized the former Secretary of the Treasury, Henry Paulson, to spend up to $700 billion to purchase distressed assets, especially mortgage-backed securities, and make capital injections into banks. This act gave the Secretary of the Treasury a sweeping new authority to unlock frozen credit markets to get the economy moving again. According to Henry Paulson, "The broad authorities in this legislation, when combined with existing regulatory authorities and resources, gives us the ability to protect and recapitalize our financial system as we work through the stresses in our credit markets," and he promised to "move rapidly to implement the new authorities."[60]

On Wednesday, November 13, 2008, Henry Paulson announced that the U.S. had changed the focus of the $700 billion financial rescue strategy by abandoning plans to buy toxic mortgage-related assets, which weighed down the balance sheets of troubled banks and Wall Street institutions. He explained that the facts had changed, and the situation had worsened. He no longer believed that purchasing assets would be the most effective use of the administration's bailout fund. Therefore, the ensuing discussion of the EESA will focus on how it was administered.

The Government introduced certain initiatives using the funding provided by the EESA. First, it established the Troubled Assets Relief Program (TARP) under the EESA with the specific goal of stabilizing the U.S. financial system and preventing a systemic collapse. The Treasury established

---

[60] Alex Johnson, "Bush signs $700 billion financial bailout bill," http://www.msnbc.msn.com/id/26987291.

several programs under TARP to stabilize the financial system. It also created the Financial Stability Program to further stabilize the financial system, restore the flow of credit to consumers and businesses, and tackle the foreclosure crisis to keep millions of Americans in their homes. They also established some programs under TARP to help achieve the required success, for example, the Making Home Affordable Program, the Capital Purchase Program (CPP), the Consumer and Business Lending Initiative, the Public-Private Investment Program, the Capital Assistance Program, the Asset Guarantee Program (AGP), the Targeted Investment Program (TIP), and the Automotive Industry Financing Program.

MAKING HOME AFFORDABLE PROGRAM

By introducing the Making Home Affordable Program (HAMP), the U.S. Government attempted to stabilize the housing market by reducing the number of foreclosures. It also attempted to bring relief to vulnerable homeowners on the brink of foreclosure. The Federal Government tried to achieve these objectives through the adoption of a number of strategies including using state and local housing agency initiatives, tax credits for homebuyers, neighborhood stabilization, community development programs, mortgage modifications and refinancing, and support for Fannie Mae and Freddie Mac. According to the Administration, more than four million homeowners refinanced their mortgages to more affordable levels, more than one million saved an average of over $500 per month through the Administration's modification program, interest rates were at record lows, home prices were rising again in many areas, and the economy was growing as a result of these programs.

HAMP, which provides eligible homeowners the opportunity to reduce their monthly mortgage payment, was a key part of this effort. The objective of introducing HAMP was to help millions of homeowners remain in their homes and prevent avoidable foreclosures. However, HAMP experienced some problems in the early stages of its introduction in February 2009. Five months after its introduction, the U.S. Treasury reported that HAMP has been able to help only 9 percent of eligible homeowners. Banks, in general, seemed reluctant to participate in this program, and the participation across banks was uneven. Eleven of the twenty-five largest participating banks were helping fewer than 5 percent of Americans headed toward foreclosure. Even Bank of America which received $45 billion in Federal Government bailout funds was helping less than 4 percent of qualified borrowers.

Some of the problems with the implementation of HAMP included delays, long wait times for responses from banks after applications were submitted, confusion as to what constituted hardship, because hardship letters were required in some cases, and the lack of completeness and accuracy of information provided by applicants. Even when the documentation of applications was complete, applicants still experienced long wait times for responses from banks. This program was for struggling homeowners who were not yet delinquent in their mortgage payments but were in imminent default. However, possibly because of the aforementioned delays, according to the Treasury Department, by the end of December 2009, the success rate of this program was an abysmal 1 percent. This program achieved this success among borrowers who were at least 60 days delinquent on their loans.

CAPITAL PURCHASE PROGRAM (CPP)

According to the U.S. Department of the Treasury, the Capital Purchase Program (CPP) is a voluntary program in which the U.S. Government, through the Department of the Treasury, invests in preferred equity securities issued by qualified financial institutions. Only viable institutions that are recommended by their federal banking regulator can participate in this program. The Treasury's intent is to provide immediate capital to stabilize the financial and banking system and to support the economy. It is vital that lending be available to families and businesses that need access to credit to pay for college, invest, and to create jobs. A necessary precursor to economic recovery is a stable, healthy financial system. The Treasury invested up to $250 billion in senior preferred shares on standardized terms. This included warrants for future Treasury purchases of common stock in U.S. banks that were healthy but desired an extra layer of capital for stability or lending.

The CPP is available to qualifying U.S. controlled banks, savings associations, and certain bank and savings and loan holding companies engaged solely or predominately in financial activities permitted under the relevant law. Financial institutions participating in the CPP pay the Treasury a 5 percent dividend on senior preferred shares for the first five years following the Treasury's investment and a rate of 9 percent per year, thereafter. Banks can repay the Treasury under the conditions established in the purchase agreements as amended by the American Recovery and Reinvestment Act, and the Treasury can sell these shares when market conditions stabilize.[61] According to the **Financial Stability Division, (a branch of the** U.S. **Department of the Treasury),** since the inception of CPP in October 2008, it has strengthened regional, small, and large financial institutions as well as community development financial institutions in over **forty-eight states, Puerto Rico and the District of Columbia.**

CONSUMER AND BUSINESS LENDING INITIATIVE (CBLI)

The poor implementation of the securitization of mortgage assets, especially those containing subprime mortgage assets, the bundling and sale in the secondary markets, and the very high foreclosure rates of subprime mortgages, contributed in part to the real estate market crisis that led to the financial crisis. The impact of this development was severe on the credit market, because it clogged the flow of funds. In spite of the criticism about the bundling and sale of securitized assets in the secondary market, the U.S. Government still believes that when banks make loans for small businesses, commercial real estate, or autos they should be able to bundle and sell those loans into a vibrant and liquid secondary market. The secondary market is expected to recycle money back to financial institutions so that they can make additional loans to other worthy borrowers.

The Consumer and Business Lending Initiative (CBLI) was designed to jumpstart the credit markets. Under the CBLI, the Treasury and the Federal Reserve were working together to provide an initial $200 billion in financing to private investors to help unfreeze and lower interest rates for loans to students, small businesses, and others. This program had the potential to unlock up to $1 trillion of new lending and unfreeze currently frozen credit markets.[62] The objective of this initiative was to support the consumer and business credit markets by providing financing to private investors to help unfreeze and lower interest rates for auto, student loans, small business loans, credit cards, and other consumer and business credit. The Treasury used $20 billion to provide credit protection for $200 billion of lending from the Federal Reserve. This program also protects taxpayer resources by limiting purchases to newly packaged, "AAA" rated loans. In addition, under this initiative, the term asset-backed securities loan facility now includes Commercial Mortgage-backed Securities (CMBS). Additionally, it increased the guarantee for Small Business Administration (SBA) loans and reduced the SBA lending fees.

PUBLIC-PRIVATE INVESTMENT PROGRAM (PPIP)

In an attempt to increase the flow of credit throughout the U.S. economy, the U.S. Government established the Public-Private Investment Program (PPIP) to coordinate the effort between the Treasury, the FDIC, and the Federal Reserve to improve the health of financial institutions holding real-estate-

---

[61] U.S. Treasury, Financial Stability Division, http://www.financialstability.gov/roadtostability/capitalpurchaseprogram.html.
[62] U.S. Treasury, Financial Stability Division, http://www.financialstability.gov/roadtostability/capitalpurchaseprogram.html.

related assets. The PPIP seeks to improve liquidity, promote price discovery, free up capital, and allow financial institutions to engage in new credit formation. The Government expects that this initiative will result in an increased amount of available capital and credit to corporations, small business owners, homeowners, and the American public. The Government believes that greater accessibility of credit in the U.S. financial system will stimulate economic growth. The Government further believes that better clarity about the value of legacy assets should increase investor confidence and enhance the ability of financial institutions to raise new capital from private investors.[63]

CAPITAL ASSISTANCE PROGRAM (CAP)

On February 26, 2009, the U.S. Government introduced the Capital Assistance Program (CAP). The main object of this program is to restore confidence throughout the financial system by ensuring that the nation's largest banking institutions, banks with assets in excess of $100 billion on a consolidated basis, had sufficient capital to cushion them against larger than expected future losses should they occur, due to a more severe economic environment. The second objective of this program is to support lending to creditworthy borrowers. Under CAP, federal banking supervisors will conduct forward-looking assessments to evaluate the capital needs of the major U.S. banking institutions under a more challenging economic environment. If that assessment indicates the need for additional capital buffers, the banks will have an opportunity to turn first to private sources of capital. In light of the challenging market environment at the time, the Treasury made government capital available immediately to eligible banking institutions through CAP to provide this buffer.

The result of the stress tests revealed that some of the largest banks were stable, whereas others needed billions of dollars in capital. On Thursday, May 7, 2009, the Federal Reserve's findings regarding the result of the stress tests on the largest U.S. banks indicated that ten of the nation's nineteen largest banks needed a total of $75 billion in new capital in order to be able to withstand losses in case the recession worsened. Some of the banks that needed more capital were: Bank of America Corp ($33.9 billion), Wells Fargo & Co. ($13.7 billion), GMAC LLC ($11.5 billion), Citigroup Inc.($5.5 billion), and Morgan Stanley ($1.8 billion). Some of the regional banks also needed to increase their capital base. Those banks were: Regions Financial Corp. of Birmingham, SunTrust Banks Inc. of Atlanta, KeyCorp of Cleveland, Fifth Third Bancorp of Cincinnati, and PNC Financial Services Group Inc. of Pittsburgh.

THE AUTOMOTIVE INDUSTRY FINANCING PROGRAM (AIFP)

In 2009, the Government introduced The Automotive Industry Financing Program (AIFP). The objective of this program was to prevent a significant disruption of the American automotive industry, which would have posed a systemic risk to financial market stability and resulted in a negative effect on the economy of the United States. The program required participating institutions to implement plans that achieve long-term viability. Participating institutions must also adhere to rigorous executive compensation standards and other measures to protect the taxpayer's interests, including limits on the institution's expenditures and other corporate governance requirements.[64] In addition, it was important to stem the debilitating trend in job losses by saving most of the jobs in the automobile industry, which is an important employer in the U.S. Some of the automobile companies were on the brink of bankruptcy, notably, General Motors and Chrysler. The Federal Government felt that it was necessary to

---

[63] Legacy Assets are assets in balance sheets whose value is uncertain or depressed, see Timothy Geithner, "My Plan for Bad Bank Assets," March 23, 2009, http://online.wsj.com/article/SB123776536222709061.html. See also U.S. Treasury, Financial Stability Division, http://www.financialstability.gov/roadtostability/capitalpurchaseprogram.html.

[64] U.S. Treasury, Financial Stability Division, http://www.financialstability.gov/roadtostability/capitalpurchaseprogram.html.

establish this program to save the industry, not only to satisfy an economic objective but also to preserve the automobile industry as a matter of national pride.

The U.S. Government also engaged in other programs such as the Asset Guarantee Program (AGP) and the Targeted Investment Program (TIP). It was under one of these programs that General Motors received $50 billion in July 2009, in exchange for a 65 percent ownership with shares as security for the investment.

Under TARP, the U.S. Government purchased preferred stock in more than 282 banks in America including all of the largest banks. For example, Bank of America Corp. and Citigroup Inc. benefitted the most from this program, each totaling $45 billion. Other banks that benefitted significantly from this program are J. P. Morgan Chase & Co. $25 billion, Wells Fargo & Co $25 billion, Goldman Sachs Group Inc. $10 billion, and Morgan Stanley $10 billion. Some of these banks made full or partial repayment of TARP funding. Some of these banks have negotiated with the Government to convert a portion of this funding to the bank's equity capital.

Did this program restore confidence in the battered U.S. banking system? Did this program achieve the desired objective of keeping money flowing through the financial system, thus ensuring that banks continued lending to companies and consumers? Opponents of this program argue that the U.S. Government had seized the opportunity provided by the financial crisis to increase its involvement in the financial markets, imitating the Government's response during the Great Depression. They argue that the financial crisis and the economic recession did not compare with the Great Depression. Unemployment was at 9.5 percent in the second quarter of 2010, all reports indicated that about $2 trillion is sitting idle in bank vaults, and businesses are not hiring. Proponents of the program argue that these efforts averted a catastrophic financial event. They state that the stock market has somewhat stabilized and is growing, the job loss rate has greatly decreased compared to the situation in 2008, and there is evidence of increased job growth. They argue that a full recovery will occur slowly as consumer demand increases and investor confidence returns. This will generate increased employment that will most likely energize the housing market into a full recovery.

OVERSIGHT OF THE TROUBLED ASSET RELIEF PROGRAM

As you can imagine, disbursing $700 billion can be complicated. The Emergency Economic Stabilization Act of 2008 established a number of oversight mechanisms. Some of these oversight mechanisms are the Financial Stability Oversight Board, the Congressional Oversight Panel, the Special Inspector General for TARP (SIGTARP), and additional requirements for both the Government Accountability Office (GAO) and the Congressional Budget Office (CBO). Each of these mechanisms has its special areas of focus.

For example, according to Section 104 of this Act, the Financial Stability Oversight Board reviews the operation of TARP to make recommendations to the Treasury for improvements and to watch for fraud and misrepresentation. It also has the power to ensure that the Treasury follows policies in accordance with the Act and the economic interest of the U.S.

The Congressional Oversight Panel reviews the state of the markets, current regulatory system, and the Treasury Department's management of TARP. The panel is required to report its findings to Congress every thirty days, starting with the first asset purchase made under the program.

The Comptroller General, director of Government Accountability, monitors the performance of the program and reports the findings to Congress every sixty days. The Comptroller General is also required to audit the program annually. The Act grants the Comptroller General access to all information, records, reports and data that belong or are in use by the program.

This Act provides for The Special Inspector General to monitor, audit, and investigate the activities of the Treasury in the administration of the program and must report the findings to Congress every quarter. The Senate must confirm this Presidential appointee. However, the Office of the Special Inspector General for TARP seems to perform similar functions as the Comptroller General.

AMERICAN RECOVERY AND REINVESTMENT ACT OF 2009

By the first quarter of 2009, the economy worsened because of the financial crisis and the economic recession that was already more than two years old. Many job losses occurred in January 2009, and the U.S. experienced its highest job loss in thirty-four years. Employers slashed 598,000 jobs, and, in three months, the U.S. lost 1.8 million jobs. Since the beginning of 2008, it had lost 3.6 million jobs. With a battered real estate market, a stock market in crisis, and the economy in a recession, President Barack Obama urged Congress to pass a bailout bill for the American people. On February 13, 2009, Congress passed the American Recovery and Reinvestment Act of 2009.

The immediate goals of this legislation were to create new jobs and save existing ones, spur economic activity, invest in long-term growth, and foster unprecedented levels of accountability and transparency in government spending. The fiscal implications of this bill were numerous. The bill provides:

1) $288 billion in tax cuts and benefits for millions of working families and businesses

2) Increases in federal funds for education and health care as well as entitlement programs (such as extending unemployment benefits) by $224 billion

3) Provides $275 billion for federal contracts, grants, and loans

4) Recipients of recovery funds must report quarterly on how they are using the money. To ensure greater transparency, the Government must provide all data relating to the disbursement of these funds on the web site, www.recovery.gov, so the public can track the disbursement and recovery of the funds.

Many of the Recovery Act projects focused on immediate jumpstarting of the economy, such as offering financial aid directly to local school districts, expanding the Child Tax Credit to $1,000, and underwriting a process to computerize health records to reduce medical errors and save on health care cost. Some provisions in the bill also targeted some long-term projects that will help improve the infrastructure development and enhancement, for example, planned investments in the domestic renewable energy industry and the weatherizing of 75 percent of federal buildings as well as more than one million private homes around the country. This bill also includes the construction and repair of roads and bridges, scientific research, and the expansion of broadband and wireless service.

Some parts of the American Recovery and Reinvestment Act of 2009 focused on providing aid to low-income workers by increasing the unemployment benefits by $25 a week, and extending them through December 31, 2009, providing job training, increasing food stamp benefits by 12 percent through fiscal 2011 and issuing a one-time bonus payment, and providing $3 billion in temporary welfare payments. The bill also provided for direct cash payments for vulnerable members of society, such as the elderly. There was a one-time payment of $250 to recipients of Supplemental Security Income and Social Security, and veterans receiving disability and pensions.[65] Taxation relief was an important part of this legislation, and it related to new tax credits, expanded child credit, expanded earned income tax credit, unemployment, expanded college credit, homebuyer credit, home energy credit, bonus depreciation for companies losing money, and government contractors, among others. In the case of bonus depreciation, if a business is losing money before or after this deduction the company is allowed to carry back the loss up to two years and get a refund on taxes paid in previous years. They may also carry it forward for up to twenty years.

---

[65] This government program provides stipends to low income persons who are either aged (65 or older), blind, or disabled.

The intent of this stimulus legislation was to create jobs and to promote investment and consumer spending. This is in consonance with the Keynesian economic theory that government spending should be used to cover the output gap created by the drop in consumer spending during a recession. The total amount provided for this bailout was $787 billion.

CREDIT CARD ACT OF 2009

In response to years of consumer complaints against credit card companies, the President signed the Credit Card Act of 2009 into law on May 22, 2009. Consumers had complained that companies that issued credit cards arbitrarily added or increased fees, increased interest rates, and changed the terms of the agreement. They further lamented the lack of transparency in the communication of actions of banks and credit card companies that provided credit. Often, the contract's unfavorable terms were embedded in the multiple pages of the contract. There were also complaints that credit card companies arbitrarily changed billing and payment due dates. This confused some consumers, and they often incurred late payments as a result. Some consumers also complained that credit card companies sometimes received payments in time but still charged the customers a late fee with an accompanying interest rate hike.

This is a very important reform as it reduces the degree of debt and subsequent default caused by excessive credit card interest rates and fees and huge unaffordable limits. It will also reduce the exploitation of consumers as the credit card companies can no longer change interest rates or impose fees arbitrarily. This Act stipulated information that a credit card company must disclose to consumers, new rules regarding rates, fees, and limits, and it standardized payment information.

The Credit Card Act provides that credit card companies must send customers a 45 days' notice before they can increase a customer's interest rate, change annual fees, cash advance or late fees, or make significant changes to the terms of a customer's credit card. If a credit card company is going to make changes to the terms of the card, the credit card company must first give the customer the option to cancel the card. If the customer takes that option, however, the credit card company may either close the account or increase the monthly payment, subject to certain limitations. For example, they may require the customer to pay off the closed account in a number of years, usually five, or they may increase the minimum payment under the terms of the account so that the customer can pay the balance on the credit card sooner. However, a credit card company does not have to send a forty-five day advance notice if the card has a variable interest rate tied to an index and the index goes up. The credit card company also does not have to provide notice before the rate goes up if the introductory rate expires and the card reverts to the previously disclosed rate or the rate increases because the customer is in a workout agreement and has not made payments as previously agreed.

Another important problem that the Credit Card Act addressed was the issue of making monthly minimum payments. Some consumers owed balances on their cards and regularly charged items to their cards but only made minimum payments. This led to huge balances over time. This sometimes led to default, especially in adverse circumstances, for example, a loss of employment by the consumer or by other family members. The Act mandates that credit card companies must indicate in their monthly statement how long it will take the customer to pay off the balance if they only make minimum payments. It will also tell you how much you would need to pay each month in order to pay off your balance in three years.

The Credit Card Act put an end to credit card interest rate increases during the first year of a customer opening an account, with some exceptions. These exceptions include a situation where the card has a variable interest rate tied to an index, or the customer took advantage of an introductory rate that must have a life of at least six months. Other situations include where the customer is more than sixty days late in paying the bill or the customer is in a workout arrangement and is not making the payment as agreed. In these situations, the rate may go up. If the credit card company raises the rate after the first year, these rates must apply only to new charges. The Act also imposed restrictions on over-the-limit transactions. Credit card companies can deny any potential charges by a customer that will take the account over the limit without permission. However, if the credit card company allows such a charge, it may not charge the customer an over-the-limit fee. If a customer opts in to allow transactions that take the account over the limit, the customer can revoke the opt-in at any time, but the credit card company is allowed to impose one fee per billing cycle.

Another restriction imposed by the Credit Card Act is the maximum total fees, annual fees or application fees that a credit company can charge in the first year. This fee must not exceed 25 percent of the initial credit limit. If the initial credit limit is $5,000, the total of all fees must not exceed $1,250. This is probably an improvement over what existed before, but the high percentage of the initial credit allowed as fees is still exorbitant and should have been reduced further. With the reduced labor hours involved in processing credit card applications and monitoring transactions because of online and computer applications, credit card companies do not spend as much as they used to in these activities.

Another restriction introduced by the Credit Card Act is the use of credit cards by underage consumers. In the absence of evidence of an underage person to make payments, a credit card can be opened only if there is a co-signer. The co-signer must agree to all credit limit increases, which is an improvement. In the past, young people and college students racked up credit cards bills mainly because they were easily available to them and often unsupervised by parents.

Finally, the Credit Card Act of 2009 focused on billing payments. It standardized payment dates and times and stipulated that a credit card company must mail or deliver the credit card bill at least twenty-one days before the payment is due. A customer's due date should also be the same date each month. For example, a payment is always due on the 15th or on the last day of the month, and the cutoff time on the due date must not be earlier than 5:00 p.m. To solve the problems of customer payments on weekends and holidays, the Act specifically provides that if the payment due date coincides with a weekend or holiday, when the company does not process payments, the consumer has until the following business day to pay. For example, if the due date is Sunday, August 15, 2010, the payment is on time if it is received by Monday the 16th before 5:00 p.m.

To protect consumers, the Act directed that any additional money in excess of the minimum payment made by a credit card customer must be applied to the account balance with the highest interest rate. For example, if a consumer owes $8,000 at an interest rate of 9 percent, $6,000 at an interest rate of 12 percent, and $4,000 at an interest rate of 5 percent and the consumer's minimum payment for the last account is $100 but the consumer pays $150, the excess of the payment over the minimum payment is $50. According to the Act, the bank must apply this amount to the account with the highest interest rate. In this case, that will be the account with the $6,000 balance and 12 percent interest rate. However, there is an exception to this provision. It relates to a purchase under a deferred interest plan. For example, no interest will be charged if paid in full by September 2010. In this situation, the credit card company may allow the consumer to choose to apply extra amounts to the deferred interest balance before other balances. Otherwise, for two billing cycles prior to the end of the deferred interest period, the credit card company must apply the entire payment to the deferred interest rate balance first.

This Act also addressed the practice of double cycle billing. In the past, some credit card companies, in determining the balance that forms the basis for calculating the interest-billing amount for a particular period, used the current balance on the credit card and the average daily balance from the previous billing period. This practice definitely led to higher amounts, especially if there were higher average daily balances in the previous period. The Credit Card Act put an end to this practice. Credit card companies can only impose interest charges on balances in the current billing cycle.

DODD–FRANK WALL STREET REFORM AND CONSUMER PROTECTION ACT, 2010

In 2009, the U.S. Department of the Treasury proposed a Financial Regulatory Reform. According to the U.S. Department of the Treasury, Americans across the nation were struggling with unemployment, failing businesses, falling home prices, and declining savings mainly because of the effects of a poor regulatory system that enabled many unfavorable developments to occur. Among others, the Treasury Department named the following negative developments. First, it identified rising asset prices, particularly in the housing market, the weak credit underwriting standards and the growing leverage throughout the system. Second, at some of our most sophisticated financial firms, risk management systems did not keep pace with the complexity of new financial products. Third, the lack of transparency and standards in markets for securitized loans helped to weaken underwriting standards. Fourth, market discipline broke down as investors relied excessively on credit rating agencies. Fifth, compensation practices throughout the financial services industry rewarded short-term profits at the expense of long-term performance. Sixth, households saw significant increases in access to credit, but pervasive the failures in consumer protection left many Americans with obligations that they did not understand and could not afford. Seventh, gaps and weaknesses in the supervision and regulation of financial firms presented challenges to the Government's ability to monitor, prevent, or address risks as they built up in the system. The Treasury made recommendations to prevent many of these problems from growing out of control and threatening the stability of our financial system in the future.

President Obama signed the Dodd-Frank Wall Street Reform and Consumer Protection Act of 2010 into law on July 22, 2010. This law was universally described as a sweeping bank regulation because of its all-embracing nature. This new law created two agencies to ensure financial stability; and established an authority for orderly liquidation of financial institutions previously considered too big to fail, should the need arise. In addition:

- It also transferred powers to the Comptroller, the FDIC, and the Federal Reserve System in an attempt to streamline banking regulation and reduce regulatory competition
- It regulated advisers of hedge funds and others, and brought the insurance industry under the regulatory control of the Treasury
- It introduced the Volcker Rule and bank regulation
- It introduced Wall Street transparency and accountability by regulating the over-the-counter swaps markets
- It attempted to mitigate systemic risk within and promoted stability in the financial system by creating the payment, clearing, and settlement supervision
- It established investor protections and improvements to the regulation of securities by revising the powers and structure of the SEC, credit rating organizations, and the relationships between customers and broker-dealers or investment advisers
- It established a Bureau of Consumer Financial Protection and amended the Federal Reserve Acts to change the New York Federal Reserve President to a Presidential appointment with the advice and consent of the Senate
- It also improved access to mainstream financial institutions
- It amended the Emergency Economic Stabilization Act of 2008, and established the Mortgage Reform and Anti-Predatory Lending Act.

FINANCIAL STABILITY OVERSIGHT

In recognition of the fact that many warning signs of the financial crisis and economic recession were either overlooked or ignored, the Dodd-Frank Wall Street Reform and Consumer Protection Act of 2010 introduced two new agencies, the Financial Stability Oversight Council and the Office of Financial Research. These two agencies must monitor systematic risk and research the state of the economy. Both agencies must clarify the comprehensive supervision of bank holding companies by the Federal Reserve.

The Financial reform law established the Financial Stability Oversight Council. The objectives of this council are to identify the risks to the financial stability of the United States from both financial and non-financial organizations, promote market discipline by eliminating expectations that the Government will shield them from losses in the event of failure, and respond to emerging threats to the stability of the U.S. financial system. This Financial Stability Oversight Council is expected to enhance the integrity, efficiency, competitiveness, and stability of U.S. financial markets, promote market discipline, and maintain investor confidence. The membership of this council includes leaders of key agencies, government departments, and quasi-government institutions involved in giving direction in the financial system, such as the Treasury Department, the Federal Reserve System, the office of the Comptroller of Currency, and the Bureau of Consumer Financial Protection. Other members of the Council include the Securities and Exchange Commission, the Federal Deposit Insurance Corporation, the Commodity Futures Trading Commission, the Federal Housing Finance Agency, the National Credit Union, and the President's appointee to represent the insurance industry. There are also five non-voting members; the Director of the Office of Financial Research, the Director of the Federal Insurance Office, a representative of the state insurance commissioners, a representative of the state banking supervisors, and a representative of the state securities commissioners.

The second agency established by the reform act is the Office of Financial Research. It charged this second agency with providing administrative, technical, and budget analysis as well as other support services to the Council and its affiliated agencies. The Director reports to and testifies before the Senate Committee on Banking, Housing, and Urban Affairs and the House Committee on Financial Services. Expected information on the testimony shall be on activities of the office, including the work of the Data Center and the Research and Analysis Center, the assessment of significant financial and market developments, and potential emerging threats to the financial stability of the country. This testimony must be delivered every year, and these reports to Congress are independent of any political influence. The Act prohibits any officer or agency of the United States from having any authority to require the director to submit the testimony for approval, comment, or review prior to the submission of such testimony. This is very important, as the Director of the Office of Financial Research must act with utmost independence for the effective delivery of the mandate of the office.

Both the Financial Stability Oversight Council and the Office of Financial Research are provided with abundant resources. First, the power of the Federal Advisory Committee Act that limits the powers of advisory committees does not apply to the Financial Stability Oversight Council. Both agencies may draw on virtually any resource of any department or agency of the Federal Government. Any employee of the Federal Government may be detailed to the Council without reimbursement and without interruption or loss of civil service status or privilege. Any member of the Council who is an employee of the Federal Government serves without additional compensation. To encourage a strong research support, the new law established a revolving fund known as the Financial Research Fund in the Office of Financial Research, within the Treasury Department. All appropriations, fees, and assessments that the Office receives are deposited into this fund. The Act permits surplus funds to be reinvested, and it is expected that this Financial Research Fund will become self-funding within two years.

ORDERLY LIQUIDATION AUTHORITY

Over the years, some financial institutions and other companies have been labeled too big to fail. Many believe that it would be a disaster for the economy if these business entities failed. Why does this belief persist? It is because these entities are so central to our macro economy. Some of them control a high percentage of the capital or recourses in a particular industry. Others employ a high percentage of workers in a particular industry or the distribution network. The general belief is that the failure of these companies may either trigger huge unemployment or negatively affect the supply network of the industry. Lehman Brothers was considered too big to fail. Many believed that its failure ignited the financial crisis. American International Group (AIG) was considered too big to fail, hence the billions of bailout money the Federal Government has showered on it. Because of AIG's imposing presence in the global insurance industry, the Government argued that if we did not bail it out, insurance the way we know it would cease to exist. What about General Motors (GM), was it too big to fail? "What's good for General Motors is good for the country," goes the old saying. If that is true, then so is the reverse: If the 100-year-old automaker were to fail then it would bring down a substantial portion of the U.S. economy with it. A GM collapse would almost instantly add tens of thousands of Americans to the unemployment rolls. Auto dealerships across the country would be at risk. A host of suppliers, from aluminum smelters to vinyl extruders to computer-chip etchers, would lose a key customer. The argument went on and on as the Government bailed out bank after bank: Bear Stearns and commercial banks such as Bank of America, Citigroup, and J. P. Morgan Chase. If the Government had allowed these banks to fail, according to them, the financial system would have tanked.

Some people lamented that we had to use taxpayers' money to bail out big businesses. A strong argument emerged suggesting that the public policy of bailing out big businesses be they banks or automobile companies was counterproductive. This opinion asserted that the Government should allow these large banks or other institutions to fail if they assume excessive risk and are unable to effectively manage such risk exposure. In a capitalist system, businesses must reap the fruit of good business operations and demise should befall them for overextending themselves and putting the whole economy and the financial system in jeopardy.

It was in response to these concerns that the Wall Street Reform and Consumer Protection Act established the Orderly Liquidation Authority for the orderly liquidation of banks, insurance companies, and non-banking financial institutions. Depending on the type of financial institution, different regulatory organizations may jointly or independently, by a two-thirds vote, determine the necessity for appointing a receiver for a financial company. For banks, in general, the relevant authority is the Federal Deposit Insurance Corporation (FDIC) or the Federal Reserve System; for broker/dealers, the Securities and Exchange Commission or the Federal Reserve System; for insurance companies, the Federal Insurance Office or the Federal Reserve System. There is a provision that the Secretary of the Treasury in consultation with the President may also make a determination to appoint a receiver for a financial company.

The Dodd-Frank Wall Street Reform and Consumer Protection Act of 2010 established the Government Accountability Office (GAO). The GAO must review and report the Secretary's decision to Congress. Within twenty-four hours of a financial institution entering into receivership under the provisions of this Act, the Secretary of the Treasury shall report to Congress, and there shall be a report to the public within sixty days. This report should contain details on the state of the economy, the impact of its default on the company, and the proposed action.

This Act further established an Orderly Liquidation Authority Panel inside the United States, the Bankruptcy Court for the District of Delaware. This court must evaluate the decision of the Secretary of the Treasury that a company is in, or in danger of default. If the Panel agrees with the Secretary, the company in question goes into receivership. If they do not agree, the Secretary can amend his or her petition and re-file it. This provision brings some legal definition to the orderly liquidation process.

Some of the other provisions of this Act that have been very favorable includes limiting the Government's liquidation obligation, which cannot exceed 10 percent of the total consolidated assets or 90 percent of the fair value of the total consolidated assets of the financial institution. Another provision is a prohibition on taxpayer funding. Taxpayers shall bear no losses from liquidating any financial company under the Act. Any losses shall be the responsibility of the financial sector and be recovered through assessments. This Act also authorized private funding for the FDIC to buy and sell securities on behalf of the company (or companies) in receivership in an effort to raise additional capital.

TRANSFER OF POWERS TO THE COMPTROLLER, THE FDIC, AND THE FEDERAL RESERVE SYSTEM

This sweeping regulatory reform abolished the Office of Thrift Supervision, permanently increased the amount of deposit insurance by the FDIC from $100,000 to $250,000, and required that each of the financial regulatory agencies represented on the Council shall establish an Office of Minority and Women Inclusion. This office shall be responsible for all matters of the agency relating to diversity in management, employment, and business activities. The Dodd-Frank Wall Street Reform and Consumer Protection Act of 2010 transferred the power of the Office of Thrift Supervision over the appropriate holding companies to the Federal Reserve System, state savings associations to the FDIC, and other thrifts to the Office of the Comptroller of the Currency. A weakened thrift charter remained. The Act made all these changes in an effort to streamline banking regulation and reduce regulatory competition.

REGULATION OF ADVISERS TO HEDGE FUNDS AND OTHER FUNDS

The bill is designed to redress the poor regulation of domestic hedge funds and to prevent future Ponzi schemes from occurring, such as the type Bernard Madoff perpetrated for decades before he was caught. Under title IV of the Reform Act, most domestic funds, managing more than $100 million, must register with the Securities and Exchange Commission as investment advisers and must comply with various disclosure requirements. In an attempt to further regulate advisers to hedge funds, different government agencies were required to study and report on various issues and report to Congress. For example, the Government Accountability Office (GAO) was to study the appropriate criteria for determining the financial thresholds or other criteria needed to qualify for accredited investor and report within three years. In addition, it was to study the feasibility of forming a self-regulating organization for private funds and report within one year. The SEC was to study short selling, including feasibility, benefits, and the costs of real-time short-sale publications, as well as a voluntary pilot program for reporting.

This bill increased the responsibility of investment advisers and hedge funds by requiring them to take necessary steps to safeguard client assets over which such advisers have custody, including without limitation, verification of such assets by an independent public accountant, as the commission may, by rule, prescribe. Had this sort of provision been in place, such schemes, as the Madoff Ponzi scheme, where investors altogether lost billions of dollars might not have existed.

INSURANCE INDUSTRY UNDER THE REGULATORY CONTROL OF THE TREASURY

We purchase insurance to cover against identifiable losses, some of which may be catastrophic if not covered by insurance. Yet, the Federal Government bailed out AIG, one of the largest companies in the world, a titan in the global insurance industry. The insurance industry undermined our expected protection against risk.

The Dodd-Frank Wall Street Reform and Consumer Protection Act of 2010 sought to bring the insurance industry under greater supervision by establishing the Federal Insurance Office within the Department of the Treasury. This act charged the Federal Insurance Office with monitoring all aspects of the insurance industry: the extent to which traditionally underserved communities and consumers, minorities, and low and moderate income persons have access to affordable insurance, except health insurance. It also makes recommendations to the Financial Stability Oversight Council about insurers that may pose a risk to the economy. This bill also helps state regulators with national issues such as administering terrorism insurance programs, and coordinating international insurance matters. In addition, the Federal Insurance Office determines whether state insurance measures are preempted by covered agreements (states may have requirements that are more stringent) and consult with the state regulators regarding insurance matters of national importance and international importance. This office may require any insurance company to submit such data as may be reasonably required in carrying out the functions of the Office.

VOLCKER RULE AND BANK REGULATION

The "Volcker Rule" is named after the former Chairman of the Federal Reserve Bank, Paul Volcker. The Volcker Rule limits any one bank from holding more than 10 percent of FDIC insured deposits. It prohibits any bank with a division holding such deposits from using its own capital to make speculative investments. This is an effort to prohibit commercial banks from participating in certain risky trading activities by limiting the size and scope of the United States' largest banks through regulation. This is expected to have a positive impact on reducing systemic risk.

WALL STREET TRANSPARENCY AND ACCOUNTABILITY

Many experts believed that the lack of adequate oversight and regulation of the derivatives markets enabled large financial institutions to assume enormous risk by recklessly buying and selling trillions of dollars' worth of over-the-counter (OTC) derivative instruments linked to subprime mortgage securities. Earlier legislation exempted the OTC derivatives market from capital adequacy requirements, among other disclosure and regulatory rules.

The Dodd-Frank Wall Street Reform and Consumer Protection Act of 2010 introduced the Wall Street Transparency and Accountability Act. This Act encourages various derivatives known as swaps, which were traditionally traded on the OTC, to be traded through exchanges or clearinghouses. This is a significant development as there will now be more information available, leading to more transparency in the derivatives market.

Regulators, market observers, and investors now have the opportunity to be adequately informed about activities and trends in the OTC derivatives market. The Act charges the Commodity Futures Trading Commission (CFTC) and the Securities and Exchange Commission (SEC) with the regulation of the derivative instrument, known as swap. The Act instituted regulations relating to reporting and recordkeeping requirements for certain swaps, requirements for registration swap dealers, major swap participants, and swap execution facilities, conflicts of interest, and margin requirements. Perhaps this new regulation will prevent a situation such as the one that took place when American International Group (AIG) was able to underwrite about $80 billion in credit default swaps (CDS) while it had only $20 billion in reserves from occurring again.

INVESTOR PROTECTIONS AND IMPROVEMENTS TO THE REGULATION OF SECURITIES

Extensive regulation to protect investors has been long overdue. Even before the financial crisis, investors had suffered from the reckless and sometimes fraudulent actions of chief executives of companies like Enron and WorldCom. There are even more investor victims as a result of Wall Street greed and excessive leverage. Bernie Madoff's multibillion dollar Ponzi scheme stands out. Acts of financial crime by corporate officers in the financial services sector is a common occurrence. In 2009, the SEC charged the former Chief Executive Officer of Countrywide, Angelo Mozilo, with insider trading and securities fraud. In 2010, The SEC charged Goldman Sachs & Co. and one of its vice presidents for defrauding investors by misstating and omitting key facts about a financial product tied to subprime mortgages as the U.S. housing market was beginning to falter. The defendants settled these charges. There were allegations that Bear Stearns directors knew that the hedge funds they were peddling were heavily invested in toxic assets. A civil investigation emerged because of the takeover of Merrill Lynch by the Bank of America. It was alleged that Bank of America did not tell its shareholders the truth about its merger with Merrill Lynch. In 2010, a bankruptcy examiner revealed that the former Chairman and Chief Executive Officer of Lehman Brothers, Dick Fuld, and his team falsified accounting records before the collapse of Lehman Brothers.

The Investor Protections and Improvements to the Regulation of Securities Act provided the long-awaited protection to investors. The Act strengthened the Securities and Exchange Commission and established two new advocates for investor protection, the Office of the Investor Advocate, and Ombudsman. It authorized a third investor protection advocate that was previously established in 2009, the Investor Advisory Committee.

The Investor Advisory Committee is charged with advising and consulting with the SEC regarding issues related to investor protection, regulating securities products, trading strategies, fee structures, the effectiveness of existing disclosure requirements, and various initiatives to protect investors. The Investor Advisory Committee must introduce initiatives to protect investors' initiatives to promote investor confidence, and the integrity of the securities marketplace. This Committee must also consult with the SEC regarding the regulatory priorities of the SEC. This Committee consists of representatives of state securities commissions, senior citizen interest groups, individual equity and debt investors, and institutional investors who are knowledgeable about investment issues and have reputations for integrity. The Committee is expected to submit its findings to the SEC and to make recommendations, including recommendations for legislative changes, to help better protect investors.

The Investor Advocate is responsible for staffing the Office to assist individual investors in resolving issues with the SEC or with any self-regulated organizations, such as the New York Stock Exchange, identifying areas in which to improve protections for individual investors, and naming the Ombudsman. According to the U.S. Government, an Ombudsman is a neutral party that helps resolve disputes between citizens and the Government. An Ombudsman has broad powers to investigate an agency's actions and make recommendations but does not have legal authority to make an agency follow its recommendations. With regard to this Act, the Ombudsman will act as a liaison between the SEC and individual investors to help resolve any issues that an investor may have with the SEC or with a self-regulated organization.

The Dodd-Frank Wall Street Reform and Consumer Protection Act of 2010 specifically authorized the SEC to issue point-of-sale disclosure rules when retail investors purchase investment products or services. These disclosures include concise information on costs, risks, and conflicts of interest. Thus, the SEC is now the proper authority to impose on brokers and dealers a fiduciary duty to ensure that the broker or dealer is acting in the client or customers' best interests. To aid brokers and dealers, the SEC is required to prepare simple and clear disclosures about the terms of the relationship between a client or customer and the broker or dealer.

The Act mandated the SEC and Comptroller General, the head of the Government Accountability Office, to conduct a number of studies aimed at ensuring or improving investor protections. The SEC must conduct studies to:

1) Evaluate existing legal and regulatory standards of care for brokers, dealers, and investment advisors to determine whether there are gaps in the protection of individual investors under these standards

2) Determine the need for enhanced examination and enforcement resources against investment advisers

3) Identify the financial literacy of investors, the methods for improving disclosures, the most useful and understandable relevant information that individual investors use in making investment decisions, methods for increasing transparency, and effective efforts to educate investors and increase financial literacy of investors to improve investor behavior

4) Identify ways to improve access by investors to registration information about registered and previously registered investment advisers, brokers, and dealers

The Comptroller General was mandated to conduct studies to:

1) Identify existing mutual fund advertising requirements and practices, the impact of advertising, and methods to improve investor protections

2) Identify and examine potential conflicts of interest between staff of investment banking and equity, and fixed-income securities analysts' functions within the same firm to determine whether any potential or real conflicts of interest may harm investors

3) Analyze the effectiveness of state and federal regulations that are intended to protect investors and other consumers from individuals who hold themselves out as individual planners

The Act increased the accountability and transparency of rating agencies. For example, the Act directed the SEC to examine credit ratings issued by each Nationally Recognized Statistical Rating Organization (NRSRO) to determine whether the NRSRO had established and documented internal processes for determining credit ratings consistent with SEC rules. There are also numerous provisions empowering the SEC regarding NRSRO's maintenance and availability of certain information. This includes the prescription of specified rules governing NRSRO disclosures of procedures and methodologies used to determine the credit ratings of structured securities, including disclosure on a publicly accessible internet site, in a central database of the historical default rates of all classes of financial products rated by an NRSRO. It also modifies the SEC powers to impose fines and censure a non-compliant NRSRO, including NRSRO's failure to guard against certain violations and conduct sufficient surveillance to ensure that credit ratings remain current.

An important provision in the Act that will protect investors by promoting enforcement and remedies is the introduction of monetary incentives for the greater protection of whistleblowers. As provided in this Act, a whistleblower is entitled to up to 30 percent of the monetary sanctions imposed in an action that results in monetary sanctions exceeding $1 million, if the whistleblowers voluntarily provided original information to the SEC that led to the successful enforcement of the action. To this end, the Act established the Securities and Exchange Commission's Investor Protection Fund to pay awards to whistleblowers and fund investor education initiatives to help investors protect themselves against securities fraud or other violations of securities laws and regulations. Furthermore, the Act prohibits acts of retaliation against an employee, contractor, or agent for providing information to the SEC. These provisions may motivate more employees to inform the SEC of negative developments in their companies. The financial reward is particularly welcome because of the corporate culture; whistleblowers easily become social outcasts who experience severe problems getting new employment. They usually become *persona non grata* within their industries, and their employers often retaliate in various ways. For example, they can retaliate by publicly disclosing uncomfortable personal details of the employee. Lynn Brewer, who was a whistleblower in the case of Enron, lost her job. Madoff did not employ Harry Markopolos, the whistleblower who uncovered Bernie Madoff's Ponzi scheme ten years before the rest of the world learned of the biggest financial crime in history. Even though no one listened to him, Markopolos would not start his car without first checking under the chassis and in the wheel wells out of fear. At night, he walked away from shadows, and he slept with a loaded gun nearby until Madoff's arrest.

BUREAU OF CONSUMER FINANCIAL PROTECTION (BCFP)

Prior to the financial crisis, banks, thrifts, and other companies in the financial services sector generally took advantage of the lack of clear regulations regarding some aspects of financial services transactions as well as the lack of accountability and transparency. This enabled them to sell mortgages and other products that were complicated and sometimes confusing to borrowers who did not have the required financial know how. These actions had disastrous results. Many of these consumers defaulted in either their credit card debts or real estate borrowings. It was obvious that in spite of the fact that there were multiple state and federal agencies that were responsible for consumer protection in the financial services industry, significant gaps and weaknesses existed in the supervisory framework for the enforcements of existing regulations. Even though, since the crisis, there have been some reforms in credit card and mortgage lending, the severity of the observed abusive practices that prevailed in the financial services sector, especially in subprime lending and non-traditional mortgages, necessitated the creation of the Bureau of Consumer Financial Protection.

The BCFP is responsible for regulating consumer financial products and services to ensure that they comply with federal law. To this end, different units in the Bureau must be responsible for research, community affairs, tracking and collecting consumer complaints, ensuring equitable access to credit, fair lending, and equal opportunity, and the promotion of financial literacy among consumers. The Bureau is located within the Federal Reserve System but must operate independently. The Fed must not interfere with matters before the Director of the BCFP. In addition, the Fed must not direct any employee of the Bureau, modify the functions and responsibilities of the Bureau, or impede an order of the Bureau.

On the advice and consent of the U.S. Senate, the President of the United States will appoint a director for the Bureau for a term of five years. The Bureau must report to the Senate Banking Committee and the House Financial Services Committee twice a year. This Bureau is subject to financial audit by the Government Accountability Office.

INCREASED GOVERNANCE AND OVERSIGHT OF THE FEDERAL RESERVE SYSTEM

The Dodd-Frank Wall Street Reform and Consumer Protection Act of 2010 requires the Federal Reserve System to constantly revise the Federal Reserve portion of the Act. Such revisions must include identifying, measuring, monitoring, and mitigating risks to the financial stability of the United States. As amended by the Act, the U.S. President now appoints the President of the New York Federal Reserve with the advice and consent of the Senate. To reduce the possibility of conflict of interest, the Act prohibits officers of any company subject to the Federal Reserve System oversight from being allowed to vote for, or serve as, a Federal Reserve president. The new law restructured the Board of Governors of the Federal Reserve System by creating the new position of Vice Chairman for Supervision. The responsibilities of this officer include developing policy recommendations to the Board of Governors regarding the supervision and regulation of financial institutions supervised by the Board. This officer must oversee the supervision and regulation of such firms and report to Congress twice a year to disclose their activities and efforts. The Vice Chairman for Supervision must also testify before the

Senate Committee on Banking, Housing, and Urban Affairs and the House Committee on Financial Services and represent the Chairman of the Board of Governors in his absence.

Because of the provisions of this financial reform act, we now expect greater accountability from the Federal Reserve System. The GAO is now required to perform several different audits of the Federal Reserve System. The Act requires, in particular, that the Federal Reserve Governance Audit examine the extent to which the current system of appointing the directors of the Federal Reserve System represents the public without discrimination on the basis of race, creed, color, sex, or national origin. Such appointments must also give due, but not exclusive, consideration to the interests of agriculture, commerce, industry, services, labor, and consumers. This audit must further identify if actual or potential conflicts of interest exist. Furthermore, the audit must identify changes to selection procedures for Federal Reserve System district banks, or to other aspects of governance that would improve public representation and increase the availability of monetary information.

The Dodd-Frank Wall Street Reform and Consumer Protection Act of 2010 tried to reduce the incidence of excessive leverage and risk exposure for financial institutions. The Act empowered the Federal Reserve System to establish prudent standards for the institutions they supervise regarding risk-based capital requirements and leverage limits, liquidity requirements, overall risk management requirements, resolution plan and credit-exposure-report requirements, and concentration limits. Among other things, the Federal Reserve may establish additional standards that are contingent on capital requirements, enhanced public disclosure, and short-term debt limits. The Fed also has the authority to require supervised companies to maintain a minimum amount of contingent capital that is convertible to equity in times of financial stress and periodically provide additional plans and reports. An example of the required plan is a plan for a rapid and orderly liquidation of the company in the event of material financial distress or failure. An example of the credit exposure report describing the nature to which the company has exposure to other companies and credit exposure cannot exceed 25 percent of the capital stock and surplus of the company.

The Federal Reserve Act empowers the Federal Reserve System to give due recognition to possible risk that can be caused by off-balance-sheet activities that create accounting liabilities. In determining capital requirements for regulated organizations, the Fed must take into consideration such activities as direct credit substitutes in which a bank substitutes its own credit for a third party, including standby letters of credit, irrevocable letters of credit that guarantee repayment of commercial paper or tax-exempt securities, and risk participations in bankers' acceptances. Other off-balance-sheet activities that the Fed must consider in determining capital requirements for regulated organizations are sale and repurchase agreements, asset sales with recourse against the seller, interest rate swaps, credit swaps, commodities contracts, forward contracts, and securities contracts. This list is not exhaustive of possible off-balance-sheet activities that the Act expects the Fed to take into consideration for this purpose.

INJECTION OF FUNDS INTO THE ECONOMY BY THE FEDERAL RESERVE SYSTEM

On November 2008, soon after the financial crisis occurred, the Federal Reserve announced it would initiate a program to purchase the direct obligations of housing-related government-sponsored enterprises (GSEs): Fannie Mae, Freddie Mac, and the Federal Home Loan Banks and mortgage-backed securities (MBS) backed by Fannie Mae, Freddie Mac, and Ginnie Mae.[66] The Fed explained that the spread of rates on GSE debt and on GSE guaranteed mortgages have widened appreciably of late. This intervention by the U.S. central bank was expected to reduce the cost and increase the availability of credit for the purchase of houses, which in turn should support housing markets and foster improved

[66] Reserve Bank, Press Release, *November 25, 2008,*
http://www.federalreserve.gov/newsevents/press/monetary/20081125b.htm

conditions in financial markets more generally. It indicated that it will purchase up to $100 billion in GSE direct obligations through competitive auctions and $500 billion in MBS will be conducted by asset managers selected via a competitive process. Eventually $1.8 trillion was injected into the economy through this monetary policy dubbed QE1.

By 2010 the US economy was in recovery despite the fear of a double dip recession. The stock market had stability and actually started growing. The banking sector and the automobile industry had stabilized. However in November 2010, the rate of unemployment was an unacceptable 10 percent. Even though interest rates remained very low, this was accompanied by unexpected, sluggish consumer demand. On November 3, 2010, the Federal Reserve announced that it would pump up to $900 billion into the economy to jump start the sluggish recovery and this exercise would be completed by the end of the third quarter of 2011.[67] In this second round of monetary stimulus, dubbed QE2, the Fed, the U.S. central bank, would buy $600 billion in long-term Treasuries over the next eight months implementing a policy known as quantitative easing. The Fed would further reinvest an additional $250 billion to $300 billion in Treasuries with the proceeds of its earlier investments.

The Fed reiterated that the pace of recovery in output and employment continues to be slow. It is believed that the sluggish consumer spending was responsible for the reluctance of businesses to hire, resulting in very slow growth in the economy. In addition, the possibility of deflation that could result from the very low inflation is of great concern to many economists. Even though this method of jumpstarting the economy was used during the Great Depression, some economists criticized its introduction on the grounds that interest rates were already low and that the risks of the Fed's purchase of additional securities outweighed the benefits. There were fears of possible hyperinflation.

The most important problem is that low consumer demand is not mostly caused by lack of availability of credit. Most consumers are not spending as much as they used to probably because they are more cautious due to the economic situation. It is believed that many banks have a lot of money which they are reluctant to lend and many businesses are not borrowing to expand their business because of the poor economic situation.

The Fed's injection of funds in the economy would be more successful if it reduced the marginal cost at which banks can fund their lending activities. If investors and consumers are seeking funds and all banks have abundant funds, then the banks' cost of borrowing will decline due to competition. This monetary policy works on the assumption that as bank rates decline, investors and consumers will be motivated to borrow. In a situation where the federal funds rate has been at 2.5 percent since 2008, borrowing rates, such as mortgage rates, are at an all-time low, and general confidence in the future economic situation is very low, the argument that the Fed's injection of funds into the economy will be futile at the best may have merit.

CONCLUSION

The U.S. Government has made significant efforts to end the financial crisis and reverse the economic recession by injecting money into the economy through various bailouts in order to mitigate the negative impact of the crisis on the middle class, the poor, and the aged. The Federal Reserve also purchased securities estimated at $2.7 trillion in two programs, QE1 and QE2 in an effort to further inject funds into the economy to stimulate demand. The Federal Reserve System initiated regulations to check and control some of the negative developments in the real estate sector, the banking sector, and capital markets, and to reduce systemic risk. Some of the actions were focused on saving the financial system and the automobile industry, whereas others were aimed at preventing a future occurrence of the financial and economic crisis.

---

[67] Annalyn Censky (2010)Fed to inject $900bn into economy, CNN,
http://money.cnn.com/2010/11/03/news/economy/fed_decision/index.htm

The actions taken have certainly stabilized the financial markets, the banking sector, and the automobile industry. With the U.S.GDP growth rate at 2.3 percent in the *third quarter of 2010, it is safe to say that the U.S. economy is beginning to recover. However, with the unemployment rate at 9.8 percent in November 2010, that is a 3.7 percent increase from the unemployment rate before the financial crisis, the economy has a long way to go before it can achieve full recovery. Because this recession has been likened to the Great Depression in several ways, it is apparent that more actions must be taken to further stimulate economic activities in the public and private sectors of the economy, in order to achieve increased employment and consumer demand.*

BIBLIOGRAPHY

Annalyn Censky, "Fed to Inject $900Binto Economy", CNN, http://money.cnn.com/2010/11/03/news/economy/fed_decision/index.htm [Sighted January 20, 2011]

Associated Press. "Congress Passes Sweeping Financial Reforms." *CBS News,* July 15, 2010. http://www.cbsnews.com/stories/2010/07/15/politics/main6681481.shtml.

———. "House Passes Tough Subprime Lending Law." *MSN,* November 15, 2007, http://www.msnbc.msn.com/id/21824966.

———."Ten of the Largest U.S. Banks Need $75 Billion." *MSN,* May 8, 2009, http://www.msnbc.msn.com/id/30619126.

Board of Governors of the Federal Reserve System. "New Credit Card Rules Effective February 22." http://www.federalreserve.gov/consumerinfo/wyntk_creditcardrules.htm.

Bottari, Mary. Prosecuting Financial Crimes: Will Anyone Bunk with Bernie? March 31, 2010. http://www.prwatch.org/node/8985(accessed December 17, 2010).

Callaway, David. "History Will Judge Lehman Brothers Mistake Harshly." *Market Watch,* September 9, 2009. http://www.marketwatch.com/story/history-will-judge-lehman-mistake-harshly-2009-09-09.

Clark, Andrew. "Paulson Abandons Plans to Buy up America's Toxic Mortgage Assets." *The Guardian,* November 13, 2008. http://www.guardian.co.uk/business/2008/nov/13/harry-paulson-banking-rescue-mortgage

Department of Treasury, Financial Regulatory Reform, A New Foundation: Rebuilding Financial Supervision and Regulation (accessed December 17, 2010). http://www.financialstability.gov/docs/regs/FinalReport_web.pdf

Drew, Alton E. "Bank's 'Too Big to Fail'? Wrong: Financial Institutions Chase Success by Taking Risks. When the Risks Don't Pay Off, It's Not the Government's Job to Bail Them Out." *Bloomberg Business Week,* February 18, 2009. http://www.businessweek.com/bwdaily/dnflash/content/feb2009/db20090218_166676.htm.

Federal Trade Commission. "High-Rate, High-Fee Loans (HOEPA/Section 32 Mortgages)." *Protecting America's Consumers,* February 2009. http://www.ftc.gov/bcp/edu/pubs/consumer/homes/rea19.shtm.

Indiviglio, Daniel. "1% Success Rate for Obama Administration Mortgage Modification Program." *The Atlantic,* December 11, 2009. http://www.theatlantic.com/business/archive/2009/12/1-success-rate-for-obama-administration-mortgage-modification-program/31700.

Irvin, Margo. "Making Home Affordable: The Waiting Game." *Huffington Post,* August 10, 2009. http://www.huffingtonpost.com/2009/08/10/making-home-affordable-th_n_256033.html.

Isidore, Chris. "Job Loss: Worst in 34 Years, Employers Slashed 598,000 More Jobs in January as Unemployment Rate Climbed to 7.6%." *CNN Money*, February 6, 2009. http://money.cnn.com/2009/02/06/news/economy/jobs_january/index.htm.

Johnson, Stacy. "What Financial Reform Means to You." *Money Talk news*, July 15, 2010. http://finance.yahoo.com/banking-budgeting/article/110085/what-financial-reform-means.

Kohlhagen, Steven W., FCIC Hearing, June 30, 2010, http://www.fcic.gov/hearings/pdfs/2010-0630-Kohlhagen.pdf (accessed December 12, 2010).

Markopolos, Harry. "Madoff Whistle-Blower: No One Would Listen." *Today Books*, March 11, 2009. http://today.msnbc.msn.com/id/35606057/38590618.

O'Carroll, Eoin. "Is General Motors Too Big to Fail, or Just Too Big?" *The Christian Science Monitor*, November 19, 2008. http://www.csmonitor.com/Environment/Bright-Green/2008/1119/is-general-motors-too-big-to-fail-or-just-too-big.

Paletta, Damian."'Volcker Rule' Stalls in Senate." February 24, 2010. http://online.wsj.com/article/SB10001424052748703503804575083823511212204.html(Sighted December 12, 2010).

Poppaw, Timothy M. "Online Automated Valuation Models or Comparable Sale Reports." January 2009. http://appraisal-network.net/avm.htm (accessed December 12, 2010).

Pro Publica: Journalism in the Public Interest, "Bailout Recipients." July 25, 2010. http://bailout.propublica.org/list/index.

Reserve Bank, "Press Release" http://www.federalreserve.gov/newsevents/press/monetary/20081125b.htm, [Sighted November 25, 2008]

SEC."SEC Charges Goldman Sachs with Fraud in Structuring and Marketing of CDO Tied to Subprime Mortgages." April 16, 2010. http://www.sec.gov/news/press/2010/2010-59.htm (Sighted December 17, 2010).

———. "SEC Charges Former Countrywide Executives With Fraud: Former CEO Angelo Mozilo Additionally Charged With Insider Trading." June 4, 2009. http://www.sec.gov/news/press/2009/2009-129.htm (Sighted December 17, 2010).

Soloan, Deborah, Damian Paletta, Jon Hilsentrath, and Aaron Lucchetti. "U.S. to Buy Stakes in Nation's Largest Banks." *Wall Street Journal*, October 14, 2008. http://online.wsj.com/article/SB122390023840728367.html.

The Library of Congress, Bill Summary & Status, 111th Congress (2009 - 2010) H.R.4173. http://thomas.loc.gov/cgi-bin/bdquery/z?d111:H.R.4173.

United States Government Accountability Office, Report to Congressional Committees, Troubled Asset Relief Program, November 2009, (Sighted December 17, 2010), http://www.gao.gov/new.items/d10151.pdf.

U.S. Government, American and Reinvestment Act of 2009. January 6, 2009. http://frwebgate.access.gpo.gov/cgi-bin/getdoc.cgi?dbname=111_cong_bills&docid=f:h1enr.pdf.

U.S. Government Printing Office, *Public Law 111- 5 - American Recovery and Reinvestment Act of 2009*.http://www.gpo.gov/fdsys/pkg/PLAW-111publ5/content-detail.html.

U.S. Government Printing Office, Public Law 111 - 203 - *Dodd-Frank Wall Street Reform and Consumer Protection Act*. http://www.gpo.gov/fdsys/pkg/PLAW-111publ203/content-detail.html.

CHAPTER 7

THE WAY FORWARD AND CONCLUSION

INTRODUCTION

The preceding chapters contain a discussion of the recent financial crisis and ensuing economic recession including the causes of the crisis, the economic background, and the local impact. In addition, we explored the effect of the crisis and economic recession on global financial markets and economies, and we looked at the actions taken to address the maladies of the crisis and recession to create jobs and prevent future financial crises and economic recessions. In conclusion, we examine the current situation in the economy and financial services sector including the stock markets and the real estate sector. As discussed, the mortgage crisis in the real estate sector ignited the financial crisis.

The path forward should include learning from those economies, such as Canada, that were able to avoid the financial meltdown and did not have a significant banking crisis or even a serious debt crisis. It is important to examine possible ways to reduce the Government deficit in order to avoid a national debt crisis such as the one that Greece and Ireland have experienced. Improving the U.S. balance of trade has not been a topic of much public discourse, but it should be. In Chapter 2, we observed the negative trend in the U.S. balance of trade, which the crisis and economic recession exacerbated. This chapter also discusses the consumers' high leverage situation and the paucity of the American personal savings rate.

AN OVERVIEW OF THE CURRENT ECONOMIC SITUATION

Despite all the actions taken by the Government to resuscitate the U.S. economy, the economic recovery has been very slow. Since September 2009, the economy has achieved positive GDP growth rates, the highest rate being the 5 percent recorded in December 2009. The declining GDP growth rate of 1.7 percent in June 2010 introduced concerns as many economists wondered if the U.S. would experience a double-dip recession. However, there was a higher GDP growth rate in the third quarter of 2010. It is safe to say that the economy is on a slow but steady recovery path. Table 7.1 contains the quarterly GDP growth rate from March 2008 to September 2010, and Figure 7.1 illustrates the trend.

Table 7.1 U.S. Quarterly GDP Growth Rate March 2008 to September 2010

Quarters	GDP Growth Rate
Mar-08	-0.7
Jun-08	0.6
Sep-08	-4
Dec-08	-6.8
Mar-09	-4.9
Jun-09	-0.7
Sep-09	1.6
Dec-09	5
Mar-10	3.7
Jun-10	1.7
Sep-10	2.6

Source: U.S. Department of Commerce, Bureau of Economic Analysis, http://www.bea.gov/national/index.htm#gdp

Figure 7.1 U.S. Quarterly GDP Growth Rate March 2008 to September 2010

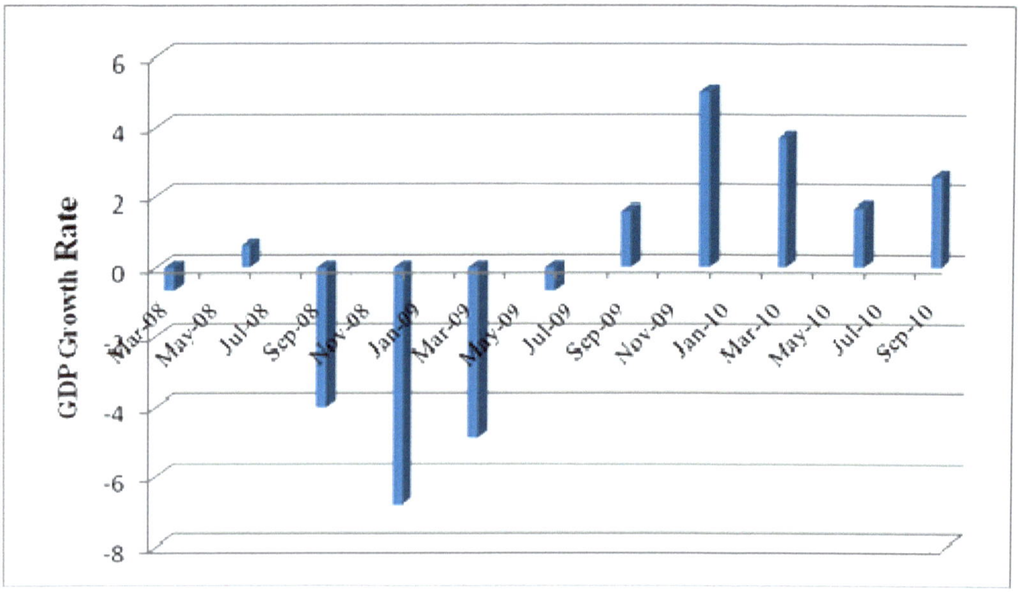

Some consider the December 2010 Job Report released by the Bureau of Labor Statistics as disappointing, and it is puzzling. In July 2010, there was anxiety about the threat of a double dip recession. The highest monthly unemployment rate of 10.1 percent during the recession occurred in October 2009. According to the report, the unemployment rate in December 2010 was 9.4 percent. The report also showed that the number of unemployed persons decreased by 556,000 to 14.5 million from 15.2 million in 2009. This is an indication of progress. See the Monthly Unemployment Rate, January 2008 to December 2010, in Table 7.2 and the graphical illustration of the trend in Figure 7.2.

Table 7. 2 U.S. Monthly Unemployment Rate January 2008 to December 2010

Month	Unemployment Percentage of Labor Force
8-Jan	5
8-Feb	4.8
8-Mar	5.1
8-Apr	5
8-May	5.4
8-Jun	5.5
8-Jul	5.8
8-Aug	6.1
8-Sep	6.2
8-Oct	6.6
8-Nov	6.9
8-Dec	7.4
9-Jan	7.7
9-Feb	8.2
9-Mar	8.6
9-Apr	8.9
9-May	9.4
9-Jun	9.5
9-Jul	9.4
9-Aug	9.7
9-Sep	9.8
9-Oct	10.1
9-Nov	10
9-Dec	10
10-Jan	9.7
10-Feb	9.7
10-Mar	9.7
10-Apr	9.9
10-May	9.7
10-Jun	9.5
10-Jul	9.5
10-Aug	9.6
10-Sep	9.6
10-Oct	9.6
10-Nov	9.8
10-Dec	9.4

Source: Data Derived from U.S. Bureau of Labor Statistics, http://data.bls.gov/PDQ/servlet/SurveyOutputServlet

Figure 7. 2 U.S. Monthly Unemployment Rate (January 2008 to December 2010)

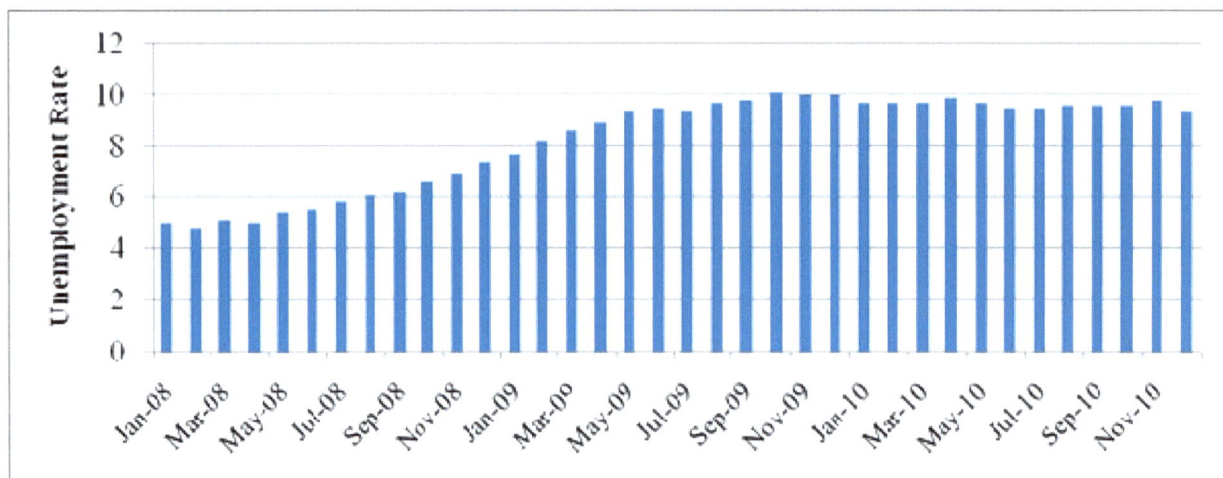

The number of people employed in non-farm employment increased by 103,000. Employment also rose in leisure and hospitality, and in healthcare sectors of the economy. However, the unemployment report was not completely pleasing. Even though the unemployment rate fell by 0.4 percentage points to 9.4 percent in December 2010, there was little change in employment in other major industries. The increase in employment in leisure and hospitality is interesting as it could be an indication of increased demand reflecting the availability of more disposal income and general consumer confidence in the economy. On the other hand, it may be seasonal, reflecting Thanksgiving and Christmas holiday travel into the U.S. from abroad and within the U.S.

According to the job report, the number of people who lost their jobs and those who completed temporary jobs dropped by 548,000 to 8.9 million. Businesses added only 113,000 jobs to their payrolls in December 2010. The Government continued to shed staff, cutting 10,000 workers. Unemployment remained high for teenagers, Blacks, and Hispanics. See Table 7. 3 for major worker group survey data.

Table 7.3 Unemployment among Major Worker Groups, December 2010.

Worker Group	Unemployment Rate
Adult men	9.4
Whites	8.5
Adult women	8.1
Teenagers	25.4
Blacks	15.8
Hispanics	13
Asians	7.2

Source: U.S. Department of Labor, Bureau of Labor Statistics, Employment Situation Summary, http://www.bls.gov/news.release/empsit.nr0.htm.

According to the Bureau of Labor Statistics' January 2011 report, the Consumer Price Index for all urban consumers (CPI-U) increased 0.5 percent in December 2010 on a seasonally adjusted basis, and the all items index increased 1.5 percent before seasonal adjustment. This is a favorable development, particularly, for a country that is trying to stimulate its economy. Mild inflation is generally accepted as a positive economic phenomenon, especially after a recession. It indicates possible increased flow of funds into the economy and increased demand. Prior to the crisis, the Federal objective was to keep the inflation rate below 5 percent.

There had been low inflation in the U.S. since the financial crisis and economic recession. In fact, the average monthly Consumer Price Index (CPI) in December 2009 was -0.4 percent, indicating a deflation. According to the Bureau of Labor Statistics, Consumer Price Index report, the average CPI over the last twelve months increased to 1.1 percent in November 2009. The index for all items less food and energy has risen 0.8 percent. The energy index has risen 3.9 percent over that span with the gasoline index up 7.3 percent, but the household energy index was down 0.2 percent.

The federal funds rate has remained at 0.25 percent since January 2009.[68] This is the rate at which depository institutions, mostly banks, borrow excess federal funds. If the banks have excess funds with the Federal Reserve Banks, they can also make unsecured loans using the reserve balances at Federal Reserve Banks.[69] This is the primary tool used by the Federal Op[70]en Market Committee to influence interest rates and the economy. Changes in the federal funds rate can affect the interest rate in such depository institutions' financial products such as certificates of deposit, savings accounts, and money market accounts. Possibly for this reason, the prime rate has also been low at 3.25 percent for the same period.[71] Depository institutions use the prime rate as the underlying rate for many financial products. Examples are credit cards, home equity loans and lines of credit, auto loans, small business loans and personal loans.

Bank failures have continued unabated. Twenty-five Federal Deposit Insurance Corporation (FDIC) banks failed in 2008. This number increased to 140 in 2009 and reached 157 in 2010. The big banks have stabilized, and many have paid back some or all of the bailout funds they received from the Federal Government. Even though there is evidence of increased credit availability, the main concern with the financial services sector is the prolonged credit crunch. The flow of credit is necessary to stimulate demand for consumer and capital goods, services, and investment in real estate.

According to the Nuwire Investor, "Commercial real estate transactions are slowly picking up and are expected to accelerate in 2011 and 2012, as sources of capital are returning slowly but steadily to the market. While lenders and potential investors remain conservative and cautious in what properties they pursue, analysts believe that as the market stabilizes, access to capital will expand from 'A' list properties in high quality, well located areas, to properties in secondary and tertiary markets."[72] To everyone's surprise, the Commercial Mortgage-Backed Securities (CMBS) market is functioning again.[73] This will further stimulate the market.

The stock market has also recovered. The stock markets reacted to investors' nervousness about the fragile economic recovery in the U.S., the high unemployment situation that has prevailed for years, and the gloomy business outlook, not to mention the fear of a possible double-dip recession. All of these have affected the recovery of the stock market. The unprecedented political divide in recent years, the passing of various stimulus bills in Congress, and the passing of the Healthcare Reform Act of 2010 and

---

[68] See Trading Economics, "United States Interest Rate," http://www.tradingeconomics.com/Economics/Interest-Rate.aspx?Symbol=USD (accessed January 10, 2011).

[69] Federal Reserve Bank of New York, "Federal Funds," August 2007, http://www.newyorkfed.org/aboutthefed/fedpoint/fed15.html (accessed January 10, 2011).

[70] See United States Department of Labor, Bureau of Labor Statistics, "Consumer Price Index Summary – 2010," January 14, 2011, http://www.bls.gov/news.release/cpi.nr0.htm.

[71] See Bankrate.com, "Prime rate, fed funds, COFI," http://www.bankrate.com/rates/interest-rates/prime-rate.aspx (accessed January 15, 2011).

[72] Daniel Beaird, "Commercial Real Estate Activity Starting to Pick Up," *Nuwire Investor*, June 17, 2010, http://www.nuwireinvestor.com/articles/commercial-real-estate-activity-starting-to-pick-up-55459.aspx (accessed January 10, 2011).

[73] See Daniel Beaird, "Deals Are on the Rise, as Capital Returns to the Market," *National Real Estate Investor*, June 17, 2010, http://nreionline.com/news/deals_rise_capital_returns_0617/# (accessed January 10, 2011).

the Finance Reform Act of 2010 were all very contentious and met with reactions of approval or disapproval by the market. Even the bailout of the automobile industry and its subsequent survival received reactions from the stock market.

The market also has shown sensitivity to developments abroad. In particular, it reacted to the debt crisis in Greece, the debt situation in Ireland, and the generally very high levels of debt in many European countries. Such negative developments in Europe led to losses in many U.S. stock market indexes. There is documented evidence of positive correlation between movements in index values of stock markets in the U.S. and such movements in many European indexes.[74]

Despite all these challenges, the U.S. stock markets have thrived recently. The DOW Jones Industrial Average increased by 35 percent between October 15, 2008, and December 31, 2010. See Figure 7.3.

Figure 7.3 DOW Jones Industrial Average Index Values 2008 to 2010

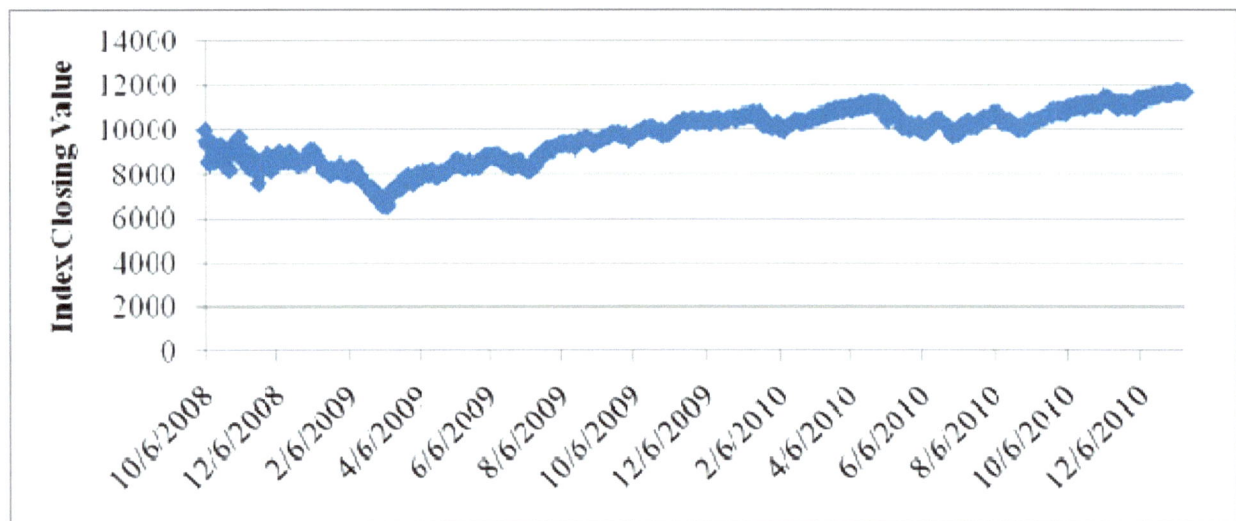

In December 2010, in the lame duck session, Congress voted to uphold and continue the income tax cuts introduced in 2001 during the presidency of George W. Bush. This decision by Congress was widely criticized by many democrats. They argued that wealthy Americans did not deserve a tax cut when the economic recovery was still very fragile. President Obama justified the continuation of the tax for two more years. He stated, "Independent experts have concluded that, taken together, this package of tax cuts will significantly accelerate the pace of our economic recovery, spurring additional jobs and growth. Our fundamental mission must be to accelerate hiring and growth while we do the things we know are necessary to insure America's leadership in an increasingly competitive world and build an economy that will provide opportunity to any American willing to work for it."[75]

Just as it is difficult to determine if and to what extent the various stimuli helped the economic recovery, it will be equally as difficult to determine in hindsight to what extent this continuation of the tax cuts positively or negatively affected the economy. Because the tax cut is for everyone, all Americans will have more money to spend in the next two years than they would have had if Congress had decided not continue the Bush era tax cuts. The richer Americans will undoubtedly have more

---

[74] See Chiaku Chukwuogor, "Stock Markets Returns and Volatilities: a Global Comparison," *Global Journal of Finance and Banking Issues* 1, no. 1, 2007, http://www.globip.com/pdf_pages/globalfinance-vol1-article1.pdf.
[75] Alex Villarreal, "Obama: Tax Cuts Compromise to Help Grow US Economy," *Voice of America*," January 8, 2011, http://www.voanews.com/english/news/President-Obama-Anticipates-Tax-Cut-Initiative-Impact-113129719.html (accessed January 16, 2011).

money. The expectation is that they will continue to spend in consumption and in business expansion. Hence, the President's optimism that the tax cut will generate employment.

WHY CANADA AVOIDED THE FINANCIAL MELTDOWN AND THE BANKING CRISIS

It is not by chance that Canada was able to avoid the financial meltdown and the banking crisis. According to Mr. Mark Carney, Governor of the Bank of Canada, in his remarks at the International Center for Monetary and Banking Studies of the Bank of International Settlement (BIS), Canada made its mistakes thirty years ago in the 1970s and 1980s. The discussion of Canada in this section is mainly based on the content of Mr. Carney's address.[76]

Canada suffered deterioration of its fiscal situation. Inflation surged to double digits and Canada experienced some bank failures.[77] Specifically, inflation in the 1970s in Canada was over 14 percent and generally over 12 percent in the 1980s. Canada's inflation rate dropped to about 6 percent in 1990 and to roughly 2 percent by 2004. Canada learned the importance of principle-based policy frameworks. The attributes of this approach include a commitment to higher and better quality capital, an active supervisory regime with close cooperation among authorities, a well-regulated mortgage market, and a limited shadow-banking sector. A shadow-banking sector refers to non-depository financial intermediaries that are involved in facilitating the creation of credit but whose members are not subject to regulatory oversight. Examples of these financial intermediaries are investment banks, hedge funds, and money market funds. According to the *Wall Street Journal*, the shadow banking system in the U.S. grew rapidly during the past decade, accumulating more than $10 trillion in assets by early 2007. The operators in the shadow-banking sector are not regulated. Hence, they do not have federally insured customer deposits and cannot borrow directly from the Government. This means that the shadow banking system does not have reliable access to short-term borrowing during times of stress.

Other measures that Canada introduced were a robust market infrastructure, better resolution mechanisms, and macro prudential instruments for the management of systematic risk. Systematic risk is "a risk of disruption to financial services that is caused by an impairment of all or parts of the financial system and has the potential to have serious negative consequences for the real economy."[78] Macro prudential policy focuses on the interactions between financial institutions, markets, infrastructures, and the wider economy. It complements the micro prudential focus on the risk position of individual institutions, which largely takes the rest of the financial system and the economy as given.[79] The Dodd-Frank Wall Street Reform and Consumer Protection Act of 2010, as was discussed in Chapter 6, significantly dealt with preventing a future occurrence of systematic risk, identifying the emergence of such risk in a timely manner and expeditiously taking action to reduce risk should it occur. However, the belief is that as embracive as this Act was some underlying causes of systemic risk remain unaddressed. An example is the problem of "too big to fail."

---

[76] See Mark Carney, "Looking back, moving forward – Canada and global financial reform," *Bank for International Settlement*, November 9, 2010, http://www.bis.org/review/r101111a.pdf (accessed November 26, 2010).
[77] Ibid.
[78] Bank for International Settlement, Committee on the Global Financial System, "Macroprudential Instruments and Frameworks: a Stocktaking of Issues and Experiences," CGFS Papers, No 38, May 2010, http://www.bis.org/publ/cgfs38.pdf.
[79] Ibid.

LESSONS FROM CANADA

Prior to the financial crisis, Canada emphasized that its banks operated on the basis of risk-based capital adequacy. In terms of the international minimum for the level and quality of capital (i.e., 4 percent and 8 percent as prescribed in the Basel 1 Accord), the Canadian banks capital requirements were set above this minimum at 7 percent and 10 percent for Tier 1 capital. Generally Canadian banks held more capital. All financial institutions were required to establish internal targets to provide an operating cushion against volatility and unexpected losses from inherent risks and to avoid breaching supervisory targets.

The Canadian bank supervisor, the Office of the Superintendent for Financial Institutions (OSFI), also demanded that banks with higher risks should further offset that risk with higher capital, of good quality, such as common equity to the tune of at least 75 percent of Tier 1 capital. This requirement ensured that banks with higher risks operated with larger cushions. This was why Canadian banks did not need any injections of Government capital during the financial crisis.

AN ACTIVE AND COOPERATIVE SUPERVISORY REGIME

The observed success of the Canadian financial system was the product of strong macroeconomic fundamentals and sound risk management by the banks themselves supported by an effective regulatory and supervisory regime. The four most important aspects of this regime are focused supervision, active supervision, coordinated supervision, and regularly reviewed and updated supervision.

FOCUSED SUPERVISION

There was a consolidation of supervision with the concentration on prudential supervision. In Canada, there are no government programs for promoting home ownership or community reinvestment. This focused supervision ensures that leverage ratios and other tests apply equally to banking and investment banking operations. The lack of government programs for promoting home ownership or community reinvestment in Canada possibly made supervision very convenient. It is important to remember that the U.S. Community Reinvestment Act of 1997 was introduced to reduce discriminatory credit practices against low-income neighborhoods—a laudable objective. As we learn a few things from Canada, we must not forgo an obvious superior political advancement but rather integrate the implications of the Community Reinvestment Act in our effort to achieve focused supervision of financial institutions.

There are several government departments, agencies, and enterprises promoting home ownership in the U.S. Yet, prior to the financial crisis, the home ownership rate in Canada was similar to that in the U.S. In Canada in 2006, 68.4 percent of the population of 8.5 million owned their own homes.[80] In the U.S. in 2007, 67.8 percent of the population of 204.9 million owned their homes.[81] Note that the number of people who owned homes in the U.S. prior to the financial crisis was twenty-four times as many those who owned homes in Canada.

Although we must seek to learn from other economies, it is important to put things into perspective. Due to historical reasons, there are possibly more recent immigrants and a higher number of low-income neighborhoods in the U.S. The political decision of Congress to encourage home ownership is good and humane. Moreover, as discussed in Chapter 6, the Dodd Frank Wall

---

[80] Statistics Canada, "2006 Census: Changing patterns in Canadian homeownership and shelter costs," June 4, 2008, http://www.statcan.gc.ca/daily-quotidien/080604/dq080604a-eng.htm (accessed January 17, 2011).
[81] U.S. Department of Commerce, Census Bureau, "Census Bureau Reports on Residential Vacancies and Homeownership," April 28, 2008, http://www.census.gov/hhes/www/housing/hvs/qtr108/q108press.pdf.

Street Reform and Consumer Protection Act put regulations into place to check unfair loan practices and some of the exploitation of the financially underprivileged. However, there is a need for focused and effective supervision to ensure that financial institutions, brokers, and those involved in the lending process respect the intentions of the Act. It is also important that potential homeowners receive approval to buy only homes that they can afford to buy. Lenders with the requisite qualifications and information should determine how much a buyer could afford to pay, thus protecting buyers from overextending themselves. Some buyers simply do not have the expertise to make this decision, and others may have the knowledge but may be overwhelmed by the desire of experiencing the American dream of owning a home to make a sound financial decision.

ACTIVE SUPERVISION

Back in the 1980s, when some regional banks failed, Canada had established a framework for early intervention. This helped supervisors to work with troubled institutions to correct problems at an early stage. Canada had earlier established board-level interaction, capital penalties, and several restrictions. All of these helped the management of these institutions focus on addressing issues in a timely manner.

COORDINATED SUPERVISION

In Canada, there is coordination and close cooperation among all the entities responsible for financial stability. There is also mandated information sharing among the entire relevant supervisors. For example, a joint micro-prudential committee, composed of the bank regulators, the central bank, the deposit insurer, the consumer protection agency, and the Department of Finance, regularly review these very important financial institutions.

REGULARLY REVIEWED AND UPDATED SUPERVISION

In Canada, it is a statutory requirement to renew the legislative and regulatory framework for the financial system every five years. In addition, Canada regularly subjects its system to rigorous external examination under the International Monetary Fund's Financial Sector Assessment Program (FSAP). The Canadian authorities also conduct regular system-wide stress tests.

WELL-REGULATED MORTGAGE MARKET

A well regulated mortgage market existed in Canada prior to the subprime mortgage crisis in the U.S. The Canadian legal system held mortgagors personally liable for their debts. Mortgage interest is not tax deductible. With respect to mortgage insurance, the publicly owned mortgage insurer, Canada Mortgage and housing Corporation (CMHC), has an explicit sovereign guarantee for losses that result from insurance failure. This guarantee covers amounts over 10 percent of the original mortgage. The CMHC effectively sets the key lending standards by the terms of government-backed mortgage insurance. All mortgagors with loan-to-value ratios of over 80 percent must have insurance on the mortgage. All borrowers must pass an income test, and insurance premiums vary with loan-to-value ratios and amortization periods. "Typical loan qualification criteria require that borrowers spend no more than 32 percent of their gross income (Gross Debt Service Ratio or GDSR) on shelter financial obligation including mortgage payments, taxes, utilities, and half of condo fees. In addition, borrowers should spend no more than an additional 8 to 10 percent (Total Debt Service Ratio or TDSR = 40 to 42 percent) of their gross income on all other financial obligation including personal loans, car loans, credit cards and other debts."[82]

In Canada, banks generally retain the risks of their underwriting, maintain standards, and hold onto credit skills. Underwriting standards are high in Canada, because banks retain most mortgages they originate. The rate of securitization of mortgages is low in Canada, only about 30 percent. These are mainly government-guaranteed mortgage-backed securities. This represented about 85 percent of total securitization. There is also little use of credit default swaps to hedge Canadian corporate risk.

LIMITED SHADOW BANKING SECTOR

In Canada, banks were the most important suppliers of credit, and they relied less on the shadow-banking sector for the supply of credit. Also in Canada, six banks dominate the concentrated banking system. In descending order of capitalization, they are Royal Bank of Canada, $74.6 million;[83] Toronto-Dominion Bank, $65.3 million;[84] Bank of Nova Scotia, $59.6 million;[85] Bank of Montreal, $32.6 million;[86] Canadian Imperial Bank of Commerce, $30.8 million;[87] and the National Bank of Canada, $11.1 million.[88] Banks in Canada are responsible for most of the country's direct and indirect finance, accounting for about 58 percent of credit provision. Other regulated financial institutions supply 14 percent of the total credit, and traditional market instruments supply the balance of 28 percent. These banks also control the securities underwriting and merchant banking in Canada. There is also less reliance in Canada on unsecured interbank transactions.

The mere size of the largest U.S. banks poses systematic risk. The four largest U.S. banks, listed in descending order of capitalization, are J. P. Morgan Chase, $174.88 billion; Wells Fargo, $170.27 billion; Bank of America, $147.46 billion; and Citigroup, $146.41 billion—combined capitalization of $639 billion. Compare this to a combined capitalization of the six major Canadian banks of $274 million. In the U.S., these four banks are considered too big to fail.

It is obvious that we can learn a few things from Canada. It is equally obvious that the two countries are different in size and have a different history, political situation, and social philosophy.

REDUCING THE PUBLIC DEBT

The war in Iraq and Afghanistan, the various bailouts and tax cuts in the last decade, and the negative income effects of the financial crisis and economic recession pushed the U.S. public debt up to unprecedented levels. The 2010 estimate of almost $14 trillion is alarming. Excessive national debt creates systemic risk in the economy. According to the Council on Foreign Relations, the debt-to-GDP ratio of Greece was 113 percent in 2009.[89] In 2010, Greece experienced a debt crisis.

The U.S. debt-to-GDP ratio in 2010 is 94.27 percent. This ratio has increased by about 38.99 percent since 1990. It is important that the Federal Government reduce the debt level to a reasonable amount. If the

[82] Canada Mortgage.com, "Home Financing Calculator," http://www.canadamortgage.com/calculators/convhighratio.cgi.

[83] Royal Bank of Canada, "2010 Annual Report, 2010," http://www.rbc.com/investorrelations/pdf/ar_2010_e.pdf.

[84] Toronto-Dominion Bank, "2010 Annual Report," http://www.td.com/ar2010/pdfs/2010%20MD&A_E.pdf.

[85] Bank of Nova Scotia, "Annual Report 2010," http://www.scotiabank.com/images/en/filesaboutscotia/25448.pdf.

[86] Bank of Montreal, "Annual Report 2010," http://www.bmo.com/ar2010/downloads/bmo_ar2010.pdf.

[87] Canadian Imperial Bank of Commerce, "2010 Annual Report,"http://www.cibc.com/ca/pdf/about/ar10-en.pdf.

[88] National Bank of Canada, "2010 Annual Report," http://www.nbc.ca/bnc/files/bncpdf/en/2/e_ri_ar2010.pdf.

[89] Roya Wolverson, "The Risk of Greek Contagion," *Council on Foreign Relations*, May 5, 2010,
http://www.cfr.org/publication/22055/risk_of_greek_contagion.html.

debt level is not controlled, it may cause another crisis in the U.S., a negative situation similar to what we experienced recently, and in addition, can lead to excessive borrowing costs for the Government, flight of investors, and depletion of inward foreign direct investment (FDI), among other things. See Table 7.4 for the growth in gross federal debt from 1990 to 2010 and the percentages of Debt-to-GDP Ratio. See Figure 7.4 for an illustration of the debt-to-GDP ratio for the same period.

Table 7.4 U.S. Public Debt as a Percentage of GDP 1990 to 2010

End of Fiscal Year	Gross Federal Debt	GDP	Gross Public Debt as % of GDP
	(Billions of dollars)		
1990	3,206,290	5,800.50	55.28
1991	3,598,178	5,992.10	60.03
1992	4,001,787	6,342.30	63.10
1993	4,351,044	6,667.40	65.26
1994	4,643,307	7,085.20	65.54
1995	4,920,586	7,414.70	66.36
1996	5,181,465	7,838.50	66.10
1997	5,369,206	8,332.40	64.44
1998	5,478,189	8,793.50	62.3
1999	5,605,523	9,353.50	58.94
2000	5,628,700	9,951.50	56.56
2001	5,769,881	10,286.20	56.09
2002	6,198,401	10,642.30	58.24
2003	6,760,014	11,142.10	60.67
2004	7,354,657	11,867.80	61.97
2005	7,905,300	12,638.40	62.55
2006	8,451,350	13,398.90	63.08
2007	8,950,744	14,061.80	63.65
2008	9,986,082	14,369.10	69.50
2009	11,875,851	14,119.00	84.11
2010 estimate	13,786,615	14.623.90	94.27

Source: U.S. Bureau of Economic Analysis, National Economic Analysis, Gross Domestic Product,
http://www.bea.gov/national/nipaweb/TableView.asp?SelectedTable=5&ViewSeries=NO&Java=no&Request3Place=N&3Place=N&FromView=YES&Freq=Year&FirstYear=1929&LastYear=2010&3Place=N&AllYearsChk=YES&Update=Update&JavaBox=no

Figure 7.4 U.S. Public Debt as a Percentage of GDP 1990 to 2010

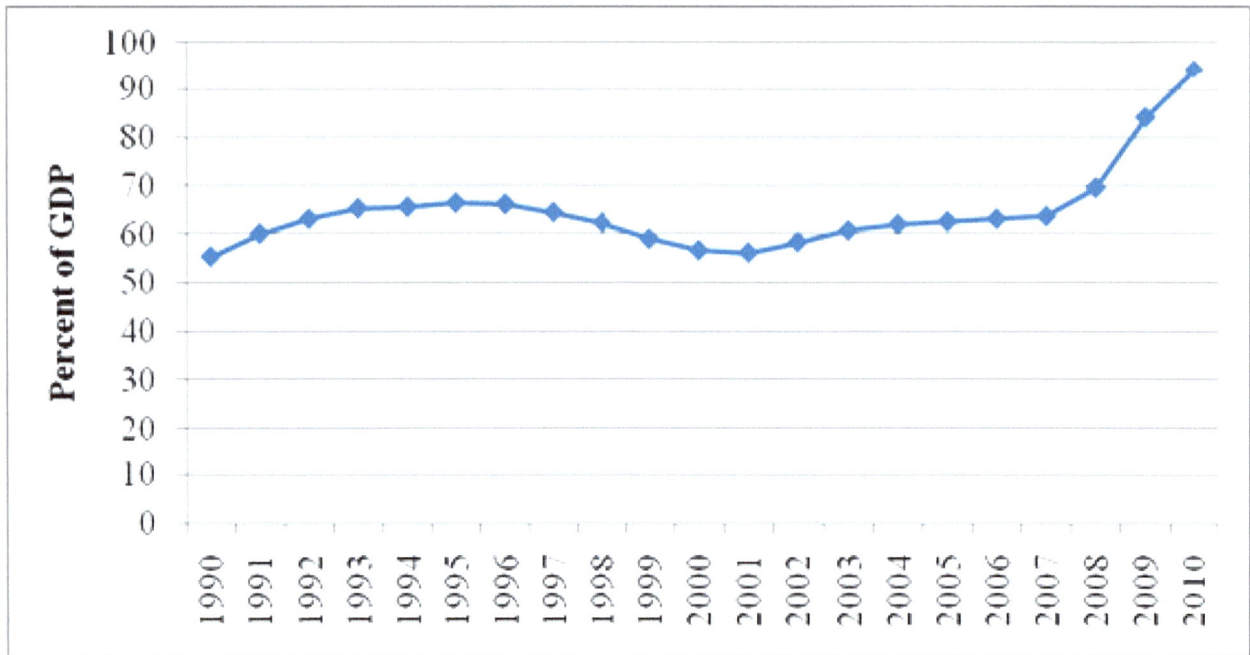

GENERAL REDUCTION IN CONSUMERS' FINANCIAL LEVERAGE—ENCOURAGE HIGHER SAVINGS RATIO

Prior to the financial crisis, many Americans had unacceptable high levels of debt leading to excessive leverage. As discussed earlier in the book, the personal savings ratio was low. The percent of personal income saved seems to be on the increase. It rose from 1.8 percent in 2007 to 5.38 percent in 2009 (see Table 7.5). The trend for the same period is illustrated in Figure 7.5.

Table 7.5 U.S. Percent of Personal Saved Income Ratio 2005 to 2009
(Billions of dollars, Quarters seasonally adjusted at annual rates)

Year	Personal Income	Personal Savings	% of Savings to Income
2005	10,488.90	12.7	0.12
2006	11,268.10	235	2.09
2007	11,912.30	214.7	1.8
2008	12,391.10	447.9	3.61
2009	12,174.90	655.3	5.38

Source: U.S. Bureau of Economic Analysis, National Economic Accounts, Comparison of Personal Saving in the National Income and Product Accounts (NIPAs) with Personal Saving in the Flow of Funds Accounts (FFAs), December 22, 2010, http://www.bea.gov/national/nipaweb/Nipa-Frb.asp

Figure 7.5 U.S. Percent of Personal Saved Income Ratio 2005 to 2009

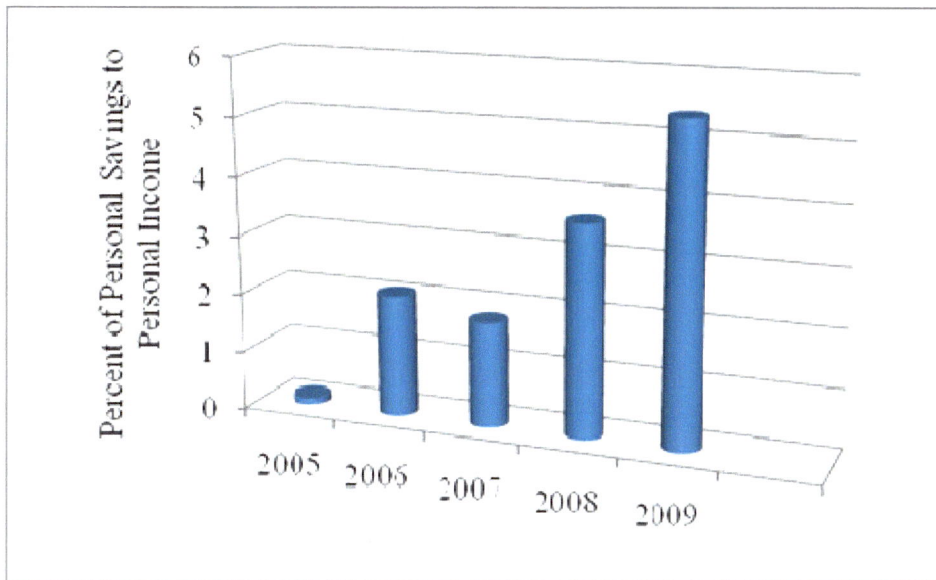

Perhaps the shocks of the financial crisis and economic recession have highlighted the importance of saving for a rainy day. Housing prices had been rising for a very long time, and the collapse of the housing market took most by surprise. The stock market had also been flourishing for a very long time. Prior to the financial crisis, there was great optimism in the investment arena that stock market returns would continue to be high and that equity values in homes would continue to flourish. Many people invested all their retirement funds in the stock market, overleveraged on their credit cards, and others refinanced their homes repeatedly. When many lost their homes to foreclosure, lost most of their retirement funds in the stock market during the financial crisis, and lost their jobs because of the economic recession, the absence of significant savings or no savings meant that they had nothing to fall back on.

The country should have exerted more effort into encouraging more cautious borrowing and increased savings. The financial reform has placed some responsibilities on the lending institutions and brokers to ensure that consumers benefit from all loan extensions and that they have the financial ability to repay the loans. Are the provisions in the financial reform act sufficient to stop the emergence of greater leverage that can contribute to the financial systemic risk? Consumers are definitely more cautious, and there is less availability of credit because of the credit crunch. Time will tell if the provisions in the financial reform act are adequate.

REDUCING THE U.S. TRADE DEFICIT

Since 1976, the United States has achieved a balance of payments deficit because the value of U.S. imports exceeded its exports. The balance of trade was just over $39 billion in December 1992, but by December 2008, it had exceeded $701 billion. Unfortunately, the balance of U.S. international goods and services has continued to deteriorate. The negative trade balance in 2009 was approximately $375 billion, and it grew to $458 billion in 2010.[90] What the U.S. could do to correct this trade imbalance is beyond the scope of this book. However, casual observations point to the need to revisit some trade agreements, tax laws, and regulations that may not be in the best interest of the U.S. Any trade agreement, tax law, or regulation that has the net effect of reducing job opportunities in the U.S. belongs to this category. Arguing that it is more

---

[90] U.S. Department of Commerce, Census Bureau, "Foreign Trade." http://www.census.gov/foreign-trade/statistics/historical (accessed January 14, 2011).

profitable for our corporations to relocate their manufacturing plants overseas because of cheaper labor costs is detrimental to the nation in the long run. With the advent of technology, higher levels of unemployment will continue to persist as machines continue to replace human beings in the workplace. In addition to this, the emphasis on lean production means employing fewer people in the workplace. Yet, there is a political momentum to educate every American with the promise of a better future. How can we assure that better future in the face of declining job opportunities?

A suggestion that is often made is that the U.S. should reinvent itself and shift its focus to high-end products to increase its exports. However, whatever advantage it finds in producing high-end goods will only be temporary. Other countries will develop those technologies with time and possibly at cheaper prices. It is important that the U.S. learns to compete better in the present global environment in the production of lower-end manufacturing products and delivery of services. There is also a need for a national conversation on how to reduce the trade deficit.

CONCLUSION

The stock market, the financial services sector, and the automobile industry have stabilized. The Federal Government bailout contributed significantly to this achievement. The economy is slowly but steadily recovering. Considering the magnitude of the economic distress, the economy would not be on this path of steady recovery if the Federal Government had not injected the various stimulus funds into the economy.

To prevent the occurrence of future financial crises and economic recessions, achieving a well-regulated financial system is a *sine qua non*. It is also important to reduce the budget deficit to an acceptable level. Moreover, it is important to educate consumers to borrow moderately. Excessive borrowing by the Government and consumers contributes to systemic risk.

BIBLIOGRAPHY

Bank for International Settlement, Committee on the Global Financial System."Macro prudential Instruments and Frameworks: a Stocktaking of Issues and Experiences." CGFS Papers No 38, May 2010. http://www.bis.org/publ/cgfs38.pdf.

Bank of Canada. "Why Monetary Policy Matters: A Canadian Perspective." http://www.bankofcanada.ca/en/ragan_paper/inflation.html (accessed November 26, 2010).

Bank of Montreal. "193rd Annual Report 2010."http://www.bmo.com/ar2010/downloads/bmo_ar2010.pdf.

Bank of Nova Scotia. "Annual Report 2010." http://www.scotiabank.com/images/en/filesaboutscotia/25448.pdf.

Bankrate.com. "Prime rate, fed funds, COFI." http://www.bankrate.com/rates/interest-rates/prime-rate.aspx (accessed January 15, 2011).

Barr, Alistair. "Brokers Threatened by Run on Shadow Bank System, Regulators Eye $10 trillion Market that Boomed Outside Traditional Banking." *Wall Street Journal*, June 20, 2008. http://www.marketwatch.com/story/big-brokers-threatened-by-crackdown-on-shadow-banking-system.

Beaird, Daniel. "Deals are on the Rise, as Capital Returns to the Market." *National Real Estate Investor*, June 17, 2010. http://nreionline.com/news/deals_rise_capital_returns_0617/# (accessed January 10, 2011).

———. "Commercial Real Estate Activity Starting to Pick Up." *Nuwire Investor*, June 18, 201. http://www.nuwireinvestor.com/articles/commercial-real-estate-activity-starting-to-pick-up-55459.aspx (accessed January 10, 2011).

Canada Mortgage.com. "Home Financing Calculator." http://www.canadamortgage.com/calculators/convhighratio.cgi.

Canadian Imperial Bank of Commerce. "2010 Annual Report." http://www.cibc.com/ca/pdf/about/ar10-en.pdf.

Carney, Mark. "Looking Back, Moving Forward – Canada and Global Financial Reform." *Bank for International Settlement*, November 9, 2010. http://www.bis.org/review/r101111a.pdf (accessed November 26, 2010).

Chukwuogor, Chiaku. "Stock Markets Returns and Volatilities: a Global Comparison." *Global Journal of Finance and Banking Issues* 1, no. 1, 2007. http://www.globip.com/pdf_pages/globalfinance-vol1-article1.pdf.

Federal Reserve Bank of New York. "Federal Funds." August 2007. http://www.newyorkfed.org/aboutthefed/fedpoint/fed15.html (accessed January 10, 2011).

National Bank of Canada. "2010 Annual Report." http://www.nbc.ca/bnc/files/bncpdf/en/2/e_ri_ar2010.pdf.

Royal Bank of Canada. '2010 Annual Report.' http://www.rbc.com/investorrelations/pdf/ar_2010_e.pdf.

Statistics Canada. "2006 Census: Changing Patterns in Canadian Homeownership and Shelter Costs." June 4, 2008. http://www.statcan.gc.ca/daily-quotidien/080604/dq080604a-eng.htm (accessed January 17, 2011).

Toronto-Dominion Bank. "2010 Annual Report." http://www.td.com/ar2010/pdfs/2010%20MD&A_E.pdf.

Trading Economics. "United States Interest Rate." http://www.tradingeconomics.com/Economics/Interest-Rate.aspx?Symbol=USD (accessed January 10, 2011).

U.S. Department of Commerce, Bureau of Economic Analysis. "National Economic Accounts." http://www.bea.gov/national/index.htm#gdp (accessed January 8, 2011).

U.S. Department of Congress, Bureau of Economic Analysis. "National Income and Product Accounts Table." December 22, 2010. http://www.bea.gov/national/nipaweb/TableView.asp?SelectedTable=5&ViewSeries=NO&Java=no&Request3Place=N&3Place=N&FromView=YES&Freq=Year&FirstYear=1929&LastYear=2010&3Place=N&AllYearsChk=YES&Update=Update&JavaBox=no (accessed January 11, 2011).

U. S. Department of Labor, Bureau of Labor Statistics. "Employment Situation Summary." January 7, 2011. http://www.bls.gov/news.release/empsit.nr0.htm (accessed January 7, 2011).

———. "Consumer Price Index Summary – December 2010." January 14, 2011. http://www.bls.gov/news.release/cpi.nr0.htm (accessed January 14, 2011).

U.S. Department of Commerce, Census Bureau. "Census Bureau Reports on Residential Vacancies and Homeownership." April 28, 2008. http://www.census.gov/hhes/www/housing/hvs/qtr108/q108press.pdf.

U.S. Department of Commerce, Census Bureau. "Foreign Trade." http://www.census.gov/foreign-trade/statistics/historical (accessed January 14, 2011).

Villarreal, Alex. "Obama: Tax Cuts Compromise to Help Grow US Economy." *Voice of America*." January 8, 2011. http://www.voanews.com/english/news/President-Obama-Anticipates-Tax-Cut-Initiative-Impact-113129719.html (accessed January 16, 2011).

Wolverson, Roya. "The Risk of Greek Contagion." *Council on Foreign Relations*, May 5, 2010. http://www.cfr.org/publication/22055/risk_of_greek_contagion.html.DEX

www.ingramcontent.com/pod-product-compliance
Lightning Source LLC
Chambersburg PA
CBHW041712210326
41598CB00007B/625